VALUATION AND DEVELOPMENT APPRAISAL

OEMCO

VALUATION AND DEVELOPMENT APPRAISAL

VALUATION
and
DEVELOPMENT APPRAISAL
(Second Edition)

Edited by

CLIVE DARLOW, BSc (Est. Man.), FRICS

1988

THE ESTATES GAZETTE LIMITED
151, WARDOUR STREET, LONDON W1V 4BN

First published 1982
Second impression 1983
Second edition 1988
Second impression 1990

ISBN 0 7282 0109 7

© CLIVE DARLOW, 1982, 1983, 1988 and 1990

Printed in Great Britain at The Bath Press, Avon

Contents

H. MARK D. NORTON MA graduated from Trinity College, Cambridge, and joined the United Africa Company. Following experience with Simpson Sears and Balfour Williamson Inc. in 1960, he became president of Larry Smith Consulting Europe, with offices in Paris, Milan, Lausanne and Madrid. He has acted as Consultant for retail store expansion programmes, urban renewal and new town retail centres, and shopping centre developments in many countries.
Chapter 6 – Market Analysis and Research

ROB SMITH ARICS is a partner of Davis Belfield and Everest, Chartered Quantity Surveyors. He is mainly involved in commercial developments, and advises clients on feasibility appraisals and budget estimates as well as contract arrangements and building procurement. His firm has developed feasibility estimating and financial appraisal programs on their in-house computer system. He prepares the firm's Cost Forecast of future building costs and tender prices and Initial Cost Estimating articles that are published in the Architects' Journal.
Chapter 5 – Development Construction Costs

DAVID J. WESTCOTT FCA is the senior tax partner in the Windsor office of Price Waterhouse, Chartered Accountants. After some thirteen years in industry, he now advises a wide range of clients regarding their taxation affairs and has a particular interest in the property development and investment aspects of taxation.
Chapter 10 – Taxation of Property Development

Acknowledgements

This book reflects the cumulative work of many cons
and experts, represented by the contributions of th
authors.

Assisted by partners, colleagues and technical staff
individual chapters present a detailed review of the
advanced valuation and development appraisal technic
The generous sharing of the authors' expertise and their co
tive knowledge will be particularly appreciated by the reade

Many other fellow professionals gave unstintingly of th
time to advise on various aspects, to review drafts and o
advice; above all to encourage.

CLIVE DARLOW BSc FRICS was for over 20 years a directo
of public property development companies. Since then he ha
combined academic appointments with active consultancy
work. His professional work has taken him to more than a dozen
countries including the United States of America, where for
2 years he was concerned with feasibility studies and the provision of development finance.
Chapter 7 – Sources and Method of Funding
        8 – Corporate and Share Capital Funding
        9 – Direct Project Funding

STUART MORLEY BSc ARICS MA DipTP is a Principal Lecturer at the Polytechnic of Central London. After graduating
in Estate Management, he worked for private sector consultants advising on implementation of large scale projects
including central area redevelopments and shopping centres.
After gaining his MA he has specialised in development work
with a particular interest in financial appraisals.
Chapter 1 – The Residual Method of Valuation

Preface

I originally conceived the idea for this book as a "crash course" for the busy practitioner who needed to acquire a more detailed knowledge of development funding. What was not fully anticipated at the time the first edition was produced was the extensive use students also were to make of the book. Their requirements have since grown significantly as syllabuses have been modified to reflect the need for the emerging surveyor to be well versed in the financial aspects of property development. This of course follows the changing nature of the work load of the profession as development has become an increasingly important aspect of its activities. Clearly this trend will be intensified as the effects of obsolescence of the 1950s and 60s projects need to be addressed through earlier than anticipated redevelopment or extensive refurbishment. Similarly the drive to regenerate the inner cities through new development and rehabilitation will bring with it new demands on the profession. In addition, technological and economic changes in many sectors of the economy are bringing with them demands for new types of larger and more sophisticated developments, which in turn require new funding applications.

Also since the first edition was published techniques of analysis, methods of funding and of course the tax regime have all been evolving. Refinements have been introduced and new methods pioneered.

We have therefore attempted to incorporate all of the new circumstances into this second edition as well as anticipating more fully the needs of the student.

In conclusion, and yet again, I record my admiration and appreciation for the professional approach of my fellow authors, in producing another edition. It is to them that all credits must be given.

London   Clive Darlow
                                                       September 1987

Introduction

Initially following World War II and the re-emergence of the economic market forces of supply and demand in the property market, developers were able to use the "back of an envelope" approach to assess potential projects. These simple calculations were often sufficient to confirm the developer's own intuition and entrepreneurial "nose" for a profitable scheme. For many years the problem was less a matter of detailed appraisal and calculation but more a question of finding a site (almost any site) and then navigating the development proposal through the labyrinthian maze of bureaucratic licences, permits, permissions, authorisations etc. Practically anything that was built could be sold, or let, such was the measure of pent-up demand for new accommodation of every description. During these earlier years of absolute shortages of most types of modern developments many developers could succeed by an elementary, even casusal appraisal, reinforced by a considerable amount of flair, not to say good luck!

If the developer had, by any chance, seriously miscalculated his sums, then the effects of rapidly escalating rental values and falling investment yields would invariably correct any such error. The increasing interest in, and involvement with, real estate investments by the ever growing battalion of the financial institutions further reinforced the demand for completed developments. But the property development sector is cyclical, generally lagging the underlying performance of the economy. After the trauma experienced by the western world's capital markets caused by the sharp escalation in oil prices, followed in 1974 by the property crash, investors attitudes changed radically. They adopted a far more cautious approach towards property and lending institutions were circumspect. As a result both required a much more detailed and thorough appraisal of projects presented to them. Having become accustomed to the more advanced investment appraisal techniques applied to the other alternative investments, such as equities and gilt edged securities, etc, the institutions demanded that the same highly professional and skilled approach be applied to property developments. This demand stimulated a much closer collaboration of cognate professionals and a mutually beneficial reciprocation of experience, knowledge and skills, in order to give clients a more thorough and analytical level of advice.

The New Era

As the economy emerged from the deep recession of the early 1980s it was accompanied by an upturn in development activity.

The quickening pace of development has been stimulated by the rapid growth in the evolving new technologies, rising standards of living, changing requirements by users of buildings and alterations to traditional demographic patterns. Market research and forecasting techniques have, as a consequence, become even more important than before.

The deregulation of the City's investment and financial markets, in 1986, has also had profound repurcussions on the way that developments are funded. Additionally many new projects have grown dramatically in cost. This has placed new demands on the accuracy of cost estimating techniques.

London has become a major international centre and offers a wide range of new financial instruments and investment vehicles. This together with the capacity to fund very large projects, through 'multi option' bank lending facilities have widened considerably the spectrum of funding alternatives. An awareness of the choice available and an understanding of the mechanics of each, is essential for those involved in the financial aspects of development.

Both investment analysts and valuers have been quick to take full advantage of the more sophisticated appraisal programmes now available, in order to evaluate the risks associated with new schemes. Familiarity with the improved methodologies will enhance the speed and quality of financial

Acknowledgements

This book reflects the cumulative work of many consultants and experts, represented by the contributions of the five authors.

Assisted by partners, colleagues and technical staff their individual chapters present a detailed review of the most advanced valuation and development appraisal techniques. The generous sharing of the authors' expertise and their collective knowledge will be particularly appreciated by the reader.

Many other fellow professionals gave unstintingly of their time to advise on various aspects, to review drafts and offer advice; above all to encourage.

CLIVE DARLOW BSc FRICS was for over 20 years a director of public property development companies. Since then he has combined academic appointments with active consultancy work. His professional work has taken him to more than a dozen countries including the United States of America, where for 2 years he was concerned with feasibility studies and the provision of development finance.
Chapter 7 – Sources and Method of Funding
       8 – Corporate and Share Capital Funding
       9 – Direct Project Funding

STUART MORLEY BSc ARICS MA DipTP is a Principal Lecturer at the Polytechnic of Central London. After graduating in Estate Management, he worked for private sector consultants advising on implementation of large scale projects including central area redevelopments and shopping centres. After gaining his MA he has specialised in development work with a particular interest in financial appraisals.
Chapter 1 – The Residual Method of Valuation

2 – Partnership Schemes and Ground Rent
    Calculations
3 – Financial Appraisals; Cash Flow Approach
4 – Sensitivity and Probability Analysis

H. MARK D. NORTON MA graduated from Trinity College, Cambridge, and joined the United Africa Company. Following experience with Simpson Sears and Balfour Williamson Inc. in 1960, he became president of Larry Smith Consulting Europe, with offices in Paris, Milan, Lausanne and Madrid. He has acted as Consultant for retail store expansion programmes, urban renewal and new town retail centres, and shopping centre developments in many countries.
Chapter 6 – Market Analysis and Research

ROB SMITH ARICS is a partner of Davis Belfield and Everest, Chartered Quantity Surveyors. He is mainly involved in commercial developments, and advises clients on feasibility appraisals and budget estimates as well as contract arrangements and building procurement. His firm has developed feasibility estimating and financial appraisal programs on their in-house computer system. He prepares the firm's Cost Forecast of future building costs and tender prices and Initial Cost Estimating articles that are published in the Architects' Journal.
Chapter 5 – Development Construction Costs

DAVID J. WESTCOTT FCA is the senior tax partner in the Windsor office of Price Waterhouse, Chartered Accountants. After some thirteen years in industry, he now advises a wide range of clients regarding their taxation affairs and has a particular interest in the property development and investment aspects of taxation.
Chapter 10 – Taxation of Property Development

appraisals especially, as new projects continue to grow in complexity, size and value.

Property development has become very competitive and the needs for enhanced skills is therefore vital for the professional team. It is therefore hoped that the following chapters will assist the reader to achieve this objective.

Contents

This book is believed to be the first to bring together these individual areas of professional expertise and concentrate them exclusively on the more numerate aspects of economic, financial, valuation, and taxation core of the development process.

By adopting the logical production sequence of the typical major development project the book commences with a thorough examination of the techniques of the site valuation through the residual method of valuation in Chapter 1, followed by an assessment of viability once the site has been acquired.

The relationship between capital return and development yield is demonstrated and the sensitive nature of the residual method to changes in key variables is discussed, with examples.

The use of the residual method to calculate ground rent and equity shares of partnership schemes is reviewed in Chapter 2. Premiums and their effect, participation clauses, yield protection and alternative sharing arrangements are all illustrated through worked examples.

Chapter 3 contains an explanation of the benefits of alternative cashflow methods of calculating development costs including the incorporation of building cost inflation and rental growth.

A re-examination of risk in financial appraisals is contained in Chapter 4. Alternative methods of sensitivity analysis and an examination of the effects on development profitability of changes in assumptions are also demonstrated.

Probability analysis and the use of Monte Carlo techniques are then reviewed.

The techniques of budget cost estimating, with worked examples, current and projected construction costs are demonstrated in Chapter 5. The various factors which influence cost estimates, the use of indices and cashflow forecasts are also discussed.

The methods used to assess the economic demand for a particular project, through the study of the relative economic and physical characteristics of a cohesive market area are discussed in Chapter 6.

In Chapter 7 the principal sources of finance for funding a development are listed and quantified. Corporate finance and share capital are summarised in Chapter 8. A detailed investigation into direct project funding, is undertaken in Chapter 9 which contrasts, by comparative examples, the many alternatives and variations thereof, in the techniques of direct property financing.

Chapter 10 concentrates on those taxes which can affect the development process. These include Value Added Tax, Corporation and Capital Gains Tax, which are illustrated by detailed examples of the calculations involved.

CLIVE DARLOW

CHAPTER 1
The Residual Method of Valuation

INTRODUCTION

The method most frequently used for appraising the viability of development schemes is generally known as the residual valuation. Although all valuers have their own way of setting out such a valuation, the basic concept is straightforward and the method simple to use. Difficulties arise not in the method itself but in estimating the amounts of the many variables that go into the valuation. This is where the expertise of the valuer is so important.

Development schemes may comprise the development of new buildings on green field or cleared sites, redevelopment of built up sites involving the demolition of existing buildings and their replacement by new buildings, the alteration extension or improvement of existing buildings (normally referred to as refurbishment of commercial buildings or rehabilitation of residential buildings), or a combination of all three. In all cases the residual valuation would be used to assess financial viability.

There are essentially three main purposes for which a residual valuation may be undertaken and to some extent they correspond to the chronological sequence of the development process:

To calculate the maximum value of a development site which a developer is considering trying to acquire. This ceiling figure (allowing the developer a reasonable profit) would then be compared with the possible sale price to see whether it is worthwhile for the site to be purchased and developed. Of course the site will not necessarily be a cleared site, in which case the appraisal will be undertaken to test the feasibility of redevelopment or conversion/refurbishment.

To calculate the expected profit from undertaking development where a site is already owned by the developer. The site value is treated as a known cost of development (it may have been acquired recently after undertaking the type of calculation mentioned above, or it may have been in the developer's ownership for some time), and the residual item of the calculation then becomes the amount of profit the development should yield. If reasonable in all the circumstances, this will encourage the developer to proceed with the proposed scheme, and if unreasonable will lead to delay or abandonment.

To calculate a cost ceiling for construction where land has been acquired (and is therefore a known cost) to ensure where possible that a reasonable profit margin is maintained. Whilst construction is under way progress will be monitored so that if viability is threatened alterations to the scheme can be considered before it is too late.

It is probable that in the course of development all three calculations will be undertaken. Firstly, if the site has to be acquired, the maximum price a developer can afford to pay (and still make a reasonable profit) must be calculated to ensure that acquisition occurs at or below this ceiling figure. Secondly once detailed plans have been agreed and land has been acquired a re-evaluation will occur, where all costs can now be allowed for with a greater degree of certainty and hence likely profit levels determined to see whether the scheme should proceed or whether it should be redesigned or perhaps even put in abeyance. Finally when tender prices are received and also whilst construction is in progress, cost ceilings could be calculated and progress monitored to ensure that a scheme which started out viable does not end up by being unviable when it is too late to do anything about it.

At these later stages in the development process, where more specific and accurate information about the project is known, more detailed calculations can be undertaken. The length of the building period and the cost of the building can be estimated more accurately enabling more detailed cashflows to be calculated and more refined appraisals undertaken as described in subsequent chapters.

It is important to remember that the appraisals which developers use to assess the viability of development schemes, are concerned solely with financial factors taking account of values and costs to the developer. They are not feasibility studies, or cost benefit studies, which would consider a much wider range of costs incurred, and benefits received, by people other than the developer himself. The developer when appraising a scheme is primarily, and above all concerned, with the value to himself of a development that he has created, and the costs incurred by him to achieve a profit. It is only if this profit is perceived to be sufficient that development will proceed.

THE BASIC EQUATION

In its simplest form, when used to assess the development value of land, the residual valuation will estimate the maximum purchase price of a site by deducting the expected total costs of development, including an allowance to cover risk and profit, from the expected price that the completed development could be sold for in the market. The residual valuation could therefore be expressed in the form of a simple equation where the answer is the residue, or sum left over, after deducting costs of development from the value of development:

	Sale price of completed development		A
less	Cost of development	B	
	Profit allowance	C	B + C
equals	Residue for purchasing land		D
i.e.	$D = A - [B + C]$		

It is important to remember therefore that in a market economy where the supply of new buildings is a small percentage of the stock of existing buildings, the value of land is determined by what can be developed on that land and the value and cost of that development. Furthermore the value of that development is not directly related to its cost of production, but is created by the interplay of market forces – namely the supply and demand for similar properties which determine market price. In respect of commercial property there will often be a user market which will determine rental levels and an owner market which will determine capital values.

It is also important to remember that although the residual valuation can be expressed as a simple equation there may be considerable difficulty in acurately estimating the component parts of the equation. For example what was simply referred to as the costs of development may encompass a variety of different elements such as demolition costs, building costs, landscaping costs, professional consultants' fees, finance costs, letting and sale fees etc. These items are all variables and accurately estimating them over a development period which may be uncertain and of many years duration is not an easy task. Furthermore with so many variables in the equation slight chanres in a few of them will almost certainly result in a wide range of answers, owing to the sensitivity of the residual valuation. This is discussed at the end of this chapter and in more detail in Chapter 4 but a very simple example will help illustrate this problem.

Assume an estimated development value of £1 m and estimated development cost, including profit allowance, of £900,000. The residual land value would therefore be £100,000, using the simple equation shown above. Suppose a more cautious developer estimates that development costs will be slightly higher – say 10% higher at £990,000, but that the estimate of development value remains the same. The residual land value now would therefore be only £10,000; a 10% difference in estimating costs would result in a 90% reduction in estimated land value!

For these reasons the Lands Tribunal are very wary of this valuation approach as ... "it is a feature of residual valuations that comparatively minor adjustments to the constituent figures can have a major effect on the result." (*First Garden City Ltd.* v *Letchworth Garden City Corporation* (1966) 200 EG 163). Generally the Lands Tribunal has rejected the residual method unless there is no simpler method of valuation available. Nevertheless the Tribunal have made it clear that, despite the above, in open market conditions the residual approach could be a precision valuation instrument:

> "it is a striking and unusual feature of a residual valuation that the validity of a site value arrived at by this method is dependant not so much on the accurate estimation of completed value and development costs, as on the achievement of a right balancing differ-

ence between these two. The achievement of this balance calls for delicate judgement, but in open market conditions the fact that the residual method is (on the evidence) the one commonly, or even usually, used for the valuation of development sites, shows that it is potentially a precision valuation instrument".
(*Clinker & Ash Ltd.* v *Southern Gas Board* (1967) 203 EG 735).

Great care must therefore always be taken in using residual valuations, and wherever possible comparable market land price evidence should always be used, at least as a check. However, for most commercial schemes this is often not possible as schemes vary in content, cost and value whereas for residential and industrial development, particularly on large regular shaped sites, a comparison method of valuation may be possible.

SIMPLIFIED RESIDUAL CALCULATION
Example 1

The purpose of this example is to examine the principal components of a simple residual calculation and how they relate to each other. Example 2 is a more detailed residual calculation itemising all the components relevant to a full appraisal.

A developer wishes to know the residual value of a site where total rental income from completed buildings is expected to be £100,000 p.a., total building costs including all fees incurred are expected to be £700,000, the building period is expected to be 2 years, and the total development period is expected to be 2·5 years.

Expected Value

Income	(1)	£100,000 p.a.
Yield @ 8%	(2)	12·5
Capital Value		£1,250,000

Expected Costs

Construction costs (inc. all fees)	(3)	£700,000
Short term finance over half building period @ say 15% p.a.	(4)	£105,000
		£805,000

Return to cover risk & profit
@ say 20% of Capital Value   (5)   £250,000   £1,055,000

Site Value

Maximum site value (on completion of development)	(6)	£195,000
P.V. £1 2·5 years @ 15% p.a.	(7)	0·7
Maximum site value today		£136,500

(1) Income

This is the income that the buildings would let for if available for letting today. Although the buildings will not be available until completed in two and a half years' time – today's rental value traditionally is usually assumed to avoid the problems of predicting the future. However in areas of strong demand, and hence competition for sites, and where there is optimism for the future, developers may project rents explicitly or "take a view" of likely future growth. This point is discussed in more detail in Chapter 3.

The net rental value is used. This assumes that all outgoings such as internal and external repairs, insurance and rates have been allowed for so that the net income (before tax) is derived comparable to other non-property investments. It is normal practice today to ensure that the tenant is responsible for bearing these outgoings so that rental values are normally quoted on a net basis, although the desirability of a landlords "hands off" approach has recently been the subject of much debate connected to the problem of obsolescence. If there are many tenants (as in a shopping centre for example) then management costs to cover rent collection, and to ensure that repairs are undertaken etc., should be deducted separately. A typical allowance would be 2·5% of total rents.

(2) Investment Yield

It is common (but not universal) practice in the commercial property market for there to be a separation between occupation and ownership of buildings. Unlike the residential market where owner occupation is common, most commercial occupants prefer to pay rent rather than acquire property outright for a capital sum. In theory their capital can be more profitably employed in their business in which they are experts, rather than being tied up in owning property, at which they are unlikely to be experts. Consequently there is a separate investment market for property which is a (small) part of the overall general investment market. Investment yields in property should therefore relate to other investment yields.

The yield of 8% has to reflect a number of factors the most important being the state of the economy and the general level of interest rates/yields; the type and the location of the property and hence its future rental growth expectations; the security of the income in terms of the tenants' continued ability to pay the rent; the life and obsolescence of the property; the management bother attached to rent collection, supervising repairs etc.; and the size of the investment (very large investments will have higher yields as fewer investors can afford the risk of having so many "eggs in one basket" or the inflexibility which would result if a smaller sum of money had to be realised by a quick sale).

The greater the rental growth expected the lower the initial return an investor would be prepared to expect. Conversely an investment where income growth is expected to be small or even zero (such as government stocks or Building Society accounts) will have a high initial yield or return to compensate. So undated government stocks (currently yielding about 10%) will give a fixed annual income of £10 for every £100 invested whilst £100 invested in prime retail or office property could (at the time of writing) give an initial annual income as low as £4–£5 (i.e. a yield of 4%–5%). But it is anticipated that this income will increase significantly at every rent review, so that in say 15 years' time the annual income might have risen to £15+. It is the skill of the valuer which is necessary to determine the appropriate yield, which can vary from 4% for prime shops to over 15% for old factories.

Having decided on an appropriate investment yield how is this used to calculate capital value? The relationship between income and capital value for freehold investments is a simple one as the income stream is assumed to be receivable in perpetuity. In the example used the initial annual income must represent 8% of the capital value. So if the capital value is X we can say that

$$\frac{8}{100} \times £X = £100,000$$

$$\therefore \quad £X = £100,000 \times \frac{100}{8} = £100,000 \times 12 \cdot 5$$

$$= £1,250,000$$

(3) Construction Costs

The individual items that go to make up the total cost of construction are examined in detail in example 2 and will obviously vary depending on the complexity and size of the development scheme. The major component of this figure is the payment to a builder for undertaking construction and it is common practice for this figure to be the tender price as at the date of undertaking the appraisal i.e. the traditional developer's assumption is to use today's rents and today's costs thereby avoiding the difficulty of predicting the future. A further justification for this approach is the crude assumption that increases in building costs will be matched by increases in rental values. The validity and the effect of this assumption is examined in Chapter 3 and as stated earlier in areas of strong demand developers may project rent and costs with a view to justify higher site values.

(4) Short Term Finance

Development schemes involve considerable capital expenditure. It is normal practice for capital to be borrowed to finance this expenditure. Traditionally the major sources for borrowing were the clearing and merchant banks but since the mid 1970's the insurance companies and pension funds became more involved in providing both short and long term finance and in some cases undertaking development themselves. This situation is constantly changing and is discussed fully in later Chapters.

     A developer works on the assumption that short term money is borrowed to finance the cost of construction, which is then repaid at the end of the development period out of the proceeds from selling the completed scheme or from raising a long term loan. As the money borrowed is a short term loan the cost of borrowing is related to the cost of short term loans generally i.e. from 0·5%–6% above bank base rate or "LIBOR" – dependant on the status of the borrower, the size of the loan and the length of time that the loan will be outstanding. At the time of writing base rate is 11% and an established development company might expect to pay up to 2% above this figure, whereas smaller, less experienced companies borrowing small amounts of money might have to pay nearer to 6% above base rate, if the money could be borrowed at all.

Some developers might have secured preferential terms on longer term loans in the past or might use internal funds generated from the profits of past developments. Nevertheless if open market site value is being determined the prevailing borrowing rate should be adopted as this reflects the opportunity cost of using this money. One exception to this is where a pension fund or insurance company might lend short term money at a preferential rate of interest (currently 9–10%) in return for acquiring the completed development at a preferential price. Normally the rate of interest used in an appraisal is related to base rate at the date the calculation is undertaken. However, if this is thought to be at an exceptionally (and artificially) high or low figure, and it is considered very probable that interest rates would change during the development period then lower or higher figures might be used, although great care should be taken in choosing an appropriate figure.

It is normal practice for builders to be paid at monthly intervals for work completed – i.e. a proportion of the total building costs. Finance is raised accordingly and interest will therefore accrue in stages, although normally it will be "rolled up" and repaid as a lump sum on completion. So payments to the builder early on will involve interest accruing at a compound rate over virtually the full building period whereas payments made near the end of the building period will incur hardly any interest.

It is therefore normal practice (certainly for an initial appraisal) to assume that the total amount is borrowed for a proportion (usually half) of the building period and this arrangement has been adopted here assuming a two year building period. The interest should be compounded quarterly. This means that a nominal rate of interest, related to LIBOR of say 14%, will be an effective cost to the developer of 14·75% p.a. i.e.

$$\left(1 + \frac{0·14}{4}\right)^4 - 1$$

which has been simplified to 15% p.a. in this example. This arrangement also assumes that the individual monthly payments are symmetrical about the midpoint of the building period i.e. that the total costs incurred during the first half of the building period approximately equate with those incurred during the last half. (This assumption is discussed at greater length in Chapters 3 and 5.) Alternative methods of calculating short term finance are to allow interest over the full period but on half the building costs, or over the full period on total building costs but at half the interest rate. Each method will give a slightly different answer.

(5) Return for Risk & Profit

Property development involves the taking of risks which can be substantial where the development is of a speculative nature, as not only will costs almost certainly alter during the development period but rental levels, investment yields and the time that it will take to let (and maybe sell) are difficult to anticipate maybe two or more years into the future. This is dramatically illustrated by the boom and crash of the early 1970's. A developer will therefore incorporate into an appraisal an overall allowance to cover himself for those risks and also to provide a profit, or return, for the time and effort involved in creating an asset. Sometimes this latter item is separately calculated as a project management allowance. The amount of this overall allowance will obviously depend on many factors such as the type of development, the size of the scheme, the length of the development period, the degree of competition (and hence optimism of the future) and whether the scheme is pre-let or forward sold. The longer the development period the more uncertain the future and therefore (other things being equal) the greater the allowance made.

This allowance might be expressed as a percentage, or mark up, on total development costs or as a percentage of the capital value created. As one item of development cost is the cost of the land and the object of the calculation is to find this figure it is easier, and therefore common practice, to express the profit allowance as a percentage of capital value. A typical allowance would currently be 15%–20% of capital value, although, depending on the size and duration of the development. lower or higher figures could be appropriate.

It can easily be shown that there is a close relationship between the two forms of percentage allowance, whether expressed of capital value or of total costs, due to the fact that development costs, plus land cost, plus profit must equal capital value. So for example if the profit allowance is 20% of capital value, then it must also be equal to 25% of total costs. This can be shown by using a simple numerical example: £100 (capital value) = £80 (development and land costs) plus £20 (profit allowance). £20 is 20% of £100 and 25% of £80. Similarly a 20% mark up on total costs is equal to approximately 17% of capital value and a 15% mark up on total costs is equal to approximately 13% of capital value etc.

(6) Residual Site Value

The maximum value for the site that the developer could afford to pay is calculated by deducting costs and a profit allowance from capital value. This indicates the site value at the date the development is completed – (i.e. the date when the development is let and capable of being sold at the capital value calculated). As the site has to be purchased and paid for before development could commence it is necessary to calculate the site value at today's date.

(7) Finance on Site Cost

Finance will be required to cover the cost of acquisition until the capital value of the completed development can be realised and all borrowing repaid. It is normal practice to allow for interest at the same rate as in (4) above and to allow for it over the full development period as the full amount of the loan will be outstanding for the entire duration of the scheme. Two and a half years has been taken in this example to allow six months from the time the site is acquired until building work could commence. During this "lead in period" the design and layout of the building will have to be settled, detailed drawings and other building contract material prepared and a contractor selected. In most cases detailed planning permission, or approval under reserved matters must be secured and Building Regulations approval obtained.

In this example, if the site was acquired for £136,500 then after two and a half years the total amount owed would be £195,000 (136,500 × 1·15$^{2.5}$). Using a discount or Present Value table converts the later sum to its present day equivalent. 0·7 is the reciprocal of two and a half years compound interest at an effective rate of 15% p.a.

DETAILED RESIDUAL CALCULATION

Example 2

The purpose of this example is to illustrate a full financial appraisal incorporating not only the principal components discussed in Example 1 but all the additional more minor, but nonetheless important, items of value and cost that should be considered in appraising the viability of a development project.

A developer wishes to estimate the development value of a site, which is for sale, close to the centre of London, with outline planning permission for 500 m² of standard unit shops with 5,000 m² of offices above. After consideration of various layouts and designs an optimum scheme is finalised which the developer feels confident would receive detailed planning permission. From knowledge of the area and the scheme proposed the developer and his advisers consider the following additional information to be realistic. All building work could commence in six months' time and take eighteen months to complete. Current building costs are estimated by the Quantity Surveyor to be:

Shops   = £350 per m²
Offices = £750 per m² (air conditioned space)

Current rental values are estimated by the letting agent to be:

Shops   = £130 per m² (standard units)
Offices = £150 per m² (air conditioned space)

The developer considers it prudent, after consultation with his agent, to allow a six month period for letting the shops and offices. A simplified time chart may therefore be drawn up to illustrate the development period. If the scheme goes ahead it could be funded from a mixture of internal finance (retained profit from previous developments) or short term bank finance, until a decision is made about whether to keep the completed building as a long term investment or to sell it and hopefully recoup a capital profit. This is discussed in more detail in Chapter 9.

The Appraisal
VALUE OF SCHEME

Income	(1)	p.a.
shops – 500 m^2 less 10% =		
450 m^2 net @ £130 m^2		£58,500
offices – 5,000 m^2 less 20% =		
4,000 m^2 net @ £150 m^2		£600,000
Total income		£658,500
Yield @ say 7% (allowing for		
purchasers costs)	(2)	14·2857
Capital Value		£9,407,000

COSTS OF SCHEME

Building Costs:	(3)		
shops – 500 m^2 gross @ £350 m^2		£175,000	
offices – 5,000 m^2 gross @			
£750 m^2		£3,750,000	
		£3,925,000	
Ancillary Costs:	(4)		
access road, car parking,			
landscaping, services etc. say		£200,000	
demolition		—	
		£4,125,000	
Professional fees	(5)		
architect, Q.S. and other			
consultants @ say 12·5%		£515,500	
		£4,640,500	

Contingencies:	(6)	
@ say 3% of total costs incurred		£139,000
		£4,779,500

Short Term Finance @ say 14% p.a.:

on total building costs ancillary costs professional fees and contingencies for say $\frac{1}{2}$ building period	(7)	£493,500
		£5,273,000
on total costs incurred on completion of building work for full length of letting delay (i.e. 6 months)	(8)	£357,000
		£5,630,000

Letting & Sale Fees:	(9)	
letting fee @ say 15% of income		£99,000
advertising and marketing @ say		£25,000
fees for selling commercial investment @ say 2% of sale price		£188,000
Total Development Cost	(10)	£5,942,000

RETURN FOR RISK & PROFIT
@ say 17% of Capital Value
(or 20% of all costs including
land)   £1,599,000

TOTAL EXPECTED COSTS	£7,541,000	£7,541,000
(incurred on completion of scheme)		
SITE VALUE (in 2·5 years' time)		£1,866,000
P.V. £1 2·5 years @ 14%.		0·72067
		£1,345,000
Less acquisition costs @ say 2·5% (11)		33,500
SITE VALUE TODAY		£1,311,500

(1) Income

Income is always calculated on the net usable floorspace a tenant can occupy. For shops there is normally little difference between net and gross areas. In this example it is assumed that there will be a parade of shop units on the ground floor of the commercial part of the scheme and so a 10% deduction has been made to allow for partition walls between the individual units and for WC's. If the shops were on two levels, a deduction could also be made for the staircase linking the two levels. For "standard sized' shop units (normally $100\,m^2$– $150\,m^2$) comparable rental evidence will often be expressed in terms of overall rent per unit shop rather than in terms of rent per m^2. Otherwise a zoning system is often used to reflect higher values at the front of a shop compared to the rear.

In office buildings there is usually a minimum of 17–20% of gross floorspace which is non-usable in rental terms. Such space would include stairs, lifts, landings, WC's, plant room and, if the building is let to more than one tenant, entrance halls. If the building is let to a single tenant then that tenant would have complete control and use of the entrance hall and it would be normal practice to include it in the net floor area, providing it was not excessively large. If individual floors are let to more than one tenant then a central corridor would have to be deducted as non-usable floorspace if it was necessary to provide one for access and fire escape purposes.

The amount of non-usable floorspace in an office building will therefore be dependent on a number of factors. In addition to those mentioned above are such factors as the age of the building and its height. Generally, older buildings will often have thick load bearing internal walls and many corridors and small rooms resulting in as much as 40% or more of gross space being deducted to give net lettable area. Taller and more modern buildings require bigger columns and more lifts and so may have a 25%–40% deduction to give nett lettable area. This is discussed in more detail in Chapter 5. From a developer's viewpoint it is vitally important to maximise the floorspace in a development and achieve the highest possible net lettable floor area, especially in Central London where rents are so high. In example 2 if the deduction was 25% rather than 20% this would mean a loss of $250\,m^2$ net lettable floorspace or an annual income of £37,500 and a capital loss of over £500,000.

(2) Yield

It is assumed that this development is in a good but not absolutely prime location. Investment value is also affected as there is a mixture of uses and it is unlikely that the building would be let to a single tenant. A building of similar size located in a prime Central London location let to a single tenant with no ground floor shop units would have an investment yield close to 5% (at the time of writing).

Purchasers acquisition costs of about 2·5% (agents fees at 1%, stamp duty at 1% and legal fees at 0·5%) would normally be deducted from the capital value if the scheme was to be sold rather than retained as an investment. Alternatively (as in this example) this could be reflected in the investment yield used. If the development were being forward funded by an institution stamp duty would only be payable on the cost of the site purchase, as the building is developed on behalf of the institution who therefore do not acquire it on completion. Similarly agents and legal fees would not be applicable here but would become an item of development expenditure as normally the developer would then be responsible for paying not only his own fees incurred but also those of the funds. See (11) below.

VAT at 15% would be payable on fees but this would normally be recoverable and so has been ignored. VAT is a complex issue and is discussed more fully in Chapter 10.

(3) Building Costs

Building costs are normally calculated on the gross internal area of the building(s) i.e. the area of the building obtained by measuring to the inside of the external walls. This total area will be slightly less than the gross external area usually used for plot ratio purposes.

(4) Ancillary Costs

These costs would normally be only a small proportion of construction costs, unless car parking was in the basement when a figure in excess of five times that for surface level parking would be incurred. For residential developments one car space per dwelling would be a normal planning requirement sometimes lowered to 75% of this level in Central London or dispensed with altogether in small awkward shaped sites. For office developments parking provision varies considerably depending on location. In Central London it is not unusual for parking requirements to be such that few if any spaces *will be allowed* by planning authorities due to congestion and the availability of public transport. In the suburbs and provinces conditions are usually much less strict and one space per 50 m² or even 25 m² might be permitted. In office parks the latter figure or lower would be the norm. Usually, from a developer's viewpoint, the more spaces that can be provided the better as the building will therefore be more attractive to potential tenants and the rent will possibly be higher.

Demolition costs are difficult to calculate as they will vary from site to site depending on the number, size and condition of existing buildings and how much of the materials are re-usable and their value. In some cases the recovery value of the materials will pay for the cost of demolition, and this is assumed here.

(5) Professional Fees

These fees are usually based on building costs but are sometimes agreed as a negotiated sum. Except for small jobs architects' scale fees for designing new buildings are 5–6% (but up to 10% for refurbishment work), quantity surveyors' about 3% and structural engineers' about 2·5%. In addition there may be other professionals involved in the design and construction, such as heating, lighting and particularly air conditioning experts, which will add further to the total for professional fees. The size and complexity of the scheme will determine the total amount to be added on for fees. A normal range would be from about 5% for a simple repetitive residential estate layout to 15% for a large complex multi-use development. VAT @ 15% will be charged but normally is recoverable. The cost of submitting a planning application will also add to the cost of all development and some developers would make a separate specific allowance for this item of expenditure.

(6) Contingencies

Some developers make allowance for contingencies, to cover the difficulties of precisely estimating building costs and the length of the building period, as a separate item; others do not, but provide a larger allowance for risk and profit. Particularly where refurbishment of an existing building is being undertaken it is advisable to provide a contingency sum as the cost of this work is very difficult to predict with unforeseen problems almost always occurring when building work is in progress. Similar unforseen problems often occur when foundations are excavated even if trial boreholes are made before building work starts.

A contingency allowance between 2% and 5% of all building and related costs incurred is usual, the actual amount depending on the stage in the development process when the appraisal is being undertaken, the degree of uncertainty about the subsoil and particularly the structure of any existing buildings that are being retained and refurbished. Where the development scheme comprises entirely of refurbishment then an allowance as high as 10% would often be adopted due to the high degree of uncertainty.

(7) Short Term Finance

The rate of interest has been taken at 2–3% above base rate/ LIBOR as an average allowance for the scheme in question, and the type of developer likely to undertake it. The annual effective rate has been calculated assuming interest will be payable quarterly. The building period has been taken as eighteen months and so finance costs are calculated over half the period, i.e. nine months. If demolition is necessary finance on this item of expenditure should be calculated over the total building period as costs will be incurred before building work can start. In practice the cost of demolition would normally be a small proportion of building costs and so little error would arise if demolition costs were added to building costs and finance allowed on the combined sum over half the building period.

Professional fees are paid at intervals during the development period. The earliest (and largest) payments, to the architect particularly, are usually made before building work commences to cover the work required to obtain detailed planning permission etc. Subsequent payments are then made at regular intervals during the building period based on a percentage of costs incurred. It is therefore arguable that finance on these fees should be allowed for longer than half the building period due to the initial payments being proportionately larger than the remainder. In practice most developers lump fees together with building costs and allow for finance over half the building period on the combined sum as it makes the calculation easier and the margin of error is small as the fees are at most only 15% of building costs. In many schemes any error is offset by the fact that slightly less than half the building costs will be incurred in the first half of the building period so that slight over-allowance on building cost finance will offset the slight under-allowance on the finance on professional fees (see Chapter 3 for discussion of the "S" curve).

(8) Letting Delay

On completion of all building work there will normally be a delay whilst the building is marketed. Once tenants have been found, legal documentation and possibly rent free or fitting out periods will further delay the receipt of income. The length of this delay will obviously be dependent on the strength of demand at the relevant time and the rent that is quoted. In a poor location during a recession the delay may be considerable. Conversely, in a prime location when demand is strong, letting may be achieved while building work is proceeding and therefore no delay will be encountered, even though an unfinished building is harder to let than one that is finished. Sometimes, to reduce risk, a prelet may be arranged before building work commences which will also eliminate delay at this stage of the development when maximum costs have been incurred, although rental concessions would probably have to be made. Nevertheless development risks would be reduced and funding would be easier and probably cheaper to obtain.

It is normal practice to make allowance for a few months letting delay dependent on the location and therefore finance will be required for *the full period* of the delay as the total costs (building costs, fees, contingencies and finance incurred during the building period) will be outstanding until the building can be sold or refinanced which normally will not be until the building has been let. This letting delay could be added to half the building period, and all the short term finance calculated in one stage, i.e. in this example interest @ 14% for 1·25 years on total building costs and fees. Whilst the answer is obviously the same it is however often useful to separate the actual cost of delay to emphasize its magnitude and significance. If the building is still unlet after say six months and the scheme has been forward sold, then in many cases the funding agreement will stipulate that the developer will be responsible for paying the rent for a further specified period or until an occupying tenant is found. In this situation the prospective profit margin will be eroded by rental payments rather than accumulating interest charges.

(9) Agents Fees

Letting and sale fees occur at the end of the development period and so finance will not have to be arranged to cover payment of these items.

Letting fees are normally based on a scale of 10% of the first year's rent where one estate agent in involved or 15%+ where two or more agents are used (common practice for larger developments). Sometimes on very large or easy to let buildings – a negotiated sum may be arranged below the level of the scale fee. The cost of advertising and the preparation of coloured brochures etc. would normally be charged as a separate item and will vary according to the marketing campaign decided on.

Allowance for sale fees will depend on a number of factors. Firstly, if the developer intends retaining the commercial building as a long term investment, then no sale fees will be paid if no sale occurs but if long term funding is necessary then funding fees will be included. Nevertheless sale fees may still be allowed even if neither a sale nor long term funding is envisaged if the object of the valuation is to calculate an open market value of the site, on the assumption that other developers will be developing for sale, either as a trading operation, or as part of a forward sale or sale and leaseback arrangement with an institution. Agents sometimes receive "notional sale commission" as part of their original introductory reward, even where the building is retained. Alternatively if the market is likely to comprise mainly institutional investor/developers, then it is unlikely that sale fees would be allowed. Similarly, if potential owner occupiers were considering developing, the maximum site value that they could afford to pay would be determined by making no allowance for sale fees. However it should be noted that in this case a separate allowance for project management fees should be made but of course there would be no letting fees to be paid or letting delay incurred.

A normal allowance for sales fees would be about 2% of the sale price (i.e. agents fees 1·5%, legal fees 0·5% and 15% VAT, which would normally be recoverable) but on a very large scheme the percentage fee may be smaller as the capital value would be much larger; the extra work involved (still one sale) would not be correspondingly greater. Similarly if one firm was involved throughout the development, in finding the site, letting and subsequently selling the completed development, reduced fees might be negotiated on costs.

(10) On Costs

Sometimes very quick or "back of the envelope" calculations need to be made and a rough and ready approach is adopted which lumps together the inputs itemised above – i.e. professional fees, finance, contingencies, letting and sale fees into one umbrella title of "on costs". In this example these items amount to approximately 50%. Clearly this is a crude approach and one that is less applicable today with the availability of portable computers, programmable calculators and desk top micros, but nevertheless it can have its uses as a check calculation if nothing else.

(11) Acquisition Costs

Estate agents' fees (about 1%), the usual legal conveyancing costs (about 0·5%), and stamp duty (1%) and VAT on these fees (recoverable) will be incurred in acquiring the site before development can commence. A (small) inaccuracy in calculating acquisition costs occurs in the method used in this example as acquisition costs will be based on £1,311,500 and not £1,345,000 as it is the former figure which represents what the developer can pay for the site. To overcome this small error either a smaller percentage could be allowed for or else, more accurately the following calculation could be undertaken:

$$\text{Net site value} = £1,345,000 \times \frac{100}{102 \cdot 5} = £1,312,000$$

DEVELOPMENT YIELD AND CAPITAL PROFIT

The previous examples have considered situations where the development value of a site is required. These calculations will show a developer the maximum price that could be paid for a site, and will in many cases be the first of many appraisals that will be undertaken to assess viability. This section examines the assessment of viability once a site has been acquired or is in the developer's ownership. In many cases this assessment will naturally be undertaken at a slightly later stage in the development process when often there is a greater degree of certainty about the scheme in terms of design and costs.

Once a site is in a developer's ownership there is less relevance in undertaking a residual calculation to work out site value, as the site has been acquired and paid for; it will be more useful to know how much profit the development is likely to make and whether this profit is reasonable or sufficient. This profit can be expressed in three basic ways – either as a residual capital sum realisable if the completed scheme was sold, or as an annual sum, expressed as a yield, if the completed scheme was retained as an investment or by the number of years it would take to eliminate the profit assuming a letting (and hence sale) were delayed. This last calculation is known as rent cover, as it is applicable to those forward funding arrangements where the developer guarantees the rent from the end of the rent void period (allowed for in the appraisal) until the scheme is income producing. Where the residual capital sum is calculated this can be expressed as a percentage of the scheme's capital value or its total development cost and then compared with the percentage allowance deemed appropriate as discussed in Examples 1 and 2. Similarly the annual sum, expressed as a yield, can be compared with the property's investment yield and the percentage difference calculated to see whether this provides an adequate mark up. Some examples will help to illustrate these approaches.

Example 3

Using the same information as contained in Example 2 and assuming the site is acquired for the sum that was shown to be the maximum the developer could afford i.e. £1,311,500 the following calculations show the amount of profit realisable, whether the scheme was sold or retained as an investment, and whether that profit is sufficient (and the same as allowed previously).

Capital Profit assuming a sale on completion

Expected Capital Value (as before)		£9,407,000
Expected total costs:		
Building costs, finance, fees etc. (as before)	£5,942,000	
Land Cost (incl. acquisition costs)	£1,345,000	
Finance on land cost @ 14% over development period of 2·5 years	£521,000	£7,808,000
Residual Capital Profit:		£1,599,000

$$\text{Profit as a \% of total costs} = \frac{1,599,000}{7,808,000} \times 100\% = 20{\cdot}48\%$$

$$\text{Profit as a \% of Capital Value} = \frac{1,599,000}{9,407,000} \times 100\% = 17\%$$

This shows that no errors have been made, because if the site was acquired for £1,311,500, a return of 17% of Capital Value would be achieved (or 20·5% of total costs) which is the assumption that was made earlier and assumed to be the minimum acceptable allowance in the circumstances of this particular development. Obviously if the site could be acquired for less than £1,311,500, or if the site was already in the developer's ownership and its existing use value was less than £1,311,500, then a higher profit margin would be made and the scheme could be said to be even more viable, although there may be an added tax liability. Conversely if the site was for sale at a higher figure, or its existing value was higher than this, a lower profit margin would result and the scheme would be abandoned, delayed or redesigned (if possible).

Rent Cover

Residual Capital Profit	£1,599,000
Rental value	£658,500
Therefore rent cover =	2·43 years

If the developer is guaranteeing the rent as part of a funding arrangement, as long as the building is let within 2·5 years a profit will still be realisable. In certain arrangements where the developer only guarantees the rent until the "profit" allowance is exhausted, the degree of rent cover is obviously vitally important from the funder's viewpoint.

As capital profit may be expressed as a percentage of capital value and as capital value is directly related to rent, it is clear that rent cover is merely a different way of looking at the same figures. It should be noted, however, that two schemes showing identical returns (when capital profit is expressed as a percentage of capital value) will have different degrees of rent cover if their investment yields are different. The higher the yield the lower the degree of rent cover; or put another way, if the same rent cover is required a higher capital profit will be needed.

Annual Profit assuming the Scheme is retained as an Investment

		p.a.
Expected annual income		£658,500
Expected total costs:		
Building costs, finance, fees, etc. (as before)	£5,942,000	
Land cost (incl. acquisition costs)	£1,345,000	
Finance on land cost @ 14% over development period of 2·5 years	£521,000	
Total costs	£7,808,000	

$$\text{Development Yield} = \frac{658{,}500}{7{,}808{,}000} \times 100\% = 8{\cdot}43\% \text{ p.a.}$$

Just as the investment yield (7% p.a.) expresses income as a percentage of capital value (or cost to an investor of acquiring the scheme) so the development yield expresses income as a percentage of total costs incurred in creating the scheme. The difference between total costs and capital value is an expression of the developer's capital profit. Similarly the difference between investment yield and development yield is an expression of the developer's annual profit. In this case it is $8.43\% - 7\% = 1.43\%$ p.a. which is a profit mark up of 20.43% (i.e. $1.43/7 \times 100\% = 20.43\%$) or the same as that shown above (after allowing for rounding errors). Alternatively the annual profit of 1.43% p.a. can be shown as being 17% of the development yield (i.e. $1.43/8.43 \times 100\% = 16.96\%$).

It is clear therefore that whether the developer's profit is expressed in annual or capital terms they are merely different ways of showing the same thing. Although, in commercial schemes, it is common practice to look to the development yield to assess a scheme's viability, problems arise if the scheme contains residential accommodation which is to be sold to potential owner occupiers. Obviously as the residential accommodation is sold there will be no annual income on this part of the scheme to enable a development yield to be calculated meaningfully.

There are two solutions to this problem, neither of which is particularly satisfactory:

(i) The overall land cost could be apportioned between the commercial and residential uses and two separate viability exercises carried out with a capital profit calculated for the residential part and a development yield calculated for the commercial part, as only that part will be retained as an investment. The advantages of this approach are that it corresponds with what will occur in practice i.e. a capital profit (hopefully) realised when the residential part is sold and a long term investment retained in the commercial scheme. It also will show how profitable *each* part of the scheme is, enabling possible changes to occur to improve performance if the viability of one part of the scheme is inadequate. Disadvantages are that apportioning the land cost between two parts of a scheme may be arbitrary particularly if the residential content is not in a separate building, and

the overall viability of the total development will not
be shown.

(ii) The scheme is appraised as a whole. The sale price of
the residential part is deducted from the total development costs and this net cost figure is used to calculate
the development yield. The advantages and disadvantages of this approach are the converse of those mentioned above. In certain situations, where the residential
part of the scheme forms a significant part of the whole,
very misleading figures are obtained for the development
yield.

In view of the above comments a more useful viability exercise
would be to examine the amount of potential capital profit
on both parts of the development and on the scheme as a whole,
rather than to calculate the amount of annual profit.

SENSITIVITY AND RISK

It was mentioned at the start of this chapter that residual
calculations were sensitive to the assumptions made and that
small changes to only one of the many variables could result
in much greater changes to the residual answer. However, particularly for commercial schemes, there is really no alternative
method to calculate the value of development sites. For residential and industrial development in "green field" situations
it is possible that there will be other sites sufficiently similar
that have been sold recently so that comparable information
of land values is available. This information would be used
either instead of undertaking residual calculations or as a
check. Land value comparables are rarely used for commercial
schemes as every site is different in terms of size, location
and the variety and density of uses that can be developed on
the site. Nevertheless useful checks can be made by examining
site value expressed as value per acre or hectare, or by examining the site value as a percentage of the schemes capital value.

For commercial developments particularly, it is imperative
that great care is used when undertaking development appraisals. This is illustrated by the following very simple examples
which show how residual land values can alter dramatically
by differential changes in the variables and how some develop-

ment schemes are more sensitive to changes in the variables than are others. The problem of sensitivity and various ways of lessening it are discussed in detail in Chapter 4.

(i) The basic residual calculation

Development A (where land cost forms a relatively large component of total costs)		Development B (where land cost forms a relatively small component of total costs)	
Value	£1,000,000	Value	£1,000,000
Cost	500,000	Cost	900,000
Land Value	£500,000	Land Value	£100,000

In Development A, land value works out as 50% of Capital Value, whereas in Development B, it is only 10%.

(ii) The Scheme's value and costs are both 50% higher than expected

Development A		Development B	
Value	£1,500,000 (+50%)	Value	£1,500,000 (+50%)
Cost	750,000 (+50%)	Cost	1,350,000 (+50%)
Land Value	£750,000 (+50%)	Land Value	£150,000 (+50%)

As value and costs of the scheme have altered by the same amount, the residual land value also alters by the same amount maintaining its relationship at 50% of CV (Development A) and 10% of CV (Development B).

(iii) The Scheme's value is 50% higher than expected, but costs are only 10% higher than expected

Development A		Development B	
Value	£1,500,000 (+50%)	Value	£1,500,000 (+50%)
Cost	550,000 (+10%)	Cost	990,000 (+10%)
Land Value	£950,000 (+90%)	Land Value	£510,000 (+410%)

Two points of interest occur here. Firstly if the scheme's value increases by more than costs increase, the residual land value increases by a much greater amount still, and it becomes a greater percentage of Capital Value. Secondly, the effect is much more marked in Development B, than in Development

A. Development B is therefore a much more sensitive calculation to changes in the variables.

(iv) The scheme's value and costs are both higher than expected but costs increase by more than value increases

Development A		Development B	
Value	£1,100,000 (+10%)	Value	£1,100,000 (+10%)
Cost	600,000 (+20%)	Cost	1,080,000 (+20%)
Land Value	£500,000 (±0%)	Land Value	£20,000 (−80%)

Although value and costs both increase, the effect on the residual land value is no change in Development A and a decrease in Development B. The change is once again more marked in Development B.

The foregoing highly simplified residual calculations clearly illustrate the dangers inherent in using this method of calculation referred to at the beginning of this chapter – namely that even slight changes or errors in only one or two of the variables can result in greatly altered answers, in this case the residual land value. Great care must be taken. These simplified examples also clearly illustrate another related point, which is that where land value forms a relatively small proportion of the finished scheme's ultimate value the calculation is at its most sensitive. Very small inaccuracies or poor estimations of just one variable can give a wide range of residual answers. A valuer advising a client in this situation needs to exercise great care in undertaking the calculation and estimating the individual components to avoid giving inaccurate advice. These calculations also, hopefully, illustrate the risk involved in speculative development particularly and why a margin of say 20% of total costs is usually allowed to cover the developer's risk and profit, so that if differential changes to costs and values occur (costs rising more rapidly than value), there is some cushioning allowance before an actual loss is made.

WORKED EXAMPLE TO ILLUSTRATE DEVELOPMENT VIABILITY AND PLANNING GAIN

A developer has assembled a development site of 10,000 m² in West London with the intention of undertaking an industrial development. The site at present contains a mixture of uses, predominantly industrial and residential, housed in old buildings some of which are in a poor state of repair, and was recently acquired in two parcels from separate owners for a total of £350,000. The local plan does not show the overall site as being proposed for redevelopment but indicates that parts of the site, which are already cleared of buildings, would be suitable for small scale residential or light industrial development. As discussions with local planning officers proceed, it becomes clear that whilst they fully support the idea of industrial development they are concerned about loss of residential accommodation and require that some new housing be incorporated into the scheme, suitably separated from the industrial part. After careful consideration, the developer revises his scheme to include a small office building of 1,000 m² along part of the frontage of the site as well as six housing units which he is prepared to construct, pay for and then transfer to the authority. This would be the subject of a S.52 agreement (Town and Country Planning Act, 1971).

(A) Assess the viability of the originally proposed industrial development.
(B) Assess the viability of the revised mixed use scheme, and indicate the problems in assessing this proposal from the LA's viewpoint.

(A) *Industrial scheme*

Assumptions
    start on site in 6 months' time
    building period of 15 months
    letting period of 6 months
    average rental value of £60 per m² (on gross internal area)
    investment yield of 9%
    building cost for average unit size say £250 per m²
    finance cost of say 14% p.a. effective (13·5% nominal)

Appraisal

	p.a.
(a) *Estimated Value*	
Income − 4,000 m² @ £60 m²	£240,000
Y.P. in perpetuity @ 9%	11·11
Capital value on completion	£2,666,500

Estimated Costs

(a) Land costs

acquisition cost		£350,000
compensation to existing		
tenants say		£20,000
		£370,000

(b) Demolition and site clearance cost

say	£50,000
	£420,000

(c) Building costs
4,000 m² @ £250 m²   £1,000,000

(d) Ancillary costs
access roads, car parking etc. say

	£100,000	£1,100,000
		£1,520,000

(e) Consultants fees
architects, QS fees @ say 10%
(of c & d)

	£110,000
	£1,630,000

(f) Contingencies @ say 3% of costs
(excl. land & demolition costs)

	36,500
	£1,666,500

(g) Short term finance @ say 14% p.a.
on land costs for 27 months

£127,000

on demolition costs for 21
months   £13,000
on building and ancillary costs,
consultants fees & contingencies ½ × 15 months plus letting

delay i.e. 13·5 months	£198,000	£338,000
		£2,004,500

(h) Letting and sale fees
    letting fees @ say 15% of
      estimated income   £36,000
    advertising, brochures etc. say
                    £5,000
    sale fees of investment @ say 2%
              £53,500   £94,500

    Total Costs   £2,098,000 £2,098,000

    Potential Capital Profit on Sale   £568,500

Viability of Development
Potential capital profit as percentage of costs

$$= \frac{568,500}{2,098,000} \times 100\% = 27 \cdot 1\%$$

Potential capital profit as percentage of value

$$= \frac{568,500}{2,666,500} \times 100\% = 21 \cdot 3\%$$

Potential development yield

$$= \frac{240,000}{2,098,000} \times 100\% = 11 \cdot 44\% \text{ p.a.}$$

    Investment Yield 9%
    ∴ Annual Profit = 11·44% − 9% = 2·44% p.a.

i.e. a mark up of $\dfrac{2 \cdot 44}{9} \times 100\% = 27 \cdot 1\%$

If planning permission were obtainable for this scheme the developer would be well rewarded for his effort assuming that he would be satisfied normally with a 20% return on costs. However, due to the additional risks involved of acquiring the site from two owners separately a higher return of say 25%

would probably be required. Nevertheless the industrial development would still be viable.

(B) Revised mixed use scheme

Assumptions for office and residential development
    4 storey office building on site area of 500 m² (i.e. plot ratio
    of 2:1) office building will be built whilst industrial estate
    is being built and will also take 6 months to let
    rental level in the area is about £130 per m²
    investment yield of 7% (i.e. not prime)
    building cost of £700 per m²
    6 residential units on site area of 500 m²
    cost of residential units – 6 @ £40,000 = £240,000

The office building and the block of 6 flats occupy a total site area of 1,000 m². The site for the industrial development is therefore reduced in size by 10% to 9,000 m² and all the cost and value figures in the original appraisal will be similarly reduced with the exception of land and demolition costs and the finance on these items.

The revised appraisal for the industrial development will therefore be as follows:

Capital value	£2,666,500
less 10%	£266,500
	£2,400,000

Costs		
Building and ancillary costs	£1,100,000	
Consultant's fees	£110,000	
Contingencies	£36,500	
Finance on above	£338,000	
Agents fees	£94,500	
	£1,679,000	
less 10%	£168,000	
Total Cost (excl. land and demolition cost)	£1,511,000	

Office Scheme Appraisal
Estimated Value

Income 1,000 m² less 20%	p.a.
i.e. 800 m² @ £130 m²	£104,000
YP in perpetuity @ 7%	14·286
Capital value on completion	£1,485,500

Estimated Costs

(a) Building costs
    1,000 m² @ £700 m²   £700,000

(b) Ancillary costs
    access road, car parking,
    landscaping etc. say   £30,000
                                    £730,000

(c) Consultants fees
    architects, QS etc. fees
    @ say 12·5%   £91,000
                                    £821,000

(d) Contingencies @ say 3%   £24,500
                                    £845,500

(e) Short term finance @ 14% p.a. – on
    building and ancillary costs and
    fees for ½ × 15 months plus let-
    ting delay i.e. 13·5 months   £134,500
                                    £980,000

(f) Letting and sale fees
    letting fees @ say 10%
        of income   £10,500
        advertising say   £3,000
        sale fees @ say 2% £29,500 £43,000

    Estimated Total Costs
    (excluding land & demolition
        costs)   £1,023,000

Overall Appraisal

Total capital value: Industrial   £2,666,500
                     Office   £1,485,500 £4,152,000

Total costs: Industrial   £1,511,000
                     Office   £1,023,000
                     Residential   £240,000
                     Land, demolition
                     etc.   £560,000 £3,334,000

∴ *Potential Capital Profit*   £818,000

Viability of Development

$$\text{Profit as percentage of costs} = \frac{818,000}{3,334,000} \times 100\% = 24 \cdot 53\%$$

$$\text{Profit as percentage of value} = \frac{818,000}{4,152,000} \times 100\% = 19 \cdot 7\%$$

If the developer was prepared to accept a 25% return on costs (20% on capital value) then the revised scheme would be just viable, although less viable than the original proposal which was unacceptable to the local authority. Would the original proposal receive permission on appeal? Would the delay be worthwhile? Assuming the developer finds the revised scheme accepable how can the authority assess whether this is the maximum gain they could achieve? On the other hand in allowing office development on this site could they be accused of "selling" planning permission?

From the authority's viewpoint, there are many problems involved in negotiating the S.52 agreement, bearing in mind that it will be wary of demanding too much "planning gain" in case no development occurs at all due to unacceptably reduced profit margins to the developer. The main problems involved for the authority are:

it cannot be certain what a developer's minimum acceptable profit margin would be, as any planning gain must be paid out of "excess" profit.

it cannot be certain what price the developer paid for the site.

it cannot be certain how much the scheme will cost to build or how much it will be worth.

it cannot be certain at what rate of interest the developer will be able to borrow money.

In any negotiations therefore the authority will be in a poor position, negotiating with one hand effectively tied behind its back. Further problems relate to whether the authority could be accused of sacrificing normal planning policies for financial gain by allowing office development in an area where office development would perhaps not normally be permitted. This could also set a dangerous precedent. Nevertheless it could also be argued that the scheme as a whole was acceptable in planning terms and shows how a forward thinking authority using initiative and bargaining skill could secure meaningful benefits (much needed new housing) in times of cash limits and cut-backs in local government spending, at no cost to rate-payers.

STUART MORLEY

For bibliography, sample computer printout and available software please see end of Chapter 4.

CHAPTER 2

Partnership Schemes and Ground Rent Calculations

INTRODUCTION

Chapter 1 discussed the use of residual valuations in assessing the capital value of development sites where the freehold interest could be acquired by a developer. In certain circumstances it is common for the freeholder of land to retain his freehold interest.

This version of the residual calculation is most commonly used in "partnership" situations, often between local authorities and developers, where one party grants a long lease (usually 125 years or longer) allowing the developer to undertake the development in the normal way but paying an annaul rent for the land rather than a capital sum. Normally the landowner would be able to exert considerable control over the development if he wished to, and in addition the ground rent receivable would be reviewed regularly to tie in with reviews of the sub leases to the occupational tenants.

This type of arrangement, albeit in a simplified form, has been used for centuries, initially by the large landed estates when their land was developed in the expansion of our major cities in the eighteenth and nineteenth centuries. It enabled a wide variety of builders to undertake residential and later commercial development on long building leases thereby ensuring that the freehold owners retained control over the form and content of building with an annual income and eventual reversion.

The central areas of many cities that were badly damaged in the second world war were redeveloped on this basis, but with the local authority as landowner. Subsequently during the last two decades it has become increasingly common for the central areas of most cities to be similarly redeveloped to provide modern shopping facilities. More recently there have been examples of partnership schemes between local authorities and private sector developers for all types of commercial and residential development and particularly as a means of undertaking industrial development in inner city locations.

The early agreements between freeholder and developer were simple landlord and tenant arrangements, often at a fixed ground rent for the length of the lease. With the advent of inflation and greater local authority involvement in implementation, these agreements are now more sophisticated often warranting the description of true partnership agreements. In place of a fixed ground rent for the duration of the ground lease elaborate arrangements are now commonplace covering risk and equity sharing, participation and yield protection.

There are a great variety of partnership agreements but a detailed discussion of their different forms, advantages and disadvantages is beyond the scope of this book. However, the main variations in the methods of financial appraisal used to assess ground rent and equity shares etc. will be discussed and a brief summary of the main advantages to local authorities and developers of using partnership agreements as a means of undertaking development are listed below to explain why their use is now so widespread.

ADVANTAGES OF PARTNERSHIP SCHEMES
From the local authorities' viewpoint, partnership agreements possess the following main advantages:

They enable developments to be initiated by the authority rather than waiting for developers to respond to plans that they have prepared. This is particularly important in some inner city locations where local authority involvement is essential to enable a developer to arrange funding.

They enable greater control to be exercised over the development itself and any future alterations during the period of the lease. This is because the control exercisable by a landlord exceeds that exercisable under Town Planning legislation.

They enable the authority in many cases to secure a safe ground rental income, to participate in the profits of development and to participate hopefully in future rental growth, which in part it will help create through the general prosperity of the area as well as the success of the scheme itself.

They enable development to be implemented using the experience and expertise of the private sector without in many cases the authority undertaking the risks of development itself. Local authorities can therefore be seen to control development and participate in its rewards, without putting ratepayers' money at risk. However, in certain locations local authorities may have to share risks to ensure participation by the private sector. This is discussed later.

They enable finance for development to be arranged which would be more difficult, if not impossible to arrange (under present legislation) if a local authority considered undertaking development itself.

From the private sector developer's viewpoint there are also a number of advantages of entering into a partnership with a local authority rather than acquiring and owning the freehold of a development site.

A local authority's powers of compulsory purchase are often essential if a large central area site in multiple ownership is to be assembled for development. The alternative of private acquisition could be time consuming, expensive and difficult if indeed it were possible at all.

The cost of acquiring and holding the site during development will not be incurred thereby lessening capital commitment and risk.

The developer is working in partnership with a local authority. Planning conflicts should therefore be lessened, more information should be available on other proposed developments etc. and planning permission should be ensured. Some commentators argue that because the local authority have a financial stake in a scheme it gives tham an incentive to act more commercially to the benefit of the private sector.

THE CALCULATION OF GROUND RENT

A fairly standard form of appraisal is shown below where a local authority wish to see a site developed in accordance with their development brief, have put it out under a competitive tender and wish to know the ground rent, equity share and return on their site purchase costs. For the purposes of simplicity or comparability the same scheme as illustrated in the previous chapter will be used (summarised below) the only difference being that, the land is assumed to have been acquired by the local authority, using its compulsory purchase powers for £1,000,000 inclusive of all disturbance costs, fees etc. The calculations for ground rent are to be based on a 125 year lease with regular (5 year) rent reviews, but with a peppercorn rent payable during the period of development.

Summary of development scheme used in previous chapter

Income		£658,500
Yield @ 7%		14·2857
Capital Value		£9,407,000
Development Costs		
Building Cost incl. fees	£4,640,500	
Contingencies	£139,000	
Finance @ 14% p.a.	£850,500	
Letting fees etc.	£312,000	
Total	£5,942,000	
Return for Risk & Profit	£1,599,000	£7,541,000
Site Valuation on completion of development		£1,866,000
Site Value today (allowing for interest charges and acquisition costs)		£1,311,500

Ground rent calculation

The basic difference between an appraisal to calculate ground rent rather than capital site value are that firstly the calculations are undertaken on an annual rather than a capital basis and secondly, from the developer's viewpoint, there are no finance charges to be incurred on site acquisition as these will be borne by the local authority unless the developer acquires all or part of the site and then hands it over at no cost to the local authority but obviously in return for payment of a reduced ground rent. A typical appraisal would be as follows assuming a 125 year ground lease is to be granted on land assembled by the local authority:

Estimated Income
expected rents from occupational
tenants   £658,500 p.a.

Estimated Costs
inclusive of building costs,
  ancillary costs, all fees and
  short term finance   (1)   £5,942,000

Development Yield
initial investment yield of say
  7·5% p.a. (or cost of long term
  leaseback finance)   (2)   0·075
annual return for risk & profit
  of say 1·75% p.a.   (3)   0·0175
annual Sinking Fund to recoup
  capital over length of lease   (4)   —
∴ Total development yield
  required 9·25% p.a.   (5)   0·0925   £549,500 p.a.

Ground Rent
∴ Ground Rent available to
  local authority (on completion
  of development)   (6)   £109,000 p.a.

Future rental growth (the equity) would typically be apportioned as follows: (7)

Local authority $\dfrac{109,000}{658,500} \times 100\% = 16\cdot5\%$

Developer $\dfrac{549,500}{658,500} \times 100\% = 83\cdot5\%$

The initial return to the local authority from its land acquisition could be shown in the following two ways:

Site Purchase Cost		£1,000,000
Interest on purchase cost during development period of say 3 years @ 11% p.a.	(8)	£368,000
Total cost on completion of development when ground rent is payable		£1,368,000
∴ Initial return to local authority	(9)	$\dfrac{109,000}{368,000} \times 100\%$ = 8% p.a.

An alternative approach would be to compare annual interest payments, incurred by purchasing the site, with annual income (ground rent):

Total cost of land acquisition on completion of development	£1,368,000
Annual interest repayments @ 11%	0·11
	£150,500 p.a.
Initial ground rent	£109,000 p.a.
∴ Initial deficit	£41,500 p.a.

This is the initial situation which will change at every rent review assuming rental growth occurs. Obviously the greater the degree of rental growth the more favourable the local authority's financial position will be also bearing in mind that the interest repayments will be fixed. It should also be emphasised that criteria other than financial criteria may be important to a local authority in assessing a scheme, and even if a poor financial return appears possible they may proceed in order to obtain other benefits. In other words they would be making an overall assessment based on a cost benefit analysis.

If either the freehold land owner, or the developer, wished to sell their interests, *on completion of the scheme*, then the following valuations might apply:

Freeholder

Ground Rent Income	£109,000p.a.
Y.P. in perpetuity @ say 7%	14·2857
Capital Value	£1,557,000

Developer

Full Rental Value	£658,500p.a.
Less Ground Rent	£109,000p.a.
Net Income	£549,500p.a.
Y.P. in perpetuity @ say 7·5%	13·3333
Capital Value	£7,326,500
Total Costs (as above)	£5,942,000
∴ Profit	£1,384,500

∴ Return on Costs

$$\frac{1,384,500}{5,942,000} \times 100\%$$

$$= 23\cdot3\%$$

Estimated Costs

(1) This is the total cost figure excluding an allowance to cover developer's risk and profit (allowed for separately) and excluding the cost of site acquisition, as obviously this cost will not now be incurred by the developer. The cost of fees (£188,000) for selling the completed investment has been included in the total cost of £5,942,000. As explained previously the inclusion of this item of expenditure will depend on the developer's intention. But if the developer does not intend to sell the completed investment then funding costs will be incurred. If the developer is a financial institution (increasingly common, particularly in partnership schemes) then again no sale will occur, as the scheme will be retained as a long term investment. However, in this situation a project management fee might well be included.

By not acquiring the freehold interest in the site a developer will save not only capital outlay but also associated legal fees, agents fees, stamp duty and finance charges. However, legal fees, agents fees and stamp duty will still be incurred on the preparation of the building agreement and acquisition of the ground lease, although these have not been shown separately in the above appraisal.

Investment Yield or Cost of Long Term Finance

(2) The total required development yield must be calculated to ensure that the developer receives sufficient return before

calculating the residual ground rent. In the original appraisal shown summarised an investment yield of 7% was used to capitalise income where the freehold investment value was required. In this example the developer will have a less attractive interest – albeit a very long leasehold interest of 125 years. Nevertheless leasehold investments are generally considered less attractive by investors as they do not have total control of the investment, there is more management, the investment is a wasting asset and rent payable will probably be reviewable on an upward only basis related to rental value rather than income. Yields tend to be slightly higher, depending on the length of lease, the covenants in the lease and the type of property. An extra 0·5% has been allowed here. Depending on the state of the property market and the availability of investments this margin could vary, and for some prime retail schemes could disappear altogether.

An alternative approach, used by developers considering retaining the completed development as a long term investment, would be to use the cost of long term finance rather than the investment yield. In many funding arrangements the leaseback 'rate of interest' would be similar to the investment yield although this will depend on how the equity and the development risks are to be shared as well as how the question of control is resolved.

Return for Risk and Profit

(3) Previously it was assumed that a developer would want a margin to cover risk and profit of about 20% on costs. Although this margin will vary according to the particular scheme and the state of the market, 20% was taken as a norm. In this example a slightly higher mark up has been used of 23·3% to give an annual return of 1·75% ($1·75/7·5 \times 100\%$ = 23·3%) for reasons explained below.

It could be argued that as this scheme is being undertaken in partnership with a local authority and the developer's outlay is reduced by the savings in land cost, the developer might be prepared to accept a slightly lower profit margin but much will depend on the arrangements regarding rental guarantees, subsequent gearing and the basis of rent reviews as discussed more fully below. While it is true that the developers *capital* outlay is reduced by the saving in land cost, additional *annual* expenditure (ground rent) will be incurred. In many situations this would be a guaranteed minimum figure (e.g. central area shopping schemes). A developer should, therefore, require a higher percentage profit margin on costs to compensate.

Sinking Fund

(4) When valuing leasehold investments, it is common practice to allow for a sinking fund to replace by the end of the lease what is, in effect, a wasting asset compared to a freehold. No allowance for a sinking fund has been made here as the lease is so long that the annual payments would be insignificantly small and in any case it would be difficult to find a company willing to enter into this type of arrangement for periods longer than about 60 years. Nevertheless the investment yield, as mentioned above, may well reflect that the investment is a wasting asset.

Development Yield

(5) The development yield required is made up of the investment yield (or cost of long term finance) and the annual return to cover risk and profit (see previous chapter). So long as the developer achieves a 9·25% yield he will be prepared to give away the remainder of annual income as a ground rent payment to the landowner (in this case local authority). Obviously the developer would like to achieve a higher yield than 9·25% but in a competitive tender situation this is the minimum figure needed to make the scheme worthwhile. It is arguable that if the developer were not in a competitive situation then a negotiated settlement might result in a higher development yield.

Ground Rent

(6) The ground rent would normally become payable after completion of the development or after a specified time limit equivalent to the estimated length of the development period. During the development period a peppercorn (or zero rent) would be paid, so that the ground rent effectively becomes payable when income is received by the developer from letting the completed scheme. In many partnership agreements, particularly central area shopping schemes, the local authority's

interest would be safeguarded by ensuring that the estimated ground rent was a minimum figure which could be increased if and when rental income from the occupational tenants increased, but could not be reduced if the scheme was less profitable than the developer expected. If the ground rent was not a minimum figure there would be a danger that the developer would overbid initially to win the nomination and then reduce the ground rent subsequently when actual costs and rents were known. Nevertheless in certain situations where tenant demand is weak and the development risks are perceived to be great, no developer may be prepared to take the risk of offering a minimum ground rent. In this situation the local authority may be faced with either having to abandon the scheme or else entering into a true partnership and sharing the development risk with the developer. Sometimes this will involve local authorities putting up some of the development costs, reducing further the developer's outlay and hence risk. In more extreme situations (e.g. nursery unit factory developments in inner city locations) the ground rent rather than being a predetermined guaranteed minimum figure, would typically be calculated on completion of development with the local authority guaranteeing the developer a predetermined return on actual costs incurred, but subject to maximum and minimum gearing, before any ground rent was payable. Alternatively local authorities may even have to take an overriding lease back from the developer and take the risk of subletting themselves. These solutions are discussed and illustrated later in the chapter.

Equity Sharing

(7) This arrangement, common in central area shopping schemes and other prime schemes, effectively means that the initial relationship between ground rent and rack rent is maintained at every rent review. Every time the rack rent increases by say 50% the ground rent would also increase by 50%. It is important to clarify the term rack rent in this context as there is a difference between rental value and rental income. From a freeholder's viewpoint the former is desirable as it ensures that ground rents are calculated as a percentage of the maximum rental income which the scheme could produce

if there were no voids or large units sublet on a premium and ground lease basis. A developer may try and resist the use of the term rental value due to the above factors and the problems which could result during future refurbishment arguing that a higher development yield (and hence lower ground rent) would result.

Although the equity sharing arrangement in the above example is a common and simple method of apportioning future rental growth it is by no means the only method. In some cases a local authority may prefer to receive a lower initial ground rent in return for a higher share of future rental growth. A developer may also prefer this arrangement in certain situations particularly if the ground rent is to be a guaranteed minimum figure as the developer will then be guaranteeing a smaller sum (less initial risk), but giving away more equity if the scheme is successful.

Local Authority's Initial Return

(8) As ground rent will not be receivable until the development has been completed, interest on land cost should be allowed until income is receivable otherwise an inaccurate return will be shown. At the time of writing the cost of local authority borrowed money is about 11% p.a. on the money markets, although the actual cost, due to pooled loan repayments, may be less, or more depending on an individual authority's circumstances.

(9) The return or yield to the local authority is calculated in the same way that the development yield was calculated in the previous chapter by relating income received divided by cost incurred to receive that income, and expressing it in percentage terms. In this case because the land was acquired at below its full development value the yield to the landowner is higher than the investment yield for the scheme as a whole. Not surprisingly therefore this scheme would be a good investment for the authority.

GROUND RENTS AND PREMIUMS

In many partnership developments local authorities prefer to receive a premium in return for accepting a lower ground rent so that this capital sum can be used to supplement their capital spending elsewhere within their area or possibly to help purchase the site itself. In an era of public sector expenditure constraints this desire may be particularly strong. This capital premium could be looked upon as being a non-site specific planning gain. Alternatively some element of planning gain could be incorporated within the development scheme similarly increasing the developer's costs and so reducing the ground rent payable. Where site value forms a large percentage of the total projects value (e.g. in high value locations, such as Central London for offices and many town centres for retail) then funding institutions will resist an unfavourable gearing where the freeholder receives more than about 10–15% of rack rental value unless the lease is not subject to upward only rent reviews. This resistance is less applicable for prime retail schemes.

A common way of achieving reduced gearing is for a premium to be paid as illustrated below. If a large proportion of the equity was receivable by the freeholder, the leaseholder could be left with an exposed top slice income in the event of a subsequent decline in rack rental income (i.e. if rents fall or there are voids) and where the ground rent is reviewable on an upwards only basis. A premium reduces gearing making the basis of rent reviews less important and consequently may lead to a reduction in development yield required.

Another solution to the problem is to have true side by side sharing of rack rental *income* which may lead to a reduction in development yield required of about 0·5 percentage points.

Revised ground rent calculation assuming a premium of £1,000,000 payable on completion of development

Estimated Income (as before)		£658,500 p.a.
Estimated Costs		
development costs (as before)	£5,942,000	
premium	£1,000,000	
Total costs	£6,942,000	
Development Yield – 9%	0·09	£625,000 p.a.
Revised ground rent		£33,500 p.a.

In this situation the apportionment of future rental growth might be:

Local Authority $\dfrac{33,500}{658,500} \times 100\% = 5 \cdot 1\%$ say 5%

Developer $\dfrac{625,000}{658,500} \times 100\% = 94 \cdot 9\%$ say 95%

It is clear that in return for receiving a premium, the initial ground rent and subsequent equity share to the local authority is reduced. Had the premium been payable at the start of development rather than on completion of development and perhaps used to help pay for site acquisition, the developer would have to allow for the cost of short term finance over the whole period, which would increase the cost, to him, of having to pay the premium earlier and so reduce the ground rent still further. Owing to public expenditure cuts and controls on capital spending introduced in the 1980 Local Government Planning and Land Act and as modified by subsequent circulars, it is now commonplace for part at least of land costs to be paid by the developer. The effect this has on the calculation of ground rent is further illustrated in the worked example at the end of this chapter.

In certain circumstances, depending on the relationship between interest rates and development yields, it might be more beneficial for the authority to maximise its ground rent and equity share and rather than accept a premium from the developer, borrow the money elsewhere at current money market interest rates (assuming that capital spending limits were not exceeded) or sell other assets which it may own to realise the capital. However, only 30% of capital receipts could be used in this way, in the year in which they were realised, due to central government constraints on capital spending. In the example used earlier if borrowing was the solution adopted the calculation would be altered as follows:

Ground Rent (as in original example)	£109,000 p.a.
less Interest on loan of £1,000,000 @ 11% p.a.	£110,000 p.a.
Net Income (deficit)	−£1,000 p.a.

But the equity share will now be: $\dfrac{109,000}{658,500} \times 100\% = 16 \cdot 5\%$

A comparison between the two alternatives therefore shows

that where £1,000,000 is obtained by way of a premium from the developer, initial income is higher (£33,500 compared to −£1,000) but the equity share is lower (5% compared to 16·5%). Which alternative is preferable to the authority will depend on other commitments, central government controls on how local authorities raise and spend money, the difference between initial yields on property investments and the rate of interest for borrowing money in the money markets, and on expectations of future rental growth of the scheme. Expectations of high rental growth may favour the second alternative. For example, if by the first rent review rents had increased by say 75% then the local authority's net income would be £57,500 (developer pays premium) compared to £80,000 (L.A. borrows externally) a reversal of the initial situation. Subsequent rental growth would further enhance the second alternative.

In the example used here the difference in interest rates and yields between the two alternatives was not great, but that will not necessarily always be the case. For example when general interest rates are very high, the cost to the authority of borrowing on the money markets would be even higher than that shown above. If the development being considered was a prime scheme with a development yield of say 6% or 7% then a much greater difference would result from a comparison of the two alternatives, as the following calculation shows.

Premium paid by developer

Estimated income		£658,500 p.a.
Estimated costs		
development costs	£5,942,000	
premium	£1,000,000	
	£6,942,000	
Development Yield – say 7%	0·07	£486,000 p.a.
Ground Rent		£172,500 p.a.

$$\text{L.A. Equity share} \frac{172,500}{658,500} \times 100\% = 26\cdot2\%$$

Capital borrowed externally by Local Authority

Estimated income	£658,500 p.a.

Estimated costs	£5,942,000	
Development yield @ 7%	0·07	£416,000 p.a.
Ground Rent		£242,500 p.a.
Interest on loan of £1,000,000		
@say 15% p.a.	0·15	£150,000 p.a.
Net Income		£92,500 p.a.

$$\text{L.A. Equity share} \frac{242,500}{658,500} \times 100\% = 36 \cdot 8\%$$

The comparison is now between an initial income of £172,500 p.a. (26·2% equity share) and £92,500 p.a. (36·8% equity share). Again assuming rents increase 75% by the first review the authority's net income will then be £302,000 in the first alternative and £274,000 in the second alternative. In contrast to the earlier set of calculations the first alternative still shows a favourable position for the authority and longer time would need to elapse for the situation to reverse. In conclusion it can be stated that, ceteris paribus, a wide margin in interest rates would favour a local authority obtaining capital by way of a premium and reduced ground rent.

PARTICIPATION

A further refinement of many shopping centre partnership agreements is a participation clause which involves the residual calculation being reworked shortly after completion of development, using actual rather than estimated figures. Due to possible inflation of costs and rents during the development period it is likely that actual rents and costs will differ from those estimated and the purpose of the participation clause is to reflect these changes in a revised ground rent and possibly equity share. This is particularly likely in many shopping centre partnership schemes due to the length of time that often elapses between the tender date, when the ground rent offer is made, and completion date when the scheme is income producing. The revised equity share will then determine the local authority's income at subsequent rent reviews. If the initial agreement stated that the estimated ground rent was to be a minimum figure (subject to upward only review and therefore a first charge out of rental income) then the object of the participation clause will be to increase the ground rent if rents have increased by more then development costs. If the reverse occurs then the initially agreed ground rent will remain as a minimum figure and any reduction in income will be suffered by the developer as this is part of the risk of development. If the scheme is not fully let at participation, then many partnership agreements allow for rental value to be used for the unlet parts, in order to obtain the total rent as mentioned earlier.

The following three examples illustrate the calculation of a revised ground rent based on different assumptions of increases in rents and costs, assuming the initial agreement (contained in the development brief) stated that at participation date any equity would be apportioned 50:50.

Calculation at participation date (shortly after completion of development)

(a)

Actual Income (say 25% higher than estimated)		£823,000 p.a.
less initial ground rent		£109,000 p.a.
Net income		£714,000 p.a.
Actual Costs (say 10% higher than estimated)	£6,536,000	
Development Yield – 9·25%	0·0925	£604,500 p.a.
Residue or Excess		£109,500 p.a.
50% of excess to L.A. (i.e. say £55,000)		
∴ *revised ground rent*		£164,000 p.a.

$$\therefore \textit{revised equity share to L.A.} = \frac{164,000}{823,000} \times 100\%$$

$$= 19\cdot9\% \text{ say } 20\% \text{ (16·5\% originally)}$$

(b)

Actual Income (+25%)	£823,000 p.a.
Less initial ground rent	£109,000 p.a.
Net Income	£714,000 p.a.

Actual Costs (+25%)	£7,427,500	
Development Yield – 9·25%	0·0925	£687,000 p.a.
Residue or Excess		£27,000 p.a.
50% of excess to L.A. (i.e. £13,500)		
∴ revised ground rent		£122,500 p.a.

$$\therefore \text{ revised equity share to L.A.} \frac{122,500}{823,000} \times 100\%$$

$$= 14\cdot9\% \quad \text{say} \quad 15\% \quad (16\cdot5\%$$

$$\text{initially})$$

A problem arises here for the developer, because the revised ground rent is higher than the previously agreed minimum figure, whereas the revised equity share is lower. According to many partnership agreements the original equity share would apply for the remainder of the lease, even though a higher ground rent is also paid, as it was stated to be a minimum figure. As the difference in this example is small (15% compared to 16·5%) the burden to the developer is not that great but in the third example below serious problems could result and some developers will resist the possibility of a minimum equity sharing arrangement.

(c)

Actual Income (+5%)		£691,500 p.a.
Less Ground Rent		£109,000 p.a.
∴ Net Income		£582,500 p.a.
Actual Costs (+25%)	£7,427,500	
Development Yield @ 9·25%	0·0925	£687,000 p.a.
Residue		−£104,500 p.a.

In this example there is no excess to share and the initial ground rent and equity share remain unaltered if the original agreement stated them to be minimum figures. The developer in this situation would therefore be faced with a reduced profit:

Developer's Income $= £582,500$ p.a.

$$\therefore \text{Actual Development Yield} = \frac{582,500}{7,427,500} \times 100\% = 7\cdot84\%$$

Assuming an investment yield of 7.5% (as before), this results in an annual return to the developer of only 0·34% (a mark up on outlay of only 4·5%). In extreme situations where there is an even wider margin between costs and rents this return could be eliminated altogether, possibly even resulting in a loss. One could argue that this is all part of the risk involved in development which the developer was prepared to accept and has to accept in all speculative development situations; that is why typically a 20–25% mark up is allowed in case this situation arises. However, whilst a large development company or institutional developer could bear a loss due to financial reserves and profits from other developments, small companies might not be able to and could go bankrupt, possibly leaving part of the development unfinished. In such situations local authorities will be under considerable pressure to allow a renegotiation of terms more favourable to the developer.

YIELD PROTECTION

Most partnership agreements, as illustrated above, allow the developer a yield protection clause to ensure that the required yield on actual development costs is received once the minimum ground rent has been paid. An alternative way of expressing this is to say that the Local Authority's ground rent is a first charge out of income, the developer's costs a second charge, the return for risk and profit a third charge, and any surplus a fourth charge being apportioned between them in some predetermined way. A refinement contained in some agreements gives the developer slightly greater protection by allowing a second and higher development yield to be used when calculating the revised ground rent at the participation date.

For example assume that, in the original tender, the developer stated that an overall 9·25% development yield would be used to derive the initial (minimum) ground rent, but that when the calculations were reworked at the participation date using actual figures a 9·75% yield would be required. In the last of the three examples shown above, no difference would result, but in the other two examples the developer would be in an improved situation. This is illustrated by using the second example.

Actual Income (+25%)		£823,000 p.a.
Less Initial Ground Rent		£109,000 p.a.
Net Income		£714,000 p.a.
Actual Costs (+25%)	£7,427,500	
Revised Development Yield 9·75%	0·0975	£724,000 p.a.
Residue		−£10,000 p.a.

Therefore the ground rent remains unaltered at £109,000 p.a. and the developer is £13,500 p.a. better off than would have been the case without the higher yield protection clause, when the revised ground rent would have been £122,500 p.a. However, it must be borne in mind that in a competitive tender, the improved position shown above may mean the developer is outbid by a competitor who is prepared to take a more optimistic (and therefore risky) view of the future.

ALTERNATIVE EQUITY SHARING ARRANGEMENTS

In some partnership schemes, particularly those involving industrial development in areas where development risks are considered by the private sector to be greater, a variety of alternative arrangements of income and risk sharing have evolved, some of which would avoid the potential problems (to the developer) mentioned in the preceding section. Three alternatives to the "four slice" method illustrated above are described as follows.

"3 Slice" Method

This method is a simplified arrangement of the typical four slice method. The ground rent is still a first charge out of income, the developer's costs still a second charge, but the remaining profit is then apportioned between the two parties in some predetermined way. The difference therefore is that the developer's profit is not a separate third charge and as a result the guaranteed ground rent will be smaller. The smaller the ground rent, the larger the authority's share of the third charge. From the local authority's viewpoint therefore it stands to receive a higher income if the scheme is more successful than expected, but will receive less if the scheme is less successful, as the guaranteed first charge is smaller. Part of the development risks are borne by the authority as can be seen clearly from the comparative diagrams and examples below.

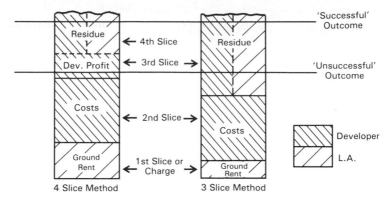

4 Slice Method   3 Slice Method

The same example as used previously in this chapter is used below for comparative purposes on the assumption that the guaranteed ground rent is £50,000 p.a. (rather than £109,000 as before), and the Local Authority now receive 50% of the equity. The calculation on completion of the scheme could now become:

	"Successful" Outcome		"Unsuccessful" Outcome	
	£	£	£	£
Actual Income		823,000 p.a.		691,500 p.a.
		(+25%)		(+5%)
Less Ground Rent		50,000 p.a.		50,000 p.a.
Net Income		773,000 p.a.		641,500 p.a.
Actual Costs	£6,536,000		£7,427,500	
	(+10%)		(+25%)	
Developers Return				
@ 7·5%	0·075	490,000 p.a.	0·075	557,000 p.a.
Residue		283,000 p.a.		84,500 p.a.
L.A.'s share (50%)		141,500 p.a.		42,000 p.a.
∴ *Total L.A. Income*		191,500 p.a.		92,000 p.a.

The comparable 4 slice method illustrated previously produced a narrower band of figures for total Local Authority Income of £164,000 p.a. and £109,000 p.a. respectively using the same assumptions of rental and cost increase. In really extreme circumstances it should be emphasised that in the example above the Local Authority's income could fall as low as £50,000 p.a. as this is the minimum guaranteed figure (first charge).

An alternative arrangement common in many industrial partnership developments would be for the scheme to be sold to an investor on completion, so that the authority received a capital sum (rather than a ground rent), but nevertheless still participating in the success or failure of the development by receiving a share of the capital profit realisable on sale.

"2 Slice" Method

There are various permutations of the 2 Slice Method. One involves the developer recovering costs and previously agreed profit as first charge with the residue going to the local authority. This arrangement is obviously more risky for the local authority as it has no first charge or minimum ground rent, and if things went badly wrong, it could end up with a small or zero income. On the other hand if the scheme was very successful, the authority would receive all the excess income. From the developer's viewpoint the risks of development are, of course, virtually eliminated unless things go disastrously wrong (i.e. if costs exceeded agreed ceiling figures). As a result of the reduction in risk it is probable that the developer would reduce his profit margin, as shown below. A further risk for the local authority is that there is now less incentive for the developer to work quickly and to carefully control costs, as

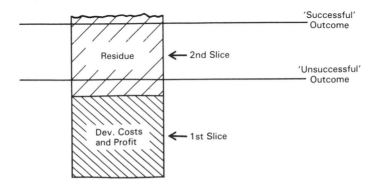

	"Successful" Outcome		"Unsuccessful" Outcome	
	£	£	£	£
Actual Income		823,000 p.a.		691,500 p.a.
Actual Costs	6,536,000		7,427,500	
Developer's Return (incl. profit) @ say 8·5%	0·085	555,500 p.a.	0·085	631,500 p.a.
Residue to LA		267,500 p.a.		60,000 p.a.

profit is virtually secure, so care must be taken in selecting a reputable developer and phrasing the legal agreement to lessen the chance of this happening.

From these figures it is clear that the local authority is now bearing a considerable part of the development risks and as a result the income it is likely to receive could vary enormously. As before this arrangement could equally well apply if the entire scheme was to be sold on completion, in which case the authority would receive a capital sum related to the success of the scheme.

For many local authorities wanting to promote small unit industrial development a common variant of the 2 slice arrangement is a *lease and leaseback*. There are many varieties even of this arrangement, some involving a developer on a fee or reduced profit basis, some where the local authority acts as developer itself.

Where a developer is involved the arrangement is similar to the two slice method described above. On completion of the development, but prior to letting the scheme to occupational tenants, the entire scheme is leased back to the local authority at a rent geared to full rental value and hopefully, from the developers viewpoint, equivalent to a prearranged return on expected costs. The authority then sublet to occupational tenants. The advantages to the authority are that it retains control over letting, will hopefully receive a profit rent (difference between the rent received from occupational tenants and the rent paid to the developer) but does not have the inconvenience of undertaking the actual development, as design and construction is the responsibility of the developer who will in return receive a profit. A further benefit is that the strength of the local authority's covenant (obviously much greater than a number of small private companies who would be the occupying tenants) should enable development finance to be obtained and at a more competitive rate. Obviously the main disadvantage is that most of the development risks are borne by the local authority.

A typical leaseback arrangement is illustrated below, again using the same scheme and assumptions as previously. The agreement provides for the leaseback rent to be 83·5% of FRV, (the equity sharing ratio used earlier in the chapter), which should give the developer an adequate return for risk and profit although in the circumstances of reduced risk for the developer a lower return might be sufficient.

	"Successful" Outcome £	"Unsuccessful" Outcome £
Actual Income (FRV)	823,000 p.a.	691,500 p.a.
Developers Return @ 83·5% of FRV	687,000 p.a.	577,500 p.a.
Residue to LA	136,000 p.a.	114,000 p.a.

There is a marked difference between these results and those of the 2 slice arrangement shown earlier. The local authority's income varies little as does the developer's but if costs are significantly higher than expected the developers return is very unattractive. However in the type of schemes being considered, the timescale is such that a fixed price building contract could probably be negotiated, thereby lessening the developers exposure. The main problem for the local authority is where some of the units remain unlet. This will not affect the rental *value*, and hence the leaseback rent, but it will obviously affect the rental *income*. If, in the above example, there were 10% voids – a far from unlikely event, then the Local Authority's income would fall by 65% from the figures shown above. Voids of more than 15% would result in a negative income to the Local Authority.

Where the local authority act as developer, the site would be leased directly to a funding institution and then leased back to the local authority to show the funding authority a suitable return on its investment. The local authority would therefore bear the total risks and organisational problems of development. A major problem of this approach and the lease-back method mentioned earlier is the capital spending implications under the 1980 Local Government Planning and Land Act.

A lease and leaseback arrangement is illustrated below using, for comparative purposes, the same basic scheme as previously, but with a developer involved only on a project management basis.

	"Successful" Outcome		"Unsuccessful" Outcome	
	£	£	£	£
Actual Income		823,000 p.a.		691,500 p.a.
Actual Costs development-				
costs	6,536,000		7,427,500	
project management fee @ say 5% of building cost	227,000		258,000	
	6,763,000		7,685,500	
Leaseback @ say 7%	0·07	473,500 p.a.	0·07	538,000 p.a.
LA Income		349,500 p.a.		153,500 p.a.
LA equity share		42·5%		22·2%

When comparing these figures with those from previous arrangements it is important to remember that here the local authority is acting as a developer and therefore shoulders all the risks. It is possible that if these risks are great, income receivable at the end of the day could be minimal as there is no safe first slice to fall back on. On the other hand if the scheme is reasonably successful the local authority should receive a higher return than in any of the previously discussed arrangements, although it is probable that the funder would want a share of this higher return (i.e. overage). Another reason for this is the leaseback rate of 7%, reflecting the improved security and reduced management problems of having the local authority as tenant. Due to Pension Fund / Insurance Company disenchantment with direct property investment the arrangement illustrated above would now more likely be arranged with a Finance House on say a 30 year mortgage with interest payment related to LIBOR. Initial return to the local authority would therefore be reduced but future return may be improved as rental growth would not be shared with the funder.

RESIDENTIAL PARTNERSHIP SCHEMES

In New Towns and Expanding Towns particularly, partnership arrangements between the public and private sectors have been common as a means of providing low income housing for sale as they enable the public sector to utilise the expertise of private sector builders whilst exerting greater control over the form of development and possibly the eventual sale price. The financial arrangements differ slightly from those described previously in this chapter as neither the local authority nor the builder retain a long term legal interest. The freehold is conveyed to the purchaser, the local authority receiving a capital sum covering the land element, and the developer receiving a capital profit covering the building element; any excess profit would be apportioned between them. A typical arrangement is shown below which would also be applicable to an industrial development if the freehold of the scheme were to be sold, on completion of development, to an investor.

Assume a local authority own a half hectare site valued at £150,000, which they wish to see developed for 15 houses. An agreement is entered into with a local builder who agrees to pay the authority £100,000 as a guaranteed sum for the land when the houses are completed, plus say 60% of the difference (if any) between the total sale price and total development costs (plus 15% profit). This agreement means that the local authority receives a guaranteed, but low, sum for its land holding in return for sharing in the profitability and risks of the development.

As the authority is sharing in the risks of development it has been assumed that the builder will be prepared to accept only a 15% return. When the houses are sold the calculations might be as follows:

	"Successful" Outcome		"Unsuccessful" Outcome	
	£	£	£	£
Actual Net Sale				
Price		1,100,000		950,000
Actual Development				
Costs				
(incl. land price of				
£100,000)	700,000		800,000	
15% profit	105,000	805,000	120,000	920,000
Residue		295,000		30,000
LA's Share (60%)		177,000		18,000
Developer's Share (40%)		118,000		12,000
∴ LA's Return (incl.				
original £100,000)		277,000		118,000
∴ Developer's Return		223,000		132,000

Where the development is "successful" the local authority achieve a much higher price for their land, £277,000 compared to the open market price of £150,000. However, if the scheme is "unsuccessful" they receive a lower price of only £118,000 with the possibility of receiving only £100,000 if the scheme was even less successful. Similarly the developer's return expressed as a percentage of total outlay (development costs + land costs) varies from 25·4% to 16·1%, whereas in a non-partnership situation where the land was acquired outright for £150,000 the return would vary from just over 46% to just over 11% – a much wider range.

WORKED EXAMPLE – to illustrate arrangements to cover site acquisition

Two years ago your client, a property development company, purchased four freehold properties now vacant for a total of £175,000. The properties have a total site area of 0·2 ha and are situated close to central London. The sites acquired form part of a site of 0·5 ha for which the local planning authority would favourably entertain an application for an office development of up to 12,500 m². The local authority own part of the balance of the site on which stand six houses. The remainder of the site they intend to acquire shortly at an estimated cost of £500,000.

Advise your clients of the ground rent and equity share you

would recommend be offered on the assumption that a 125 year lease was granted to your clients and they conveyed their valuable freehold interest to the local authority for a nominal consideration. Although the LA will use their CPO powers to complete the land assembly, due to expenditure cuts they require an immediate premium of £500,000 from your clients to cover the cost of site acquisition.

Assumptions

No information as to whether £175,000 represents today's market value of client's site. So a residual valuation must be undertaken to determine the overall site value and ∴ value of client's 0·2 hectares.

Fringe central London rents – say £150 m²
Investment yield (freehold) – say 7% (7·5% long leasehold)
Building costs – say £750 m²
Short term finance – say 14% p.a. (effective)
Building period say 18 months
Letting period 6 months
Pre-building period 6 months

Calculation of overall total site value

Expected Capital Value of development

12,500 m less say 20%		
– 10,000 m² @ £150 m²		£1,500,000 p.a.
Y.P. perpetuity @ say 7%		14·3
		£21,450,000

Expected Costs

Demolition etc. – minimal – say	£15,000	
Building & ancillary costs 12,500 m² @ say £750 m²	£9,375,000	
Architect's & Q.S. fees @ 12·5% on £9,375,000	£1,172,000	
	£10,547,000	
Contingencies @ say 3%	£316,500	
	£10,863,500	

Finance @ say 14% for ½ building period plus letting delay i.e. 15 months		£1,933,500	
		£12,797,000	
letting fees @ 15% FRV	£225,000		
Advertisements etc. say	£50,000		
Sale (of investment) fees @ say 2%	£429,000	£704,000	
Total		£13,501,000	
Developer's return for risk & profit @ say 17% capital value		£3,646,000	£17,147,000
Site Value on completion			£4,303,000
P.V. £1 say 2·5 years @ 14%			0·721
			£3,102,500
Less acquisition costs @ 2·5%			77,500
∴ *Site value today*			£3,025,000

If site value can be apportioned equally on an area basis (this will depend on frontages, access etc. to both sites)

$$\text{client's site value} = \frac{2}{5} \times £3,025,000$$

$$= £1,210,000$$

Value of the client's land ownership is therefore £1,210,000 which greatly exceeds the price paid for the land plus interest incurred over two years. In any ground rent calculation, if the client conveyed a freehold interest for a nominal consideration, then the opportunity cost of £1,210,000 plus the interest it could earn over the period of development must be taken into account by way of a reduced ground rent, as the alternative available to the LA would be to acquire the land for this sum, which could then be invested to earn interest over the development period. Similarly as the premium of £500,000 is payable immediately the developer will have to borrow this amount and incur interest charges over the whole development period.

Ground Rent Calculation

Expected Income		£1,500.000 p.a.
Expected Costs		
Development costs (ex profit)	13,501,000	
Developer's land value	1,210,000	
Opportunity cost in interest earned on land value 2·5 years @ 14%	469,000	
Premium	500,000	
Finance on premium 2·5 years @ 14%	194,000	
	£15,874,000	
Development Yield		
Investment yield @ say	7·5% p.a.	
Annual return for risk & profit (say 20% mark up)	1·5% p.a.	
ASF ignore as 125 year lease	—	
Total required yield	9% p.a.	0·09 £1,428,500 p.a.
∴ *Ground rent*		£71,500 p.a.

As the developer is effectively paying most of the land costs the resultant ground rent payable to the local authority would therefore be small and the equity share that this suggests will also be small. Typically it might be:

$$\frac{71,500}{1,500,000} \times 100\% = 4·8\%$$

As a result the local authority would try and ensure that the ground rent was a guaranteed minimum figure and negotiate a participation clause so that when the building was completed and, hopefully, fully let, revised calculations based on actual rents and costs might improve their position.

This is probable due to the elements of fixed costs (i.e. land value and premium) as shown below.

Actual Income (15% increase)		£1,725,000 p.a.
Actual Costs		
Development costs (15% increase)	15,526,000	
Developer's land value	1,210,000	
Interest on land value	469,000	
Premium	500,000	
Interest on premium	194,000	
	£17,899,000	
Development Yield @ 9%	0·09	1,611,000 p.a.
		£114,000 p.a.
Less initial ground rent		71,500 p.a.
∴ excess		43,500 p.a.
Say 50% of excess to LA (i.e. say £22,000)		
∴ *revised ground rent*		93,500 p.a.
∴ *revised equity share* = 5·4%		

These are the terms that the developer could afford to agree. However, if these terms are to be negotiated between the client and the local authority, rather than resulting from a competitive tender, then a more favourable outcome to the developer might be possible depending on the bargaining skills of the two parties.

STUART MORLEY

For bibliography, sample computer printout and available software please see end of Chapter 4.

CHAPTER 3

Financial Appraisal – Cashflow Approach

INTRODUCTION

The traditional residual method of evaluating development schemes, as described in Chapter 1 is the method most commonly used in practice. This has been so for a long time despite its relative crudity and the problems involved in its use described at the beginning of the first chapter. However, with the advent of larger property development companies and the growth in importance of financial institutions all of whom have much greater resources at their disposal, together with the increasing sophistication, ease of use, and reduced cost of computers and programmable calculators, more sophisticated techniques of appraisal and analysis are available and increasingly being used to supplement but rarely supplant the traditional residual. In some respects it can be argued that these cashflow approaches are no more than more sophisticated and potentially more accurate refinements of the residual technique. The basic method of deducting development costs and a profit allowance from total development value to give site value remains unaltered, it is merely that a cashflow approach gives a potentially more detailed calculation of the scheme's total costs through a more accurate assessment of building costs and hence of finance costs. This is discussed and illustrated in the next part of the chapter. However, the method of cashflow appraisal also has the facility to extend the amount of information provided by appraising a scheme's viability, thus enabling a developer to make decisions with a greater degree of accuarcy and to compare the viability and return from property development with alternative investments.

DIFFERENCE BETWEEN THE TRADITIONAL RESIDUAL AND CASHFLOW APPRAISALS

The basic difference between the simple residual method previously described and the cashflow method is, that in the latter method as the title suggests, all development costs and in particular building costs, are divided up into monthly, quarterly or yearly amounts, the net cashflows calculated and short term finance allowed for separately each period. In the basic residual method the simplifying assumption was made that money borrowed for example at the start of development will incur interest over the whole period whereas money borrowed towards the end of development will incur little or no interest; On average therefore it is assumed that interest will be incurred on total costs over half the period. In some cases this assumption will be reasonably accurate although even if the outgoings in each period are identical (most unlikely) there will still be an error in making this simplifying assumption. This results from the fact that money borrowed accumulates at a compound rate of interest rather than at a simple rate.

Of much greater importance is the build up of building costs. Most schemes conform to an "S" curve as shown below and discussed more fully in Chapter 5. This means that at the start of building work there is a gradual build up of expenditure normally reaching a peak after about 60% of the contract has elapsed with a tailing off towards the end. In a "typical" project

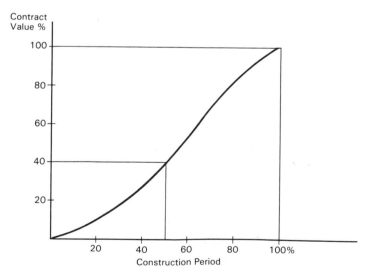

Construction Cashflow

therefore about 40% of building costs will have been incurred by the half way stage rather than 50% as assumed in calculating finance in the traditional residual. As something like 60% of building costs are incurred in the latter half of the project this will reduce interest accumulations, as money will not need to be borrowed for so long. Similarly as the cash outlay in the early stages of the contract will be low this too will mean lower interest accumulations. On the other hand professional fees (particularly architects fees) will be front loaded, which will increase interest payments.

APPROPRIATENESS OF A CASHFLOW APPROACH

Owing to the incidence of costs during the building contract as briefly explained above, it can be argued that a cashflow approach should provide more accurate information and therefore enable a more accurate appraisal to be undertaken even on relatively simple and straightforward developments. Furthermore it enables examination of the amount and timing of inflows and outflows to see if changes here and there could improve profitability as well as help determine the optimum available form of finance that should be employed. However, it is most useful in more complex schemes, discussed below, where for example parts of a scheme are let/sold before others are completed and also in developments where greater information about the scheme is required as a cashflow approach can more easily accommodate additional refinements such as allowing for inflation.

Allowing for inflation in appraisals, which involves a prediction of the future, is a controversial subject and for reasons explained later does not find favour with some developers. Nevertheless if a developer does want to examine the effects on profitability of different assumptions about cost inflation and rental growth the cashflow approach enables this to be done more accurately. For example if a quantity surveyor estimates that building costs will increase by say 5% over the next 12 months but by 8% over the following 12 months and maybe 10% over the final 12 months of a 3 year development period this would be difficult to accommodate accurately in a traditional residual approach.

Similarly the sensitivity of the proposed development to changes in these assumptions can be carried out more easily and accurately by using a cashflow approach. Taxation and its implications could be built into the appraisal and the total debt outstanding at any point in the development process, the total payback period and the date of peak cash outlay can also be shown easily, none of which are possible with the traditional residual method.

Apart from these general benefits certain types of development almost necessitate a cashflow approach.

A residential estate development will mean that some houses will be sold whilst, or even before, other houses are built. During the latter part of the development therefore, in particular, there will be complex cashflows with money coming in and money going out. Without oversimplifying the situation the traditional residual will be unable to cope with this situation; but by treating each cashflow separately a solution is relatively straightforward.

A central area shopping centre development will incorporate not merely a variety of different sized shops and stores, totalling maybe 20–30,000 m² in all, but possibly a multi storey car park, offices, flats, sports leisure facilities or other civic amenities as well. These schemes are larger, complex and take rather longer to build than smaller more straightforward buildings. The scheme is likely to be phased, some parts will be finished before others, some parts will be let before others and the cashflows are most unlikely to be equal.

An industrial estate will mean that parts of the estate will be finished before others, and so some factories or warehoues will be let, and therefore revenue producing, whilst others are being built. A further complication may be that some factories could be sold to owner occupiers rather than let so that much larger cash inflows will occur. On other parts of the estate, sites, rather than completed buildings, might be ground leased after the basic infrastructure has been provided, resulting in smaller but earlier cash inflows. An accurate appraisal of such a scheme would only be possible by using a cashflow approach.

New town development, expansion schemes of existing towns or programmes of expenditure by UDC's will mean phased implementation over many years – maybe decades – resulting in complex cashflows and the involvement of public and private sector agencies and finance. A cashflow approach would clearly be necessitated.

There are therefore many instances when a cashflow approach not only provides more information about the development but also provides a more accurate and detailed appraisal. However, it must be stressed that it would be a fallacy to say that a cashflow approach is always suitable or always more accurate than a traditional residual. Whilst it is true that it can allow more accurately for the incidence of costs and returns and therefore the actual interest incurred, the end result is only as accurate as the information used. If the timing of payments and receipts is uncertain then an arbitrary or inaccurate assumption will result in an answer no more, and possibly less accurate, than that obtained by using a traditional residual.

Where schemes are straightforward, where development periods are short, where interest rates charged on borrowed money are low and where appraisals are being undertaken at early stages in the development process, possibly before a site has been purchased and an architect and quantity surveyor appointed, there will be little point in adopting a cashflow approach. But later on when consultants have been appointed and plans of the development are at a more advanced stage, more detailed and accurate information will be available, which may make a cashflow appraisal more applicable.

ALTERNATIVE APPROACHES TO CASHFLOW APPRAISALS

Three alternative cashflow approaches to development appraisal, are described below and compared with a traditional residual approach. All three cashflow approaches accurately allow for the incidence of short term finance but each has particular benefits in certain circumstances and these are discussed. One method is then developed to show the usefulness of this approach in making allowances for future inflationary changes in both costs and income and the effect these assumptions have on the residual answer. The examples used are deliberately simplified in that details of building costs, architects and QS fees, letting fees and marketing costs, site preparation and landscaping costs and contingencies are not shown individually. They are merely totalled into outgoings per period of the development process. Similarly any initial delay (before building work could commence) needed to obtain detailed planning permission, the appointment of a contractor etc. has been ignored.

The purpose of the following examples, therefore, is to illustrate the basic method of cashflow appraisal and its difference to the simple residual, not particular refinements which might confuse the basic differences in approach. At the end of this chapter however a more detailed worked example is used to combine and illustrate all the points mentioned in this chapter. In that example a breakdown of total outgoings per period is shown.

Example:

Value a site on which a shop and office development is proposed. Total outgoings inclusive of all fees but exclusive of short term finance are £500,000 for the first year and £650,000 for the second year payable quarterly in arrears. The breakdown of costs, for the purpose of this example, is assumed to be as follows:

First Year
Period 1 – £100,000   Period 2 – £120,000
Period 3 – £130,000   Period 4 – £150,000

Second Year
Period 5 – £150,000   Period 6 – £175,000
Period 7 – £175,000   Period 8 – £150,000

(Although in practice building contractors would be paid monthly and a quantity surveyor would therefore normally prepare a monthly cashflow, for appraisal purposes quarterly periods would normally be used on the assumption that interest would accumulate on this basis.)

It is envisaged that the shops will be let (at £80,000 p.a.) before the offices are finished and the total completed scheme (total income £160,000 p.a.) could be sold for £2,290,000 (7% yield) once the offices are let, which is estimated to be three months after building work is completed. Finance is obtainable at 4 per cent per quarter (17 per cent p.a.) and a return to cover risk and profit at 20 per cent of capital value is desired.

TRADITIONAL RESIDUAL APPROACH
Expected Capital Value

Income		£160,000 p.a.
YP in perpetuity @ 7%		14·3
Capital value		£2,290,000

Expected Costs

Building costs, fees etc.	£1,150,000	
Short term finance @ 17% p.a.		
— on total costs for half building period of 2 years	196,000	
— letting delay – assume letting delay of offices is offset by letting shops before completion	—	
	£1,346,000	

Return for risk and profit @ 20% of Capital Value	458,000	1,804,000
Site value on completion		486,000
PV £1 2 years* @ 17%		0·7305
Site value today (less acquisition costs)		£355,000

The problems incurred by using this approach are clear. Firstly how to allow for the unequal incidence of costs and resulting interest charges, and secondly how to allow for the fact that the scheme is not all let at the same time, some income being received whilst costs are still being incurred.

* In all four comparable examples any initial delay in securing detailed planning permission and appointing a contractor has been ignored.

PERIOD BY PERIOD CASHFLOW APPROACH

The first cashflow method calculates accumulating short term debt on a period by period basis, so that at any point during the development process the total outstanding debt and the amount of interest owed is shown. The basis of calculating is this: at the end of the first three monthly period, £100,000 must be borrowed to pay the contractor. By the end of the second period, therefore, when a further £120,000 is borrowed, three months' interest on £100,000 is added to the total debt so that it equals £224,000. This amount then incurs interest, so that at the end of the next period the outstanding debt is the amount owed at the start of the period (£224,000), plus one period's interest (£8,960) plus the latest loan of £130,000 i.e. a total of £362,960 etc. On completion of the development when the offices are let and the scheme could be sold (as a fully let investment) the total outstanding debt is £1,276,935 (including interest charges of £206,935 – obtained by totalling the figures in column e).

Period (3 mths)	Total Costs a £	Income b £	Net flow c = a − b £	Capital outstanding from previous period d £	Interest @ 4% e £	Capital outstanding f = c + d + e £
1	(100,000)		(100,000)			(100,000)
2	(120,000)		(120,000)	(100,000)	(4,000)	(224,000)
3	(130,000)		(130,000)	(224,000)	(8,960)	(362,960)
4	(150,000)		(150,000)	(362,960)	(14,518)	(527,478)
5	(150,000)		(150,000)	(527,478)	(21,099)	(698,577)
6	(175,000)		(175,000)	(698,577)	(27,943)	(901,520)
7	(175,000)	20,000	(155,000)	(901,520)	(36,061)	(1,092,581)
8	(150,000)	20,000	(130,000)	(1,092,581)	(43,703)	(1,266,284)
9		40,000	40,000	(1,266,284)	(50,651)	(1,276,935)

The completed development, 27 months after the start of the scheme, is sold for £2,290,000. The outstanding debt obtained from the cash flow table above is £1,276,935. The site value may now be calculated.

Capital value		£2,290,000
Outstanding debt	£1,276,935	
Return for risk and profit @ 20% CV	458,000	1,734,935
Therefore site value in 27 months' time		555,065
PV £1, 27 months @ 17%		0·7026
Therefore site value today (less acquisition costs)		£389,989

It will be noted that in the calculations to obtain the net cash-flow any income received is deducted from costs so that interest is incurred on the net cost as that would be the amount borrowed. In some developments the situation may arise where income received per period exceeds costs incurred and the net flow is positive. In this case it would be common practice to allow interest in the same way on the assumption that this surplus can be invested to earn interest at the same rate as is being charged for borrowed money. Some writers argue that this may not be possible and in any case only net of tax interest will be receivable. However, the difference is likely to be small in most developments and the debate is not considered further here.

NET TERMINAL VALUE (NTV) APPROACH

The second approach, commonly referred to as Net Terminal Value by economists, is an extension of the simple residual approach (where compound interest is allowed for on total outgoings for half the building period). In the table below it will be seen that compound interest is allowed for on total cost incurred in each period for the time that this money has to be borrowed, i.e. until the scheme is sold (or refinanced). This means that each period's loan is effectively treated separately, with interest rolled up (or accumulating at a compound rate) until the completed development is sold. It is clear from the table below that the same outstanding debt figure is derived, but the result is produced rather more quickly than in the preceding example. The final part of the appraisal, to calculate the site value today, is obviously identical to that shown above.

Period	Net flow (as before) £	Interest until completion @ 4%	Net outlay on completion £
1	(100,000)	1·36857	(136,857)
2	(120,000)	1·31593	(157,912)
3	(130,000)	1·26532	(164,492)
4	(150,000)	1·21665	(182,497)
5	(150,000)	1·16986	(175,479)
6	(175,000)	1·12486	(196,850)
7	(155,000)	1·0816	(167,648)
8	(130,000)	1·04	(135,200)
9	40,000	1·0	40,000
			£1,276,935

DISCOUNTED CASHFLOW (DCF) APPROACH

The third method differs from the first two insofar as the total debt outstanding on completion of the scheme is not calcu-

Period		Net flow £	PV £1 @ 4%	Present value of cashflow (Total today) £
1		(100,000)	0·96154	(96,154)
2		(120,000)	0·92456	(110,947)
3		(130,000)	0·88900	(115,570)
4		(150,000)	0·85480	(128,220)
5		(150,000)	0·82193	(123,290)
6		(175,000)	0·79031	(138,304)
7		(155,000)	0·75992	(117,788)
8		(130,000)	0·73069	(94,990)
9		40,000	0·70259	28,104
	Return for risk and profit	(458,000)	0·70259	(321,786)
	Sale price	2,290,000	0·70259	1,608,931
	Site Value Today (less acquisition costs)			£389,988

lated. Instead a true DCF approach is used, converting all costs as they occur into present day equivalents, so that the value of the site today is immediately shown as the summation of the figures in the final column.

The calculations are in effect very similar to those in the preceding example, except that the PV £1 table is used rather than the Amount of £1 table, i.e. the cashflow is discounted backwards to arrive at a present value rather than accumulated forwards to make a valuation at the end of the project's life before discounting the resultant site value.

ADVANTAGES AND DISADVANTAGES OF THE ALTERNATIVES

It is clear that all three cashflow approaches produce identical answers for site value – £390,000 compared to £355,000 obtained by the traditional residual.

The first method (period by period approach) possesses two main advantages over the other two. First, the actual amount owed at any point during the development process is immediately shown. After one year £527,478 is the total outstanding debt, for example. This is not immediately shown by either of the other methods. Second, if a change in interest rate occurs during the development process (a not uncommon event) this can easily be incorporated into revised figures for the remainder of the loan simply by continuing the calculations on a period by period basis at the new interest rate. This method is probably most used in residential developments – where sales are phased and it is important to know the precise point at which the loan is repaid – or where changes in interest rates are expected. However, it is clear from the example above that where the development is split up into many periods the calculations are laborious, unless of course a computer is used.

The second method (NTV approach) has two possible advantages over the first. It is considerably quicker, and as a logical extension of the traditional residual approach it is possibly easier to understand. But it does not have the flexibilities of the period by period approach.

The third method (DCF approach) has both advantages and disadvantages. If site value is to be calculated it is marginally the quickest method, and it is the only method which enables the internal rate of return to be calculated (see below). However, there are important disadvantages, since the calculations do not relate to the process of development as it evolves. They do not show a developer what the accumulated debt is on completion of the development, for example. This is important if the scheme is to be retained as an investment and refinanced by way of a mortgage or leaseback, or if a partnership scheme is envisaged, with a peppercorn rent payable during the building period. Once a site has been purchased a developer might also wish to know the profit that will be received if the scheme is sold rather than refinanced. The DCF approach would only show today's value of the future profit, rather than the actual sum likely to be received. In terms of calculating the development yield and examining the profit in percentage terms this would not matter, however, since all methods give the same answer.

PROFITABILITY AND ITS MEASUREMENT

In the first chapter profitability of the scheme, examined above, would have been assessed as follows:

Capital Profit   £458,000
Capital Value   £2,290,000 (annual income = £160,000)
Total Costs   £1,832,000 (including land cost and interest on land cost)

$\therefore$ Return

$$= \frac{458,000}{2,290,000} \times 100\% = 20\% \text{ of Capital Value}$$

or

$$= \frac{458,000}{1,832,000} \times 100\% = 25\% \text{ of Total Costs}$$

$\therefore$ Development Yield $= \dfrac{160,000}{1,832,000} \times 100\% = 8\cdot73\%$ p.a. (25% mark up on investment yield of 7%)

These measures of profitability or return are somewhat crude as they have to reflect a number of different factors, predominantly the degree of risk and the length of time before profit (if any) is realised. So if one scheme took 4 years to develop and another 2 years – a developer would obviously want a greater profit from the first scheme as compensation for the extra time before any money was earned. But how much extra profit?

An alternative approach using the DCF method described above would be to determine what discount rate would equate total costs (excluding the profit allowance) to total capital value. This discount rate or internal rate of return (IRR) would therefore reflect the scheme's profitability relative to the actual incidence of costs and income and show the rate of return earned on funds invested in the project. This rate of return could then be compared with the rate of interest on borrowed money; the minimum acceptable return would be the interest rate on borrowed money plus an acceptable margin for the degree of risk involved. The main advantage of this approach over the traditional approaches previously discussed is that the effect of time the developer has to wait before profit is received has been accounted for separately, so that the margin to be considered relates solely to the degree of risk involved.

The following example illustrates how the IRR is calculated. Whilst the DCF method is essentially the same as shown above, the major problem now is that it is the discount rate that has to be found whereas previously cashflows were discounted at the rate of interest payable on borrowed money. The approach is therefore an iterative one – picking two trial discount rates which hopefully will be on either side of the correct rate and interpolating between the two answers (net present values) to work out the correct rate. Whilst this may look tedious the use of computers simplifies the calculation enormously.

The correct discount rate must therefore be between 7% and 8% and is obviously much closer to 8% than 7%. An approximation of the correct figure is obtained as follows:

difference between NPV's = 62,968 + 6,500 = 69,468
The 1% difference in discount rates which gives this differ-

Example:

Period	Net flow (as before) £	PV £1 factor @ 7%	PV £1 factor @ 8%	Present value of Cashflow @ 7% £	Present value of Cashflow @ 8% £
0	(390,000)	1	1	(390,000)	(390,000)
1	(100,000)	0·9346	0·9259	(93,460)	(92,590)
2	(120,000)	0·8734	0·8573	(104,808)	(102,876)
3	(130,000)	0·8163	0·7938	(106,119)	(103,194)
4	(150.000)	0·7629	0·7350	(114,435)	(110,250)
5	(150,000)	0·7130	0·6806	(106,950)	(102,090)
6	(175,000)	0·6663	0·6302	(116,602)	(110,285)
7	(155,000)	0·6227	0·5835	(96,518)	(90,442)
8	(130,000)	0·5820	0·5403	(75,660)	(70,239)
9	40,000	0·5440	0·5002	21,760	20,008
9	2,290,000	0·5440	0·5002	1,245,760	1,145,458
Net Present Value				62,968	(6,500)

ence of 69,468 in NPV's can be apportioned to give the required discount rate (a slight error occurs in this method of apportionment as the interest rates lie on a curve rather than a straight line as assumed here for ease of calculation. As long as the interest rates are not far apart any errors will be small and insignificant).

$$either \ 7 + \frac{62,968}{69,468} = 7·90643\%$$

$$or \ 8 - \frac{6,500}{69,468} = 7·90643\%$$

∴ true annual discount rate $= (1 + 0·0790643)^4 - 1 = 35·6\%$
say $= 36\%$

If the cost of borrowed money was assumed to be 17% p.a. then an IRR of 36% p.a. shows a considerable margin to cover risk and profit of over 100% and indicates that the original assumption of a 25% total mark up on costs for a project taking just over two years to complete was rather excessive. As the development period was relatively short the IRR calculation indicates that a smaller mark up would have been acceptable still giving a reasonable rate of return. Most developers, who use this approach, would consider an IRR of 20–25% to be acceptable, depending on the cost of borrowed money.

RENTAL GROWTH AND COST INFLATION – SHOULD PREDICTED VALUES BE USED IN APPRAISALS?

All the appraisals illustrated so far in this chapter and in Chapter 1 have been undertaken using costs and rents current at the time the appraisal was undertaken with no estimation being made of what might happen to those assumptions during the development period. In Chapter 1 it was briefly mentioned that the traditional assumption was that even if rents and costs changed they would change at similar rates and so the effects would cancel themselves out and in any case it was both dangerous and difficult to predict the future; it was better to use current figures of which there was some certainty rather than future estimates which were less certain. The possibility of future changes was crudely taken account of by using a contingency sum and modifying the allowance for risk and profit.

These traditional assumptions predate the present era of an economy where inflation appears to be ever present even at relatively low levels (at the time of writing) and so all that a developer can now be certain of is that whatever happens in the future, current estimates probably will be proved wrong. It can almost be guaranteed that rental levels, capital values and building costs will change in the future even over the short term. Although not yet widespread it is becoming more common for some development companies and the institutions to approach development appraisal in a more sophisticated manner not just by using cashflow appraisals but also by building into appraisals assumptions about the future. When the market is optimistic and user demand is strong some developers, keen to acquire sites, may well use predicted rents and costs to justify higher site values as shown below. There are dangers in this approach and it is certainly true that any answer is only as good as the inputs used to derive it.

Nevertheless this fact should not be an excuse for ignoring what might occur in the future and the consequences that might result. No appraisal, whether it is a simple residual or a detailed cashflow appraisal should be done in isolation; it should form part of a series of sensitivity analyses at the very least, (see Chapter 4) therefore attempting to account for likely changes in costs and rents helps to give a better picture of a scheme's viability.

Nevertheless some developers are wary of making predictions for the reasons now discussed.

Some companies lost money or went bankrupt as a result of the boom and subsequent crash in the early/mid 1970's when it was common practice, due to the initial euphoria at the time, to predict greater rises in rents than in costs or, as in some cases, merely to predict rises in rents. As rents had risen continuously over the previous 25 years and had risen rapidly in the boom conditions of the early 1970's there was perhaps some justification for this practice but many developers and their advisers were guilty of excessive optimism and paid the price.

Many developers consider it is difficult and dangerous to predict the future maybe two or three years hence and think that the present relationship between costs and values is just as likely to be correct as any future relationship. It is certainly true that predictions are difficult to make accurately and have in the past often been notoriously inaccurate. Nevertheless more research into the property market, rental growth trends and the movement of tender prices and building costs is now undertaken by the larger estate agency and quantity surveying firms and financial institutions – research which fifteen years ago was non-existent. Much more is now known about the property market, and the dangers of predicting rental growth and particularly cost inflation have been reduced. However, for a trader developer aiming to sell a scheme on completion these dangers are greater than for an institutional developer aiming to create a long term investment. An institution can afford to ride out any short term hiccups in the property market. If rental growth predictions for the development period turn out to have been optimistic in the short term, it is possible that by the first rent review any shortfall will have been largely made up and in the longer term the investment may not suffer. For the traditional development company, selling or refinancing on completion, this could be disasterous.

A final argument sometimes voiced against using forecasted values and costs is that rises in costs will be roughly balanced by rising rents and therefore the residual answer will be unaffected. Of all the reasons for not using forecasted figures this is probably the weakest for two reasons. Firstly, as the following chart shows, it is unlikely that costs and rents will change at the same rate. Whilst it is true that changes in tender prices will often bear a close relationship to changes in rental and capital values, as a rise in capital values will stimulate more development activity and therefore more building work and hence increased profit margins, there is no such relationshp between inflation in the cost of materials and labour and the change in value of buildings. Secondly even if costs and values did increase at the same annual rate a higher residual value would result, as the following example shows, because most developments tend to be let and sold at the end of the development period, therefore benefiting from growth in values throughout the whole period, whereas building costs are incurred and paid at stages during the development period. In many cases where letting occurs when the scheme is completed, annual rental growth considerably less than that of annual cost inflation will still give a similar residual answer to the traditional approach of using present day values and costs.

One final point worth making is that if calculations are undertaken assuming money is borrowed at prevailing short term money market interest rates these high rates of borrowing are partly caused by short term expectations about inflation, and repayments will be made in depreciated pounds. If an interest rate allowing for inflation is used it is logical that estimates of actual amounts that will have to be borrowed (and later repaid) should also be made. If present day figures are used it would be logical to allow for an interest rate net of inflation to avoid a pessimistic and mathematically illogical answer.

There is therefore a strong case for carefully building estimates of rental growth and cost inflation into development appraisals even if only as part of a detailed sensitivity analysis. But where is this information to come from and how reliable are forecasts likely to be? Forecasting building cost inflation is relatively well established and is undertaken by the Building

Cost Information Services of the RICS and by some of the major firms of Quantity Surveyors (see Chapters 4 and 5). Changes in building costs are likely to be less volatile than changes in rent and are obviously directly related to changes in labour

Change (% per annum) on previous reading for rents, building costs and tender prices.

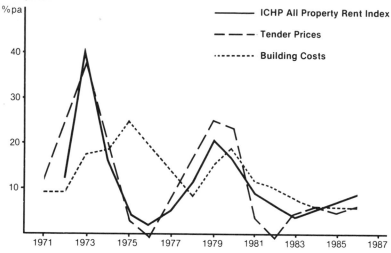

Sources: Investors Chronicle/Hillier Parker Rent Index. Davis Belfield & Everest.

costs (wages) and materials costs which can be forecasted one or two years ahead fairly accurately. Rental values are determined by the interaction of supply and demand and are much more difficult to predict. Nevertheless prediction is possible providing detailed information is obtainable regarding the supply of floorspace currently available and that likely to come on the market over the short term. This should be reasonably accurate up to two or three years in the future as future supply will come from schemes currently under construction. Further into the future, forecasting is more hazardous as it relies on schemes with planning permission but not yet started and schemes in the pipeline but without planning permission. The demand side is even less easy to predict as it will relate to the strength of the economy, both local and national, technological change and transport infrastructure changes etc. At national level forecasting is easier than at the local level and some firms attempt forecasting one or two years ahead. For example Hillier Parker regularly publish forecasts for shop and industrial rents. The former forecast uses a relationship between rents, retail profits and disposable income governed by the formula for 1986 of

$$SR_t = 0\cdot271\,P_{t-1} + 0\cdot726\,DI_t + 15\cdot092$$

Where SR_t = ICHP Shop rent index in year t

P_{t-1} = retail profits of one year earlier derived from a series produced by Phillips and Drew for stores profits

DI_t = disposable income in yeart t, as published by C.S.O.

The above formula produces a high correlation coefficient between actual and expected shop rents of $r = 0\cdot926$ which suggests a good fit as shown in the diagram below. Forecasts for retail profits are published by Phillips and Drew and fore-

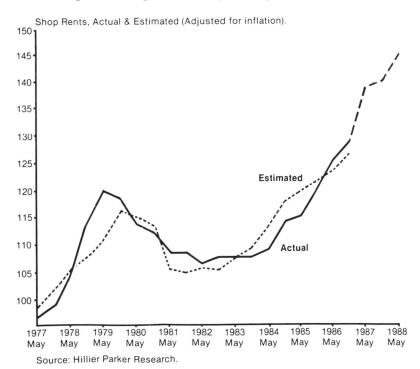

Shop Rents, Actual & Estimated (Adjusted for inflation).

Source: Hillier Parker Research.

Valuation and Development Appraisal

casts for personal disposable income are published by the Henly Centre, Laing and Cruickshank and Phillips and Drew.

THE EFFECTS OF USING PREDICTED VALUES FOR COSTS AND RENTS

The following example illustrates the effect rising costs and rental values have on the residual site value; the calculations are simple extensions of those used earlier. The same figures are used as before but costs are assumed to rise by 3% per quarter (approximately 12·5% p.a.) and rents by 1·5% per quarter (approximately 6% p.a.). Obviously the method can be further extended to allow for combinations of different rates of increase over the development period and no particular significance is meant by the assumptions made in this example.

Period	Today's estimate a £	Cost growth factor @3% b	Inflated estimate $c = a \times b$ £	Today's estimate d £	Income growth factor @1·5% e	Inflated estimate $f = d \times e$ £	Net cashflow inflated estimate $f - c$ £
1	(100,000)		(100,000)				(100,000)
2	(120,000)	1·045	(125,400)				(125,400)
3	(130,000)	1·076	(139,880)				(139,880)
4	(150,000)	1·109	(166,350)				(166,350)
5	(150,000)	1·142	(171,300)				(171,300)
6	(175,000)	1·176	(205,800)				(205,800)
7	(175,000)	1·212	(212,100)	20,000	1·093	21,860	(190,240)
8	(150,000)	1·248	(187,200)	20,000		21,860	(165,340)
9				20,000		21,860⎱	44,380
				20,000	1·126	22,520⎰	

The cost growth factor assumes inflation to the middle of each quarterly period. This is a simplification because in reality the contractor would be paid monthly and inflation would increase each monthly payment. It could therefore be argued each monthly payment should be calculated separately and then added together to give the quarterly total. This approach is obviously more accurate but can lengthen the amount of calculations considerably, although the use of a computer makes this a relatively easy task.

However, a counter argument could be used that there will be a delay in paying the contractor of probably one month (two weeks for the issue of the architect's certificate and a further two weeks for payment itself). In addition there would normally be a 3–5% retention allowance, deducted from each monthly payment – half of which would be repaid on completion and half six months later.

A considerable degree of refinement to cashflow appraisals can therefore be made and many of these are incorporated in the various software programmes now available in the market. However, to explain the basic method here a number of necessary simplifications have had to be made:

It has been assumed that rent is fixed three months before the tenant takes possession, allowing time for negotiating and drawing up the lease. In some schemes, particularly during a downturn in the market, a longer period of time could be justified – reflecting increased letting delays, the time taken to print brochures, rent free periods for fitting out etc. It is assumed rents are payable quarterly in advance and that once rent is agreed it will of course be fixed until the first review (usually every 3–5 years). The shops are let in period 7 (21 months) the offices in period 9 (27 months).

Period	Net flow (as before) £	Interest @ 4% per Qtr	Net outlay by completion £
1	(100,000)	1·36857	(136,857)
2	(125,400	1·31593	(165,017)
3	(139,880)	1·26532	(176,992)
4	(166,350)	1·21665	(202,390)
5	(171,300)	1·16986	(200,397)
6	(205,800)	1·12486	(231,496)
7	(190,240)	1·0816	(205,763)
8	(165,340)	1·04	(171,954)
9	44,380	1	44,380
			£1,446,486

Capital value

£44,380 × 4 × 14·3 (YP)		£2,538,500
Less: net outlay	£1,446,486	
return for risk/profit		
@ 20% CV	£507,700	£1,954,186
Site value		£584,314
PV of £1 27 months @ 17% p.a.		0·7026
Site value today (less acquisition costs)		£410,539

TRADITIONAL RESIDUAL USING PROJECTED COSTS AND RENTS

Clearly the traditional residual method of valuation becomes even more inappropriate when rental and cost projections are to be incorporated into an already complex appraisal and a number of simplifying assumptions have to be made. In this following calculation it has been assumed that rental growth over one and threequarter years would be allowed for which is the average amount allowed above. Inflation of building costs has been taken to the midpoint of the building period, assuming therefore that increased costs thereafter are offset by less inflation before that point. Depending on the incidence of costs this assumption may or may not be very inaccurate.

Expected Capital Value

Present estimate of income	£160,000 p.a.
Rental growth over say	
1·75 years @ 1·5% per quarter	1·11
Future estimate of income	£177,500 p.a.
YP in perpetuity @ 7% say	14·3
Capital value	£2,538,000

Expected Costs

Present estimate of building costs, fees etc.	£1,150,000
Inflation in building costs averaged over say half building period – 1 year @ 3% per quarter	1·126

Future estimate of building
  costs etc.   £1,295,000

Short term finance @ 17% p.a.
  – on total costs for half
    building period   £220,000

£1,515,000

Return for Risk and Profit
  @ 20% of capital value   £508,000 £2,023,000

Site value on completion   £515,000
PV £1 2 years @ 17%   0·7305

Site value today (less acquisition
  costs)   £376,000

The main conclusion to be drawn from these calculations is that in many cases by not allowing for cost and rent inflation a potential underestimate, or conservative estimate, of site value may be obtained, for in this example, even if costs inflate at twice the rate of rents, a higher site value is still obtained. Where similar rates of increase are expected for both costs and rents, obviously much greater differences will result. Great care must be used in these projections, but the evaluation gives a more detailed picture of what is likely to occur during the development process and should at the very least be incorporated in any sensitivity testing of a development project (see Chapter 4). Put another way, the projected cashflow appraisal above illustrates that in this example if the site were purchased for the originally determined value, a considerable safety margin is available, compared to the 20.5% profit on cost initially assumed, before the return to cover risk and profit is eroded.

A measure of this safety margin is shown in the traditional way below assuming the site were purchased for £390,000:

Capital value   £2,538,500 (annual income
                      £177,520)

Total Costs
  from cashflow   £1,446,500
  Land cost   390,000

Interest on land cost
@ 17% p.a. over
27 mths   165,000   2,001,500
Capital Profit   £537,000

$$\therefore \text{Return} = \frac{537,000}{2,538,500} \times 100\% = 21 \cdot 2\% \text{ of Capital value}$$

$$\text{or} \quad = \frac{537,000}{2,001,500} \times 100\% = 26 \cdot 8\% \text{ of total costs}$$

$$\therefore \text{Development Yield} = \frac{177,520}{2,001,500} \times 100\% = 8 \cdot 87\% \text{ p.a. } (26 \cdot 7\%$$

mark up on investment yield of 7%)

WORKED EXAMPLE OF A PHASED INDUSTRIAL DEVELOPMENT

The following worked example examines in a more detailed and realistic way how a cashflow approach could be applied to a complex development.

An industrial developer, has asked for advice on the price he should pay for a 2·5 hectare development site, which is for sale at £400,000 with outline planning permission for 12,500 m² of factory space. The site, although partially cleared, still contains a number of old dilapidated buildings which the local planning authority wish to see redeveloped to provide modern buildings to attract additional employment into the area.

Initial research suggests the following:

(a) Owing to the supply/demand relationship in the area and the general economic climate a phased development programme over a 4 year period seems desirable. This would allow 6 months to obtain detailed planning permission, and select a suitable builder etc., a further 6 months for demolition of the existing buildings, site clearance and the provision of new roads and services etc. followed by a 2·5 year building period with phased completions as follows:

first 12 months   1,000 m² completed every 3 months
next 6 months   1,250 m² completed every 3 months
final 12 months   1,500 m² completed every 3 months

In addition to this gradual build up in completions you also recommend that a further 3 month period should be allowed for letting each phase when completed, and that on completion of the whole scheme 3 months should be allowed to achieve a sale of the completed investment.

(b) Development costs would be itemised as follows:

demolition   – £50,000
estate roads & services   – £30,000 per hectare
building costs   – £200 per m² current costs (incl. access roads & car parking)
cost inflation   – 2% per 3 months (8·25% per annum)
architects & QS fees   – 12% with half total fee paid before work starts on site, rest paid @ 6% of cost every 3 months
letting fees   – 20% of initial annual rent to allow for two letting agents and cost of advertising and bro-chures etc.
investment sale fees   – 2% of sale price
short term finance   – 3·5% per 3 months (14·75% per annum)

(c) Current rental value   – £36 per m²
Expected rental growth   – zero growth for first 12 months
                               – 1% per 3 months (4% p.a.) over next 18 months
                               – 2% per 3 months (8·25% p.a.) thereafter
Investment Yield   – 99%

The developer has stated that he would require a return of 17% of Capital Value and would like your advice on site value using both current costs and rents and expected future costs and rents with some justification of these future figures.

Answer

As this development scheme is phased with lettings occurring whilst subsequent phases are being built, a cashflow approach is necessitated. Two cashflow appraisals both on a quarterly basis are shown below, the first using current figures, the second using projected figures. In the first appraisal the calculation of building costs is straightforward – for the first four building periods the cost will be 1,000 m² × £200 = £200,000; for the next two periods it will be 1,250 m² × £200 = £250,000; for the final four periods it will be 1,500 m² × £200 = £300,000. The combined total of building costs and demolition/new roads and services will therefore be £2,625,000 (see table below) and the total of architects and QS fees will be £315,000 (£2,625,000 × 0·12), a quarter is assumed to be paid after 3 months and a further quarter paid after 6 months.

The calculation of rents is not quite so straightforward. The first payment will occur 3 months after the first (3 month)

Period (mths)	Demolition, estate roads & building costs £	Architects & QS fees £	Letting fees Sale fees & return for risk & profit £	Total Outlay £
3		79,000		79,000
6		79,000		79,000
9	50,000	3,000		53,000
12	75,000	4,000		79,000
15	200,000	12,000		212,000
18	200,000	12,000	7,200	219,200
21	200,000	12,000	7,200	219,200
24	200,000	12,000	7,200	219,200
27	250,000	15,000	7,200	272,200
30	250,000	15,000	9,000	274,000
33	300,000	18,000	9,000	327,000
36	300,000	18,000	10,800	328,800
39	300,000	18,000	10,800	328,800
42	300,000	18,000	10,800	328,800
45			10,800	10,800
48			100,000	950,000
			850,000	
	2,625,000	315,000	1,040,000	3,980,000

phase has been completed. As rents are paid quarterly in advance the first payment will therefore be $0.25 \times 1{,}000\,\text{m}^2 \times £36 = £9{,}000$, and letting fees will be $1{,}000\,\text{m}^2 \times £36 \times 20\% = £7{,}200$. Three months later another $1{,}000\,\text{m}^2$ phase will have been completed and let so that total income received will then be £18,000 (£9,000 + £9,000). After 45 months all the buildings will be let and total quarterly income will be $0.25 \times 12{,}500\,\text{m}^2 \times £36 = £112{,}500$. Capital value will therefore be $£112{,}500 \times 4 \times \dfrac{100}{9} = £5{,}000{,}000$. Sale fees will be 2% of this figure i.e. £100,000 and developer's return @ 17% will be £850,000. The cashflow appraisal will therefore be as shown below:

Period	Total outlay £	New income £	Total income & sale price £	Net cash flow £	P.V. £1 factor @ 3·5%	Present value £
3	(79,000)			(79,000)	0·9662	(76,300)
6	(79,000)			(79,000)	0·9335	(73,700)
9	(53,000)			(53,000)	0·9019	(47,800)
12	(79,000)			(79,000)	0·8714	(68,800)
15	(212,000)			(212,000)	0·842	(178,500)
18	(219,200)	9,000		(210,200)	0·8135	(171,000)
21	(219,200)	9,000	18,000	(201,200)	0·786	(158,100)
24	(219,200)	9,000	27,000	(192,200)	0·7594	(146,000)
27	(272,200)	9,000	36,000	(236,200)	0·7337	(173,300)
30	(274,000)	11,250	47,250	(226,750)	0·7089	(160,700)
33	(327,000)	11,250	58,500	(268,500)	0·685	(183,900)
36	(328,800)	13,500	72,000	(256,800)	0·6618	(170,000)
39	(328,800)	13,500	85,500	(243,300)	0·6394	(155,600)
42	(328,800)	13,500	99,000	(229,800)	0·6178	(142,000)
45	(10,800)	13,500	112,500	101,700	0·5969	60,700
48	(950,000)		5,500,000	4,050,000	0·5767	2,335,600

Gross Site Value	490,600
less acquisition costs @ 2·5%	12,300
Net Site Value	478,300

A further appraisal allowing for expected increases in costs and rents is shown on pages 94–96. To simplify the presentation of the cashflows a separate table is shown for the calculation of income on page 94.

Rental growth has been calculated to the start of the 3 month period allowed for letting. The first letting of $1{,}000\,\text{m}^2$ is achieved after 18 months and therefore the rent will be fixed after 15 months. As no increase in rental values is expected during the first twelve months only 3 months growth @ 1%

Period	New income (present rental value of £28 m²) £	Growth factor	New income (projected rental values) £	Total income & sale price £
15				
18	9,000	1·01	9,090	9,090
21	9,000	1·02	9,180	18,270
24	9,000	1·03	9,270	27,540
27	9,000	1·041	9,370	36,910
30	11,250	1·051	11,820	48,730
33	11,250	1·062	11,950	60,680
36	13,500	1·083	14,620	75,300
39	13,500	1·1045	14,910	90,210
42	13,500	1·127	15,210	105,420
45	13,500	1·15	15,520	120,940
				5,642,000

(4% per annum) has been allowed for. When the rate of rental growth increases to 2% per 3 months (8·25% per annum) the calculations become more complicated. For example the growth factor shown in the above table for 39 months is calculated as follows:

Growth factor – 6 periods @ 1% (no growth in previous
   4 periods)   1·062
Multiplied by Growth Factor – 2 periods @ 2%   1·04

∴ Growth factor – 8 periods   1·1045

Calculation of the capital value of £5,642,000 is also complicated because when the entire scheme is sold as an investment its reversionary potential must be considered. The early phases were let more than two years previously, since when growth in rental values is expected to have occurred. Whilst total income received at completion is £483,800 (£120,940 × 4) the Full Rental Value of the scheme is £517,500 (12,500 m² × 36 × 1·15). The first reversion can be expected in about 2·5 years time (assuming 5 year rent reviews) and increases in income will occur every subsequent three months. The calculation of capital value is lengthy but is otherwise a straightforward reversionary calculation and for that reason is not shown here.

The complete cashflow appraisal will therefore be as follows:

Period	Demolition, estate roads & building costs a £	Inflation factor @ 2% (8·25% p.a.) to middle of period b	Inflated building costs c = a × b £	Architects & QS fees d £	Letting & sale fees & return for risk & profit e £	Total inflated outlay f = c + d + e £
3				94,600		94,600
6				94,600		94,600
9	50,000	1·05	52,500	3,150		55,650
12	75,000	1·071	80,300	4,820		85,120
15	200,000	1·093	218,600	13,120		231,720
18	200,000	1·115	223,000	13,380	7,270	243,650
21	200,000	1·139	227,800	13,670	7,340	248,810
24	200,000	1·16	232,000	13,920	7,420	253,340
27	250,000	1·183	295,750	17,750	7,500	321,000
30	250,000	1·207	301,750	18,100	9,460	329,310
33	300,000	1·231	369,300	22,160	9,560	391,020
36	300,000	1·255	376,500	22,590	11,700	410,790
39	300,000	1·281	384,300	23,060	11,930	419,290
42	300,000	1·306	391,800	23,510	12,170	427,480
45					12,420	12,420
48					112,800 ⎱	1,071,900
					959,100 ⎰	
			3,153,600	378,430		

Period	Total inflated outlay £	Total projected income £	Net cashflow £	PV £1 factor @ 3·5%	Present value £
3	(94,600)		(94,600)	0·9662	(91,400)
6	(94,600)		(94,600)	0·9335	(88,310)
9	(55,650)		(55,650)	0·9019	(50,190)
12	(85,120)		(85,120)	0·8714	(74,170)
15	(231,720)		(231,720)	0·842	(195,110)
18	(243,650)	9,090	(233,560)	0·8135	(190,000)
21	(248,810)	18,270	(230,540)	0·786	(181,200)
24	(253,340)	27,540	(225,800)	0·7594	(171,470)
27	(321,000)	36,910	(284,090)	0·7337	(208,440)
30	(329,310)	48,730	(280,580)	0·7089	(198,900)
33	(391,020)	60,680	(330,340)	0·685	(226,280)
36	(410,790)	75,300	(335,490)	0·6618	(220,030)
39	(419,290)	90,210	(329,080)	0·6394	(210,410)
42	(427,480)	105,420	(322,060)	0·6178	(198,970)
45	(12,420)	120,940	108,520	0·5969	64,780
48	(1,071,900)	5,642,000	4,570,100	0·5767	2,635,580

Gross Site Value   395,480
less acquisition costs @ 2·5%   9,890
Net Site Value   385,590

ASSESSMENT OF MAXIMUM PRICE PAYABLE

The site is for sale at £400,000. The two appraisals produce site values either side of this figure. Using present day figures suggests a value of £478,000 and using projected figures suggests a value of £386,000. Should the developer proceed to purchase at £400,000? Does the developer have more confidence in one appraisal than in the other? Are the cost and rental value projections reasonable or unduly pessimistic? Further examination also suggests that minor changes to the scheme's phasing would improve profitability and justify a higher acquisition cost. Similarly if each phase was sold as soon as it was let (or sold to individual owner occupiers) rather than waiting until the whole scheme was finished before selling as one large investment, then the net cash outflows would be reduced and viability improved.

Are the projections used reasonable? This question is dealt with in more detail in the following chapter but a brief examination of past trends suggests that they are certainly not unreasonable. Analysis of building cost increases over the past few years shows that recently costs have risen by about 5–6% per annum (see analysis in Chapter 4). Forecasts from reliable sources suggest increases slightly above this average rate over the next two years. So allowing for annual increases of 8·25% over the next four years seems reasonable.

Analysis of rental increases for prime industrial premises shows that over the country as a whole an average rate of growth of about 10% p.a. has been achieved since 1965 (Investors Chronicle/Hillier Parker Rent Index) but only about 4% p.a. over the last five years (and no increase at all in the North of England or Scotland).

Recent low rates of rental growth have been due to the aftermath of the economic recession, which reduced demand for space, and high levels of supply of accommodation, in part resulting from a high rate of development activity in the late 1970's. The assumption made in the above appraisal was that there would be no growth for the next twelve months and thereafter the situation would improve, as surplus supply diminished, so that in two and a half years time longer term average figures of about 8% p.a. would be achieved. In the light of a very brief analysis this appears possible but a local survey into the balance between supply and demand would still be necessary. Although increased research and data collection makes forecasting more accurate great care needs to be taken as over short time periods rents can vary enormously. Developments are mainly concerned with short term trends unlike investments which are often held for long time periods where short term fluctuations may cancel each other out.

CONCLUSION

Once again the extreme sensitivity of most financial appraisals is clearly demonstrated by the effect on site value of different rental growth assumptions. It should be abundantly clear that some form of sensitivity analysis must be undertaken ideally combined with a full probability analysis which not only examines different assumptions for each variable, particularly rents and costs, but their likelihood of being achieved. The result is a much more detailed picture of a development's viability enabling a developer to make better, more informed decisions. An examination of the problems of sensitivity and some of the methods available to provide more information about development viability is contained in Chapter 4.

STUART MORLEY

For bibliography, sample computer printout and available software please see end of Chapter 4.

Financial Appraisal – Sensitivity and Probability Analysis

INTRODUCTION

A residual valuation is a method of valuation which provides an estimate of site value or development return by using estimated figures for the variable elements occurring in a development such as rents and costs etc. Because there are so many variables in this method of valuation great care must be taken in its use as small changes in one or more of these variables can often exert a disproportionate effect on the residual answer. Attention was drawn to this problem in Chapter 1 and illustrated with some very simple examples. It was also pointed out that for this reason the Lands Tribunal treats residual valuations with a great deal of scepticism.

Due to the inherent sensitivity of this method of valuation and also due to the general risks in undertaking a speculative development, developers make an allowance of approximately 20% on top of estimated costs to help cover themselves and to help ensure they receive some profit at the end of the day. This chapter examines the problem of sensitivity and the effect on developers profit margins in some detail and looks at ways of improving the relatively unsophisticated nature of residual valuations so that a more complete picture of a scheme's financial viability can be shown thus making decision-making an easier and more informed procedure.

In Chapter 3 forecasting was discussed as a method of improving the sophistication of the residual and this could be described as the first step in examining a scheme's sensitivity, by looking at how the residual answer altered depending on whether present day or future estimates were used for the main variables of rent and cost. Many developers and their advisers are still sceptical of forecasting for a number of reasons that were briefly discussed. However, it is clear that even if present day figures are used these are still estimates as they relate to a future, and therefore uncertain, situation. The more complex a scheme and the longer it takes to build, the more uncertain it will be as each variable in the residual valuation will possess a greater possibility for change.

THE MAIN VARIABLES

Most financial appraisals of the type illustrated in previous chapters contain at least seven major variables each of which must be estimated and each of which must therefore be subject to change in the future. An examination of these variables and their likelihood of change is made below, illustrated by using the financial appraisal from Chapter 1 reproduced in simplified form later in this chapter.

Rent

Along with investment yield this is probably the most important variable as small changes in rent will exert the greatest change on profitability or residual site value. For example in the appraisal reproduced later in this chapter a small 10% reduction in rent would reduce the residual site value by about 40%! Accurately estimating rental levels is therefore crucial but difficult. It is difficult because it is unlikely that there will be sufficiently close direct comparables of recent lettings even to act as a base estimate before any forecasting is attempted.

For example are the comparables of similar size, age, and condition? Are they in the same location and do they possess the same level of finish and facilities? Was the rent achieved typical or exceptional due to special circumstances which made the prospective tenant pay over the odds or were there substantial rent free periods giving a misleading view of rental levels? Obviously the experience and skill of the valuer will overcome some of these problems, but nevertheless they will reduce the degree of certainty of any rental estimate.

Further problems arise because the development will not be available to let until some date in the future (typically two to three years for many commercial schemes) and so some estimate of what will happen during that period will have to be made even if it is not specifically made by projecting the rent to an expected future level. In the past rents have not increased in any uniform way but tend to move in cycles due in part to the cyclical nature of the economy and of the development process itself. It may well be that a development started during an upturn in the cycle (boom) may be completed during the seemingly inevitable downturn (recession).

The following figure illustrates this point very clearly showing how the degree of rental growth has varied markedly from

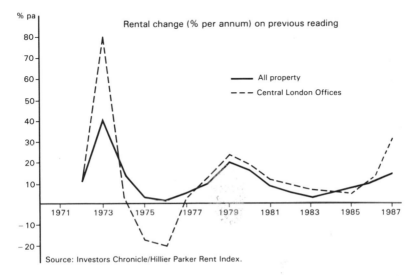

Source: Investors Chronicle/Hillier Parker Rent Index.

year to year. Furthermore much more dramatic changes have occurred and are likely to continue to occur for particular properties in particular locations as is also shown by the variation in rental growth achieved by central London offices.

Investment Yield

As for rents small changes in yield levels can have dramatic effects on residual calculations. Again using the same appraisal as an example – if a yield of 7·5% instead of 7% were used, a seemingly slight change, then the site value would be reduced by about 27%. Investment yields can alter significantly during a two or three year development period as the following figure shows, even though for prime properties they have been more stable over the last few years.

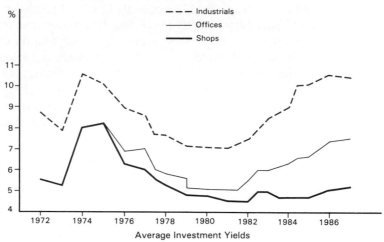

Average Investment Yields

Source: Investors Chronicle/Hillier Parker

Construction Cost

Construction costs are probably less difficult to predict over the short term than rental levels but can nevertheless be subject to substantial change. This change can be due to two different factors.

Firstly tender prices may change between the appraisal date and tender date just before the start of construction. Tender prices will vary due to inflation in building costs and the amount of work available. In a recession where the amount of building work decreases, it is possible that building costs will increase but tender prices may stabilise or increase at a lower rate, as profit margins are cut in a more competitive climate.

However, as the period of time between appraisal date and tender date is normally twelve months at the most and usually no more than six months, forecasting can be made with a reasonable degree of accuracy.

Secondly material and labour costs may change once building work has commenced. Unless a fixed price contract has been agreed (possible for short contracts), then inflation in material and labour costs will be borne by the developer. Recent changes in tender prices and building costs are illustrated below and discussed in greater detail in Chapter 5.

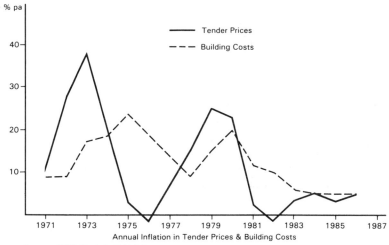

Sources: BCIS. Davis Belfield & Everest

Building Period

The length of time taken to construct a scheme can usually be estimated fairly accurately but sometimes delays occur due to such factors as strikes, shortages of building materials or the discovery of archaeologically important remains when the foundations are being excavated. Delays in completing the building will increase total costs due to inflation in building costs and increased finance charges (both on building costs and land costs) as money will have to be borrowed for a longer period.

Letting Period

Similarily letting delays will increase finance costs as the full amount of the loan required to finance the cost of construction will be outstanding, and therefore incurring interest, over the full period needed to let the building. Finance charges on land acquisition will also be increased as the period from land acquisition to completion and disposal will be extended. Long delays will significantly increase overall costs particularly when interest rates are at high levels.

Development Period

The development period incorporates the building and letting period and also the time taken before construction commences. During this period planning permission must be obtained (possibly both outline and detailed). There may be delays either in awaiting the local authority's decision, or, if they are not happy with the proposals, in further discussion, negotiations over planning gain possibly, and the preparation of a new submission. Not only will this lead to delay but possibly to a change in the size and composition of the scheme. The appraisal could therefore change considerably. There may also be delays in builders submitting tenders, in deciding on which tender to accept, and before the selected builder actually goes on site and starts work.

Finance Interest Rate

Interest rates for short term borrowing from banks can be subject to great change over short time periods as the following table shows. For example over the 15 years from 1971 to 1986,

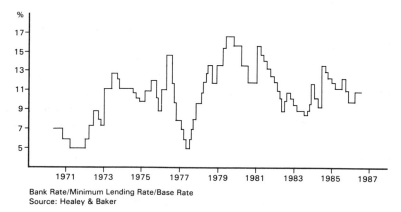

Bank Rate/Minimum Lending Rate/Base Rate
Source: Healey & Baker

Bank Base Rate, to which much short term borrowing is related, altered repeatedly from lows of 5% in early 1972 and late 1977, to highs of 15% in 1976 and 1981 and 17% in late 1979 and early 1980.

Floorspace

Rental (and hence capital) value and building costs are obviously based on the size of the development. As stated above if outline planning permission has not been obtained at the appraisal date the size of development cannot be certain and this will compound any uncertainty mentioned previously. But even if outline planning permission has been obtained fixing the gross floor area (and hence easing the task of calculating building costs) some uncertainty may well exist about net floor areas, on which rents are based. If the development is an office building will net floor area be 80% or 75% of gross floorspace for example? This will depend on the constraints of the site and ability of the architect to design as efficient a building as possible. In the appraisal below if the net office floor area achievable was only 75% of gross floor area rather than 80% as assumed, this would reduce the development value of the site by about 23%, a significant reduction.

Fees

Fees are payable at various stages of the development process – when the site is acquired, when the scheme has been designed, whilst it is being built, after it has been let and when it has been sold or funded. These fees may well be negotiated and therefore differ from the scale fees laid down by the respective professional institutions, leading to an element of uncertainty, and in some cases a developer may be unsure of how many consultants he may need to employ, i.e. specialists on air conditioning for example, so increasing uncertainty. But as the total of all fees likely to be incurred do not normally amount to a very large sum, any errors in estimation should not materially affect the outcome.

In conclusion it is important to stress that in property development all of these variables can alter individually either in similar or sometimes in different directions. In fact as shown clearly in the figure below the important variables of building cost and rent often do not move in the same direction although care must be taken in comparing such general average figures. The combination of these changes could lead to large variations in the residual value. Furthermore as stated earlier, in many cases only a slight change in just one variable can dramatically alter the residual value.

It is therefore essential that any detailed financial appraisal must contain some form of sensitivity analysis to illustrate how sensitive the appraisal is to changes in its variables. There are a number of different methods of approaching this, varying

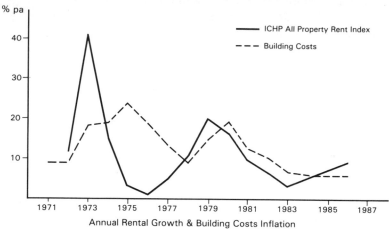

Annual Rental Growth & Building Costs Inflation
Sources: as above

in their sophistication, the stage in the development process at which they are undertaken and the information it is desired for them to provide. The methods described here are all illustrated by using the financial appraisal from Chapter 1 reproduced in simplified form below.

Value of Scheme		*p.a.*
Income		£658,500
Yield @ 7%		14·2857
Capital Value		£9,407,000

Costs of Scheme		
Land cost (incl. acquisition costs)	£1,345,000	
Building Cost (incl. ancillary costs)	£4,125,000	
Professional fees	£515,500	
Contingencies	£139,000	
Short term finance @ 14% p.a.		
land cost	£521,000	
bldg. etc. cost	£493,500	
letting delay on building costs	£357,000	

Agency fees
   letting and marketing   £124,000
   sale of investment   £188,000

Total Development Cost   £7,808,000 £7,808,000

Return for risk and profit   £1,599,000

$\begin{bmatrix} 17\% \text{ of Capital Value} \\ 20\cdot5\% \text{ of Total Costs} \end{bmatrix}$

METHOD 1 – SIMPLE SENSITIVITY TESTING

In the above appraisal the developer estimated that a return to cover risk and profit of £1,599,000 was required which represented 17% of the value of the completed development or approximately 20% of total outlay. On this basis the valuation of the site was £1,345,000 (including acquisition costs). The first form of sensitivity analysis would be to examine how changes in individual variables affected site value to enable the developer to make a more informed decision before purchasing the site. This type of simple analysis will give an indication of how sensitive the particular calculation is and should be looked at as an extension of the analysis contained at the end of Chapter 1. One form of this analysis might be to draw up a matrix of site values resulting from small changes to rent and yield as shown below. Other relationships (e.g. value and cost) could obviously be looked at similarly. (See computer printouts at the end of this chapter for further examples.)

Matrix of Site Values			
Estimated Rental Value of office space £ per m²	*Investment Capitalisation Rate* 6·75%	7%	7·25%
145	1·38 m	1·18 m	1·0 m
150	1·54 m	1·35 m	1·16 m
155	1·72 m	1·51 m	1·31 m

The following analysis assumes that the site can be, and subsequently is, acquired for £1,345,000 (including acquisition cost). It examines how sensitive the profit margin is to changes in the principal variables and therefore will show the developer how different changes in each variable separately affect the residual answer indicating how sensitive the profit margin is, and which variables are capable of exerting the greatest change on the scheme's viability. The developer can then ensure that their values are estimated with as much accuracy as is possible. Those variables which do not affect profitability greatly can therefore be estimated with less research so that time and effort can be put to greatest use.

Change in Variable *±10%*		*Return for risk and profit* *Amt. £*	*% of CV*	*Change in profit* *%*
Rent	+	2·51 m	24·0	+57·0
	−	0·69 m	8·0	−57.0
Yield	+	0·76 m	9.0	−52·5
	−	2·62 m	25·0	+64·0
Bldg. Cost	+	1·03 m	11·0	−35·5
	−	2·16 m	23·0	+35·5
Finance rate	+	1·45 m	15·5	− 9·0
	−	1·74 m	18·5	+ 9·0
Bldg. period	+	1·51 m	16·0	− 6.0
	−	1·69 m	18·0	+ 6·0
Letting period	+	1·55 m	16·5	− 3·0
	−	1·65 m	17·5	+ 3·0
Pre-bldg. period	+	1·59 m	17·0	− 1·0
	−	1·61 m	17·0	+ 1·0
Land Cost	+	1·41 m	15·0	−11·5
	−	1·78 m	19·0	+11·5

The table shows how the developer's profit is likely to alter with small (10%) changes in each of the variables. It is very clear that rent, investment yield and (to a lesser extent) building costs are by far the most sensitive variables, with a 10% change in rent or investment yield altering profit by more than five times as much. The majority of development projects will show similar characteristics although the degree of sensitivity will vary, except that in some cases, where land acquisition forms a much larger share of total development value (here it is only 14%), land cost could also be an important and sensitive variable.

It is also necessary to emphasise that although the short

term rate of interest, for example, does not appear to be a crucial variable, as a 10% increase in the rate only reduces profit by about 9%, the chances of such a change occurring are normally much greater than a similar change in rents. Put another way, as was shown previously, it is not unusual for interest rates to change markedly during the period of development whereas a large change in rents (particularly downwards) is less likely. This rather simple method of sensitivity testing does not consider the probability or likelihood of these changes occurring. This failing is remedied in Method 3.

As rent, investment yield and building cost are the most sensitive variables a developer must therefore pay particular care in estimating them as accurately as possible. In some cases the developer may decide to go further.

Rather than waiting until the development is completed before letting it, a prelet could be negotiated before the development starts. This eliminates any letting delay, fixes a definite rent and would probably make raising finance easier and possibly cheaper. On the other hand the start of development may be delayed whilst the prelet is arranged. Assuming that it is in fact possible to achieve a prelet, if the rent is then fixed, and substantial rental growth and cost inflation occur in the vicinity during the development period then the developer may suffer a double penalty, at least until the first rent review. For this reason developers will try and overcome the problem by some form of indexation during the development period or by arranging a rent review at the date of occupation, although it is probable that some concession will have to be given to the tenant to reflect his early commitment.

Similarly it is now common practice to prefund certain types of developments by agreeing, prior to commencement, to forward sell the finished and let development to an investor at an agreed yield. Whilst this of course eliminates any delay in finding a purchaser when the scheme is finished and maximum costs are incurred, it also gives the developer the guarantee of a certain price, but the investment yield agreed will reflect this and will be higher (see Chapter 9). The developer's resultant profit could be substantially reduced, but then risks have also been reduced and the cost of short term finance will probably be available on more favourable terms.

Finally, where the building period is relatively short (12–18 months maximum) and competition between contractors is strong, it should be possible to arrange a fixed price contract which means a higher tender price is agreed (reflecting the builder's estimate of future inflation), but subsequent increases in building costs should be avoided. Fixed price contracts are discussed in greater detail in Chapter 5.

The following table illustrates sensitivity in a different and more useful way and is widely used by developers. The table shows the scheme's downside risk where the development just breaks even. If rents fall by nearly 18% then no profit will be made. In numerical terms this would mean office rents of just under £124 m² rather than £150 m² (as estimated in the appraisal) and shop rents of about £107 m² rather than £130 m². An investment yield increasing from 7% to 8·5%, not at all impossible, particularly considering how yields have altered over the last few years (see Average Investment Yield diagram), would have a similar effect. Alternatively the finance rate would have to increase to an almost unheard of 29% p.a. or the building period would have to more than double to nearly 4 years. An increase of 300% in the letting period may appear improbable, but in a severe economic recession a letting period of two years may seem less improbable.

Variable	Change in variable to eliminate profit	New value of variable (approx.)	Original value of variable
Rent	17·5%	£124 per m² (office rent)	£150 per m² (office rent)
Yield	21%	8·5%	7%
Building cost	28·5%	£960 per m² (office cost)	£750 per m² (office cost)
Finance rate	105%	29%	14% p.a.
Building period	153%	3·75 yrs	1·5 yrs
Letting period	295%	2 yrs	0·5 yrs
Pre-building period	953%	5·25 yrs	0·5 yrs
Land cost	87%	£2·4 m	£1·3 m

The method of analysis illustrated above is basic but it does provide a developer with additional useful information about a scheme's viability and sensitivity to changes in estimates. It shows which are the key variables, the degree of sensitivity and what extreme conditions have to occur before profit margin is completely eroded. What it fails to consider is the rather more likely occurrence of combinations of a number of variables changing simultaneously rather than in isolation and secondly the probability of these changes occurring. The second and particularly the third method described below overcome these criticisms.

METHOD 2 – SCENARIOS

The second method examines how a *combination* of changes in the components of an appraisal affect the residual value, whether it is the site value or the developer's profit or development yield. In this case, to maintain consistency the developer's profit is the residual value used and tested for sensitivity, and the example is the same as used previously. Three scenarios are examined, optimistic, realistic and pessimistic, to determine how the developer's profit is affected. The values for each variable in the three scenarios have been chosen to illustrate the method and are not definitive estimates. In practice professional judgement will be crucial in selecting reasonable estimates based on expert advice, good records and knowledge of the market. This is discussed in more detail in Method 3.

Variable	Optimistic scenario	Realistic scenario	Original estimate	Pessimistic scenario
Rental growth	7% p.a.	5% p.a.	—	3% p.a.
Investment yield	6·75%	7%	7%	7·25%
Building costs increase	6% p.a.	7·5% p.a.	—	9% p.a.
Finance rate	12% p.a.	14% p.a.	14% p.a.	16%
Building period	18 mths	18 mths	18 mths	18 mths
Letting period	no delay	6 mths	6 mths	9 mths
Prebuilding period	6 mths	6 mths	6 mths	9 mths
Contingencies	3%	3%	3%	3%
Land cost (incl. acquistion costs)	£1·35 m	£1·35 m	£1·35 m	£1·35 m

Valuation and Development Appraisal

The three scenarios have been chosen to give an idea of what might happen if things go as expected, or go better or worse than expected. They are not meant (here) to represent complete extremes of circumstances which a developer could face, but situations which could reasonably occur. Even so a developer would be unlucky if he encountered the combination of adverse circumstances contained in the pessimistic scenario. Whilst the pessimistic value of each variable in isolation does not appear extreme the combination of pessimitic values for most of the variables renders the scheme unattractive although still showing a small profit.

The problem with this approach, whilst being an improvement on the first method is that little account has been taken of the probability of the selected values of all the variables occurring together. Whilst it is possible for the pessimistic and optimistic scenarios to occur, and far more pessimistic scenarios actually occurred during the slump of the mid-1970's for example, a developer might consider it unlikely that such a combination would occur. In which case either a less extreme view might be taken involving such pessimistic views on only some of the variables or else a proper probability analysis undertaken such as in method 3 below. Nevertheless the results of this sensitivity analysis show the developer that this scheme is a sensitive one as relatively small changes in each variable will dramatically alter the profit margin. Also of interest is the fact that in the realistic, and therefore most expected scenario, even though a safe view of rental growth vis à vis cost inflation has been taken (possibly even a pessimistic view) profit margins are slightly improved when compared to the original appraisal.

	Optimistic scenario	Realistic scenario	Original estimate	Pessimistic scenario
Developer's return	£3·5 m	£2 m	£1·6 m	£0·5 m
% of CV	31·6%	19·2%	17%	5·8%
% of total costs	46·1%	23·8%	20·5%	6·2%
Increase over original estimate	120%	25%		−65%

This method suffers from two main problems; *firstly* it is unlikely but not impossible, that the optimistic or pessimistic values for each variable would combined together to give the optimistic and pessimistic profit levels shown, and *secondly* no information is provided on the likelihood or probability of these estimates occurring. For example are all three scenarios equally likely or is the realistic scenario much more likely than the other two? Equally important, how probable is the pessimistic outcome? If it is considered to have say only a 5% chance then maybe a developer would consider that the risk of a substantially reduced profit was not too significant. But if it had a 20% chance then this would be serious and the scheme might then be rejected. So a refinement of this method would be to consider the probability of these scenarios being achieved.

Further extensions and refinements of this method, by incorporating realistic optimistic and pessimistic values for *each* variable and then combining these values to give a wider range of possible results may overcome the first problem mentioned above but do not tackle the question of probability of these estimates being correct. Method 3 therefore introduces the concept of probability into the estimated values of each variable so that not only is a range of values estimated for each, but an attempt is made at assessing the probability of each value occurring.

METHOD 3 – PROBABILITY AND SIMULATION

The two previous methods provide a developer with a degree of additional information namely about how the outcome of a particular devlopment might vary according to changes in individual variables either independently (method 1) or in combination (method 2). Both these methods therefore provide information about uncertainty – the uncertainty of an expected outcome. They help inform the developer how well the project will do in the light of uncertain forces. What they do not do is inform the developer about the degree of risk in the project, which can only be achieved if a probabilistic model is used. The second method is capable of modification into a crude probabilistic model, as briefly mentioned, if the likelihood of each of the three point estimates being achieved can be assessed.

Some writers equate risk with uncertainty, but the majority view is that uncertainty is defined as being where the likelihood of occurrence is unknown whereas risk is where the probability of outcomes can be estimated. The contention here is that risk or probability analysis is a significant advancement on the methods discussed previously providing of course that the appraiser is confident that some measure of probability can be made for the values of individual variables or combination of variables being achieved. This can only be made with a detailed knowledge of the present and future state of the market, and from previous experience of what outcome is likely and the chances of things going wrong.

Probability

It is one thing to say an event is very likely, fairly likely or alternatively not very likely to occur, it is another thing to try and quantify these subjective descriptions, which will be given different interpretations by different people. To overcome this problem of subjectivity statisticians use a scale of probability ranging from zero (absolute impossibility) to 100% or one (absolute certainty). An event which might be described therefore as being very likely might be given a value of say 80% or 0·8 and one which is fairly likely say 50 or 60%, i.e. 0·5 or 0·6.

This ability to ascribe probability factors to the estimated values in a development appraisal is the first step in providing more detailed information about quantifying risk. For example assume that in an appraisal a developer was reasonably confident about the values he has assumed and considers that each value has an 80% chance of being correct (a very high degree of confidence) and that none are mutually determined. Probability analysis will show that if there are say seven variables the likelihood of all the forecasts together being correct will be slight. There would be only a 21% chance $(0·8^7 \approx 0·21)$ that the answer given by combining them together would be correct. Therefore the expected profit level could be described as being dependent on a rather unlikely coincidence. A lower but more reasonable degree of confidence in the value of each variable of say 60% will result in only a 2·8% chance that the answer given by combining them would be correct!

Rather than estimate one value for each variable and assess the degree of certainty attached to it as above, an alternative approach, is to take say a 3 point estimate and assess the probability of each estimate proving correct, so that a weighted average best estimate can be derived. The example of building costs from the appraisal used in Method 2 will be used to illustrate the development of this technique. In Method 2 building costs were assumed to increase at either 6%, 7·5% or 9% per annum. If it was considered that the present rate of inflation was more likely to increase than decrease during the next 2–3 years then it might be reasonable to estimate that there was say a 60% probability of the increase being 7·5% p.a., a 30% probability of it being 9% p.a. and a 10% probability of it being 6% p.a. In which case the expected value would be the sum of all the expected values weighted by their chance of occurring, i.e.

$$\left(7{\cdot}5\% \times \frac{60}{100}\right) + \left(9\% \times \frac{30}{100}\right) + \left(6\% \times \frac{10}{100}\right)$$

which equals 7·8% p.a. and not 7·5% p.a. which appeared to be the best estimate.

However, this best estimate of 7·8% p.a. could equally have been derived from a different risk profile of say a 40% probability of the increase being 7·5% p.a., a 40% probability of it being 9% p.a. and a 20% probability of it being 6% p.a. Clearly some additional refinement must be introduced to differentiate between them, as even relying on the expected weighted value only portrays part of the picture because, whilst the best estimate is the same the spread of risks is not. The latter risk profile suggests greater uncertainty with more chance of cost inflation being higher or lower than the best estimate.

The solution is therefore to construct a full range of possible values for each variable, from extremely pessimistic to extremely optimistic, and estimate the likelihood (probability) of each value occurring. A simulation exercise can then be undertaken to combine these values as shown below. Once again the cost variable is used as an example. The three values of possible cost inflation are now extended into a range of values. To do this requires two things – an analysis of past trends and an examination of expected inflation in the economy and its effect on building costs.

Valuation and Development Appraisal

Whilst Chapter 5 also examines this, a brief analysis here of trends and forecasts will show probability factors could be used based on easily available information. The following table provides an analysis of building costs and tender prices over the period 1970–1986 together with estimates until the end of the decade.

	TENDER PRICES	BUILDING COSTS
	Annual increase over previous year	*Annual increase over previous year*
1970		
1971	12·5%	9%
1972	27%	9%
1973	37·5%	18%
1974	19%	18·5%
1975	2·5%	23·5%
1976	−0·5%	18·5%
1977	7·5%	13%
1978	15%	9%
1979	24·5%	15%
1980	23·5%	19·5%
1981	2·5%	12%
1982	−1%	10·5%
1983	3·5%	6·5%
1984	5·5%	5·5%
1985	4%	5·5%
1986	5·5%	5·5%
Prediction 1987–1990	8% p.a.	6–7% p.a.

Source: Davis Belfield & Everest

A number of points are very clear from this table:

- Tender prices vary between low and high extremes more than building costs reflecting the amount of work available and hence the size of contractors' profit margins.
- The 'boom' periods of the early and late '70's are clearly reflected in the rapid increases in tender prices in those years and similarly the "slumps" that followed those "booms" are reflected in very low increases.

- Increases in building costs reflect general inflation in the economy and bear little direct relation to the change in tender prices. 1974, 1975 and 1980 were all years of high rates of inflation in the economy.

Information on both tender prices and building costs will be necessary as in the example used previously a 6 month period was assumed to elapse before tenders are received and a further 18 months for the building period itself. Total construction costs are likely to be determined by movements in tender prices over a short period from the date of the appraisal, and by movements in building costs over the rather longer period after the tender price has been accepted. Taking account of the above information a range from +5% p.a. to +10% p.a. would currently seem appropriate and probability factors could be assessed as shown below.

Construction cost inflation per annum	Probability of occurrence		Cumulative probability of that value or less
+5%	10%	0·10	0·10
+6%	25%	0·25	0·35
+7·5%	40%	0·40	0·75
+8·5%	20%	0·20	0·95
+10%	5%	0·05	1·0
	100%	1·0	

These assumptions can be illustrated graphically in the form of frequency/probability distributions. Two forms are shown below. The first displays the information in the form of a histogram showing the probability of individual values of construction cost inflation being encountered. The second portrays the cumulative distribution of construction cost inflation and therefore shows the probability of inflation being less than or greater than a specified rate.

Simulation – The Method
The method of selecting and combining values for each variable involves using the statistical device of Monte Carlo simulation. There are three stages.

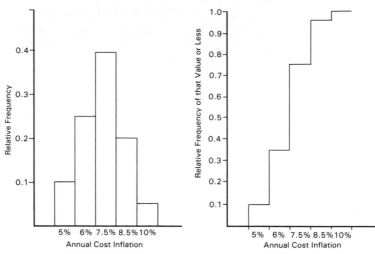

(1) A range of values for each variable, from extremely pessimistic to extremely optimistic is estimated together with
the likelihood (i.e. probability) of each value occurring as
illustrated above for construction costs. A simplified probability table assuming the same scheme as previously, is
shown below. A value with say a 10% chance of occurring
means that it has 10 chances out of a total of 100. So in
the case of construction cost inflation +5% p.a. inflation
will be given the numbers 1–10, and +6% p.a. inflation
will be given the numbers 11–35 etc.

Variable	Range	Probability	Probability numbers (out of 100)
Rental growth	0%	15%	1– 15
(rate of annual	+ 3%	20%	16– 35
increase during	+ 5%	40%	36– 75
development)	+ 7%	20%	76– 95
	+10%	5%	96–100
Investment yield	6·5%	5%	1– 5
	6·75%	15%	6– 20
	7%	50%	21– 70
	7·25%	20%	71– 90
	7·5%	10%	91–100

Variable	Range	Probability	Probability numbers (out of 100)
Construction cost	+5	10%	1– 10
inflation per	+6	25%	11– 35
annum	+7·5	40%	36– 75
	+8·5	20%	76– 95
	+10	5%	96–100
Finance rate	12% p.a.	5%	1– 5
	13% p.a.	25%	6– 25
	14% p.a.	40%	26– 65
	15% p.a.	25%	66– 90
	16% p.a.	10%	91–100
Building period	15 mths	20%	1– 20
	18 mths	50%	21– 70
	21 mths	20%	71– 90
	24 mths	10%	91–100
Letting period	0	20%	1– 20
	3 mths	20%	21– 40
	6 mths	40%	41– 80
	9 mths	15%	81– 95
	12 mths	5%	96–100
Pre-building	3 mths	20%	1– 20
period	6 mths	60%	21– 80
	9 mths	20%	81–100

(2) An appraisal is then undertaken with randomly selected values for each variable. These values are selected, accounting for probability, as follows. A number between 1 and 100 is randomly selected and that number will therefore determine which value, within the range of values for that variable, is used in the appraisal. For example referring to rental growth in the probability table above if 22 is the number randomly chosen, as this lies within the range 16–35, it will give a value for rental growth of +3% p.a. If the subsequent random numbers are say 53, 14, 80, 42, 77 and 68, the variables selected for this appraisal will be as follows:

Rental growth	Investment yield	Construc-tion cost inflation	Finance rate	Building period	Letting period	Pre-building period
+3% p.a.	7%	+6% p.a.	14%	18 mths	6 mths	6 mths

(3) This procedure is repeated over and over again each time providing a residual value for the appraisal. Sometimes different combinations of each variable will produce the same answer, so that a pattern builds up of returns and their chance of occurrence as shown below.

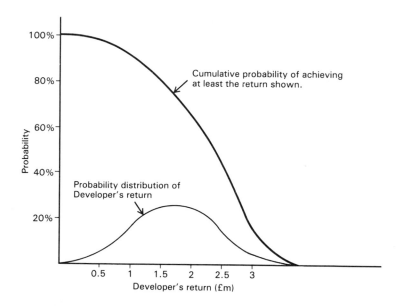

A Monte Carlo simulation was carried out on the development scheme discussed previously and with the probability assumptions shown in the table. The results based on 1000 runs were as follows.

Simulation No's: 1 & 2

	Capital value (£)	Total costs (£)	Profit (£)	Return on CV %	Return on TC %	Change in profit %
1	9·4 m	8·7 m	0·7	7·8	8·4	−54
2	11·2 m	8·2 m	3 m	26·8	36·6	87·2

Result of 1000 runs

	Mean	Standard deviation
Capital value	£10·2 m	£0.61 m
Total cost	£8·3 m	£0·36 m
Profit	£1·9 m	£0·65 m

Return on CV = 18·8%
Return on TC = 23·2%
Change in profit from original appraisal = 20·3%

Assuming that profit in this simulation is normally distributed,* a 95% prediction interval (±2 standard deviations) for a single result for profit is:

£0·6 m, £3·2 m

This means that the developer can be virtually certain that profit from this development scheme will not be less than £0·6 m and not more than £3·2 m.

Whether this risk is acceptable is up to the individual developer. Each developer will have different criteria in assessing the degree of risk that is acceptable, but at least this method of probability analysis provides the developer with sufficient information on which to make a decision and obviously provides a much clearer picture than was possible with the previous methods discussed.

A developer might for instance be faced with two alternative schemes as illustrated below, only one of which could be undertaken. Scheme B initially appears to be the more attractive development as when "best estimate" appraisals are undertaken it gives a higher level of profit. But after undertaking a probability analysis the picture is not so clear. Scheme B has a greater chance of making a substantial profit but a greater chance of making a loss. Whilst the mean value of expected profit is higher than in Scheme A the developer can be less

* The distribution resulting from a Monte Carlo simulation is often assumed to be a normal distribution as this simplifies the analysis which can be carried out. However this is only true if the variables used in the simulation are independent of each other but in a development appraisal this will not usually be the case and so slight errors will occur.

certain of achieving it. Whether the chance of higher profits in Scheme B will outweigh the greater certainty attached to the returns in Scheme A will be up to the developer, but at least the developer will have available a much clearer picture to enable this crucial decision to be made.

It is probable that institutional developers, for example, would take a safer or more conservative view of development risks than the traditional property company and so would only proceed with schemes with a narrower range of likely returns even if the most likely return was lower (curve A below). The

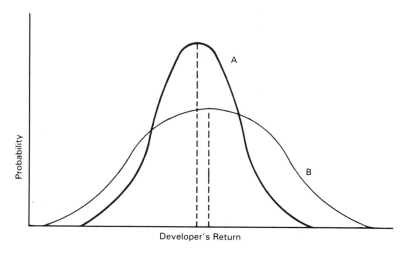

Developer's Return

development represented by curve B would be more of a gamble and might appeal to certain types of property companies. One further point to mention is the magnitude of the amount of money involved. Obviously if the scheme is risky but is small and therefore does not involve large sums of money being at risk, a developer's view of the risks involved may well be different than for a large and costly scheme. Similarly a large development company might be prepared to shoulder risks which a small company could not afford to, in case a loss resulted in bankruptcy.

The type of simulation exercise described in Method 3 is obviously extremely laborious if undertaken manually and is only really suitable for use with a computer. Many programmes involving a Monte Carlo random number selection technique are available (see the printout at the end of this chapter for an example) which enable the discounted cashflow exercise to be repeated many hundreds of times each based on a selection of the variables (seven in this case). The more calculations the better (100 would really be the absolute minimum) as this enables a more accurate and smooth probability curve to be drawn up.

Because a computer is used even greater realism can be incorporated by for example adopting different probability factors for each variable for each year of the development. This might mean a narrower range of probabilities in earlier years than in later years as there should be a greater degree of certainty over what will happen over the next year than what will happen in two or three years time.

CONCLUSION

It will be argued by some people that the type of simulation exercise described above is fine in theory but falls down in practice because of the difficulty and inaccuracy of estimating, firstly the range of values for each variable and secondly their probability of occurrence. There is some truth in this criticism and like all forecasting the accuracy of the answer is only as good as the accuracy of the inputs, however sophisticated the method itself is. Nevertheless over the last ten years great strides have been made in the property world in data collection, data analysis and forecasting. Research, within the major property firms particularly, has become a growth industry and will continue to increase and improve.

Finally, it should be emphasised that residual valuations are open to criticism due to the wide range of answers that can be obtained with only minor modification to the main variables. As a result the Lands Tribunal are very sceptical of accepting residual valuation evidence. Whilst it is clear from the foregoing pages in this and previous chapters that this criticism is well founded, it should be equally clear that this problem is greatest when only one best estimate appraisal is undertaken. The object of cashflow appraisals, forecasting, sensitivity analysis and particularly computer aided probability analysis is to overcome these criticisms and provide a more detailed and clearer picture of development viability. Some form of sensitivity or probability analysis should always be undertaken.

STUART MORLEY

COMPUTER BASED APPRAISAL PROGRAMMES

Many surveying firms, institutions and property companies have their own in house development appraisal software specially written for them. Similarly the Polytechnic of Central London (in common with many other Polytechnics and Universities) has developed its own development appraisal software which has been used for many of the calculations in Chapters 1–4.

Nevertheless there are a number of software packages available on the market and three of the most commonly used are listed below.

Interproperty Systems (IPS)
22 College Hill
London EC4

Greenlys
35 Piccadilly
London W1

Stephen Sykes Associates
Tanglewood
Vauxhall Lane
Tunbridge Wells
Kent

An example from Greenlys is reproduced below to illustrate the type of package widely used.

The Program has four main components:

(i) A residual valuation to calculate either site value or profit with up to four property types in any one appraisal.
(ii) A sensitivity analysis assessing the effects of changes in the yield, rental value or building cost of the main property type in the development.
(iii) A Monte Carlo analysis which provides:
    (a) the probability of achieving different profit levels
    (b) the expected profit
    (c) the probability of achieving a loss
    (d) the internal Rate of Return
(iv) A simplified cash flow statement with choice of equal spread or S-curve assumptions for building cost.

RESIDUAL VALUATION

DATE: 18/09/87
ADDRESS:

SITE PURCHASE

```
SITE(NET)                                              3225136
STAMP DUTY              ( 1.00%)                          32251
LEGAL FEES             ( 0.50%)                          16126
AGENTS FEES            ( 1.00%)                          32251
                                                       --------
GROSS SITE COSTS                                        3305764
```

DEVELOPMENT COSTS

```
BUILDING COST  20000 SQ. FT. AT  80.00 PER SQ.FT.  TYPE 1   1600000
BUILDING COST   5000 SQ. FT. AT  35.00 PER SQ.FT.  TYPE 2    175000
BUILDING COST   3500 SQ. FT. AT  40.00 PER SQ.FT.  TYPE 3    140000
BUILDING COST   5000 SQ. FT. AT  25.00 PER SQ.FT.  TYPE 4    125000
PROFESSIONAL FEES(12.50%)                                   255000
CONTINGENCY            ( 5.00%)                             117250
ANCILLARY                                                    50000
                                                           --------
TOTAL CONSTRUCTION COSTS                                   2462250
```

FINANCE COST

```
SITE FINANCE        30 MONTHS AT 12.00%                    1136906
BUILDING FINANCE    18 MONTHS AT 12.00%                     228317
VOID FINANCE         6 MONTHS AT 12.00%                     437459
                                                           --------
TOTAL FINANCE COSTS                                        1802682
```

LETTING COSTS

```
LETTING FEE AT 15.00% ERV                                   87900
PROMOTION COSTS                                             50000
                                                           --------
TOTAL LETTING COSTS                                        137900
```

FUNDING EXPENSES

```
DEVELOPER'S LEGAL COSTS  ( 0.50%)                           47389
DEVELOPER'S AGENTS COSTS ( 1.50%)                          142167
                                                           --------
TOTAL FUNDING COSTS                                        189556
```

```
TOTAL COSTS                                               7898152
```

RESIDUAL VALUATION (cont'd)

```
RETURNS
-------
TOTAL INVESTMENT VALUE                                        9477778

TYPE 1
------
ERV-  16000 SQ. FT. AT   30.00 POUNDS PER SQ.FT.              480000
INVESTMENT YIELD=                            6.00%
INVESTMENT VALUE=                                            8000000

TYPE 2
------
ERV-   4500 SQ. FT. AT   10.00 POUNDS PER SQ.FT.               45000
INVESTMENT YIELD=                            6.00%
INVESTMENT VALUE=                                             750000

TYPE 3
------
ERV-   3000 SQ. FT. AT   12.00 POUNDS PER SQ.FT.               36000
INVESTMENT YIELD=                            8.00%
INVESTMENT VALUE=                                             450000

TYPE 4
------
ERV-   5000 SQ. FT. AT    5.00 POUNDS PER SQ.FT.               25000
INVESTMENT YIELD=                            9.00%
INVESTMENT VALUE=                                             277778

RESIDUAL PROFIT                                              1579627
% OF COST =                                 20.00 %
YIELD ON COST=                               7.42 %
NET AREA AS % OF GROSS=                      85.07 %

ALL INTEREST COMPOUNDED QUARTERLY, ON BUILDING HALF RATE
RATE OF VAT ON FEES =  0.00%
RATE OF VAT ON BUILDING AND ASSOCIATED COSTS =  0.00%
ASSUMES  0.00% OF FUNDING FEES PAID UP-FRONT
```

SENSITIVITY ANALYSIS

```
THIS TABLE GIVES RESIDUAL LAND VALUES OVER A RANGE OF ERVS AND YIELDS
TO GIVE A PERCENTAGE PROFIT ON COST OF 20.0% AND COST/SQ.FT. OF    80.00(TYPE 1)

YIELD %    ERV= 25.00        27.50        30.00        32.50        35.00
5.50        2,828,598    3,229,142    3,630,066    4,030,610    4,431,152
5.75        2,652,741    3,035,737    3,418,732    3,801,727    4,184,723
6.00        2,491,379    2,858,353    3,225,136    3,591,919    3,958,893
6.25        2,342,987    2,695,084    3,047,181    3,399,277    3,751,373
6.50        2,205,849    2,544,403    2,882,767    3,221,131    3,559,494

THIS TABLE GIVES RESIDUAL LAND VALUES OVER A RANGE OF ERV AND BUILDING COSTS
TO GIVE A PERCENTAGE PROFIT ON COST OF 20.0% AND YIELD OF  6.00%(TYPE 1)
COSTS/SQ.FT. ERV= 25.00     27.50        30.00        32.50        35.00
70.00        2,678,681    3,045,655    3,412,628    3,779,602    4,146,576
75.00        2,584,839    2,951,813    3,318,787    3,685,761    4,052,735
80.00        2,491,379    2,858,353    3,225,136    3,591,919    3,958,893
85.00        2,397,537    2,764,511    3,131,485    3,498,459    3,865,433
90.00        2,303,887    2,670,670    3,037,644    3,404,617    3,771,591
```

```
THIS TABLE GIVES RESIDUAL PROFITS OVER A RANGE OF ERVS AND YIELDS
WITH SITE COST OF     3225136 AND COST/SQ.FT OF    80.00(TYPE 1)
YIELD ERV=25.00        27.50           30.00           32.50           35.00
5.50    879 (11.2 %)  1586 (20.1 %)  2292 (29.0 %)  2999 (37.8 %)  3706 (46.6 %)

5.75    569 ( 7.2 %)  1245 (15.8 %)  1920 (24.3 %)  2596 (32.8 %)  3272 (41.2 %)

6.00    285 ( 3.6 %)   932 (11.8 %)  1580 (20.0 %)  2227 (28.1 %)  2874 (36.2 %)

6.25     24 ( 0.3 %)   645 ( 8.2 %)  1266 (16.0 %)  1887 (23.9 %)  2508 (31.6 %)

6.50    218-( 2.8-%)   379 ( 4.8 %)   977 (12.4 %)  1574 (19.9 %)  2171 (27.4 %)
```

```
THIS TABLE GIVES RESIDUAL PROFITS OVER A RANGE OF ERVS AND BUILDING COSTS
USING SITE COST OF     3225136 AND YIELD OF  6.00%(TYPE 1)
COSTS ERV=25.00        27.50           30.00           32.50           35.00
70.00   559 ( 7.4 %)  1206 (15.9 %)  1854 (24.3 %)  2501 (32.7 %)  3148 (41.1 %)

75.00   422 ( 5.5 %)  1069 (13.8 %)  1717 (22.1 %)  2364 (30.4 %)  3011 (38.6 %)

80.00   285 ( 3.6 %)   932 (11.8 %)  1580 (20.0 %)  2227 (28.1 %)  2874 (36.2 %)

85.00   148 ( 1.9 %)   795 ( 9.9 %)  1443 (18.0 %)  2090 (25.9 %)  2737 (33.9 %)

90.00    11 ( 0.1 %)   658 ( 8.1 %)  1306 (16.0 %)  1953 (23.8 %)  2600 (31.7 %)
```

MONTE CARLO ANALYSIS

Probability	Rent /Sq.Ft.	Building Cost	Building Period	Void Period	Yield %	Interest˙ %
0	25.00	75.00	16	0	5.75	10.00
.125	26.25	76.25	17	2	5.81	10.50
.25	27.50	77.50	17	3	5.88	11.00
.375	28.75	78.75	18	5	5.94	11.50
.5	30.00	80.00	18	6	6.00	12.00
.625	31.25	81.25	19	8	6.13	12.75
.75	32.50	82.50	20	9	6.25	13.50
.875	33.75	83.75	20	11	6.38	14.25
1	35.00	85.00	21	12	6.50	15.00

MONTE CARLO ANALYSIS(250 CYCLES) SITE COST 3225136

Profit		Frequency	Percentage
-484125 TO	-170398	3	1.2
-170397 TO	143328	10	4.0
143329 TO	457054	15	6.0
457055 TO	770780	38	15.1
770781 TO	1084506	27	10.8
1084507 TO	1398232	32	12.7
1398233 TO	1711959	31	12.4
1711960 TO	2025685	17	6.8
2025686 TO	2339411	31	12.4
2339412 TO	2653137	23	9.2
2653138 TO	2966863	15	6.0
2966864 TO	3280589	8	3.2

EXPECTED PROFIT   =   1446069

LOSS PROBABILITY %   =   2.80

EXPECTED PROFIT %   =   18.33

EXPECTED IRR   %   =   19.95

GREENLY'S INDEX(0-10)=   7.67

ESTIMATED CASH FLOW STATEMENT (000) (S-curve assumption)

MONTH	LAND	BLDG	FEES ETC	SALE	NCF	PV-NCF	INTEREST	BALANCE
0	-3225.1	0.0	-80.6	0.0	-3305.8|	-3305.8|	0.0	-3305.8
1	0.0	0.0	0.0	0.0	0.0|	0.0|	0.0	-3305.8
2	0.0	0.0	0.0	0.0	0.0|	0.0|	0.0	-3305.8
3	0.0	0.0	0.0	0.0	0.0|	0.0|	-99.2	-3404.9
4	0.0	0.0	0.0	0.0	0.0|	0.0|	0.0	-3404.9
5	0.0	0.0	0.0	0.0	0.0|	0.0|	0.0	-3404.9
6	0.0	0.0	0.0	0.0	0.0|	0.0|	-102.1	-3507.1
7	0.0	0.0	0.0	0.0	0.0|	0.0|	0.0	-3507.1
8	0.0	0.0	0.0	0.0	0.0|	0.0|	0.0	-3507.1
9	0.0	0.0	0.0	0.0	0.0|	0.0|	-105.2	-3612.3
10	0.0	0.0	0.0	0.0	0.0|	0.0|	0.0	-3612.3
11	0.0	0.0	0.0	0.0	0.0|	0.0|	0.0	-3612.3
12	0.0	-13.9	-2.9	0.0	-16.8|	-15.0|	-108.4	-3737.4
13	0.0	-41.3	-8.6	0.0	-49.9|	-44.1|	0.0	-3787.3
14	0.0	-67.6	-14.0	0.0	-81.6|	-71.5|	0.0	-3868.9
15	0.0	-92.1	-19.1	0.0	-111.1|	-96.4|	-113.9	-4093.9
16	0.0	-114.0	-23.6	0.0	-137.6|	-118.3|	0.0	-4231.5
17	0.0	-132.8	-27.5	0.0	-160.3|	-136.5|	0.0	-4391.8
18	0.0	-148.0	-30.6	0.0	-178.7|	-150.7|	-127.1	-4697.7
19	0.0	-159.2	-33.0	0.0	-192.2|	-160.6|	0.0	-4889.8
20	0.0	-166.1	-34.4	0.0	-200.4|	-165.9|	0.0	-5090.3
21	0.0	-168.4	-34.9	0.0	-203.2|	-166.7|	-146.7	-5440.2
22	0.0	-166.1	-34.4	0.0	-200.5|	-162.9|	0.0	-5640.7
23	0.0	-159.3	-33.0	0.0	-192.3|	-154.7|	0.0	-5833.0
24	0.0	-148.2	-30.7	0.0	-178.8|	-142.6|	-169.1	-6180.9
25	0.0	-133.0	-27.5	0.0	-160.5|	-126.8|	0.0	-6341.5
26	0.0	-114.2	-23.6	0.0	-137.8|	-107.8|	0.0	-6479.3
27	0.0	-92.3	-19.1	0.0	-111.4|	-86.3|	-190.0	-6780.6
28	0.0	-67.8	-14.0	0.0	-81.9|	-62.9|	0.0	-6862.5
29	0.0	-41.6	-8.6	0.0	-50.2|	-38.2|	0.0	-6912.7
30	0.0	-14.2	-52.9	0.0	-67.1|	-50.5|	-205.5	-7185.4
31	0.0	0.0	0.0	0.0	0.0|	0.0|	0.0	-7185.4
32	0.0	0.0	0.0	0.0	0.0|	0.0|	0.0	-7185.4
33	0.0	0.0	0.0	0.0	0.0|	0.0|	-215.6	-7400.9
34	0.0	0.0	0.0	0.0	0.0|	0.0|	0.0	-7400.9
35	0.0	0.0	0.0	0.0	0.0|	0.0|	0.0	-7400.9
36	0.0	0.0	-277.5	9477.8	9200.3|	6548.6|	-222.0	1577.4

```
TOTAL  -3225.1  -2040.0   -830.3   9477.8   3382.3|  1184.4| -1804.9   1577.4

INTERNAL RATE OF RETURN = 19.95%
```

ESTIMATED CASH FLOW STATEMENT (000) (equal spread assumption)

MONTH	LAND	BLDG	FEES ETC	SALE	NCF	PV-NCF	INTEREST	BALANCE
0	-3225.1	0.0	-80.6	0.0	-3305.8	-3305.8	0.0	-3305.8
1	0.0	0.0	0.0	0.0	0.0	0.0	0.0	-3305.8
2	0.0	0.0	0.0	0.0	0.0	0.0	0.0	-3305.8
3	0.0	0.0	0.0	0.0	0.0	0.0	-99.2	-3404.9
4	0.0	0.0	0.0	0.0	0.0	0.0	0.0	-3404.9
5	0.0	0.0	0.0	0.0	0.0	0.0	0.0	-3404.9
6	0.0	0.0	0.0	0.0	0.0	0.0	-102.1	-3507.1
7	0.0	0.0	0.0	0.0	0.0	0.0	0.0	-3507.1
8	0.0	0.0	0.0	0.0	0.0	0.0	0.0	-3507.1
9	0.0	0.0	0.0	0.0	0.0	0.0	-105.2	-3612.3
10	0.0	0.0	0.0	0.0	0.0	0.0	0.0	-3612.3
11	0.0	0.0	0.0	0.0	0.0	0.0	0.0	-3612.3
12	0.0	-107.4	-22.2	0.0	-129.6	-115.7	-108.4	-3850.3
13	0.0	-107.4	-22.2	0.0	-129.6	-114.6	0.0	-3979.9
14	0.0	-107.4	-22.2	0.0	-129.6	-113.5	0.0	-4109.4
15	0.0	-107.4	-22.2	0.0	-129.6	-112.5	-119.4	-4358.4
16	0.0	-107.4	-22.2	0.0	-129.6	-111.4	0.0	-4488.0
17	0.0	-107.4	-22.2	0.0	-129.6	-110.4	0.0	-4617.6
18	0.0	-107.4	-22.2	0.0	-129.6	-109.3	-134.6	-4881.8
19	0.0	-107.4	-22.2	0.0	-129.6	-108.3	0.0	-5011.4
20	0.0	-107.4	-22.2	0.0	-129.6	-107.3	0.0	-5141.0
21	0.0	-107.4	-22.2	0.0	-129.6	-106.3	-150.3	-5420.9
22	0.0	-107.4	-22.2	0.0	-129.6	-105.3	0.0	-5550.5
23	0.0	-107.4	-22.2	0.0	-129.6	-104.3	0.0	-5680.1
24	0.0	-107.4	-22.2	0.0	-129.6	-103.3	-166.5	-5976.2
25	0.0	-107.4	-22.2	0.0	-129.6	-102.3	0.0	-6105.7
26	0.0	-107.4	-22.2	0.0	-129.6	-101.4	0.0	-6235.3
27	0.0	-107.4	-22.2	0.0	-129.6	-100.4	-183.1	-6548.1
28	0.0	-107.4	-22.2	0.0	-129.6	-99.5	0.0	-6677.7
29	0.0	-107.4	-22.2	0.0	-129.6	-98.5	0.0	-6807.3
30	0.0	-107.4	-72.2	0.0	-179.6	-135.3	-200.3	-7187.2
31	0.0	0.0	0.0	0.0	0.0	0.0	0.0	-7187.2
32	0.0	0.0	0.0	0.0	0.0	0.0	0.0	-7187.2
33	0.0	0.0	0.0	0.0	0.0	0.0	-215.6	-7402.8
34	0.0	0.0	0.0	0.0	0.0	0.0	0.0	-7402.8
35	0.0	0.0	0.0	0.0	0.0	0.0	0.0	-7402.8
36	0.0	0.0	-277.5	9477.8	9200.3	6548.6	-222.1	1575.5

| TOTAL | -3225.1 | -2040.0 | -830.3 | 9477.8 | 3382.3 | 1183.2 | -1806.8 | 1575.5 |

INTERNAL RATE OF RETURN = 19.92%

BIBLIOGRAPHY

J Ratcliffe, *An Introduction to Urban Land Administration*, Estates Gazette 1978

D Cadman & L Austin-Crowe, *Property Development*, E & F N Spon 1983 (2nd ed)

W Rees (ed), *Valuation – Principles into Practice*, (3rd ed) Estates Gazette 1988. Ch 13 Development properties by J Ratcliffe & N Rapley

B Jolly, *Development Properties & Techniques in Residual Valuation*, Property valuation handbook CALUS, CEM 1979

A Baum & D Mackmin, *The Income Approach to Property Valuation* (2nd ed), Routledge & Kegan Paul 1981

W Britton, K Davies & A Johnson, *Modern Methods of Valuation*, Estates Gazette 1984

Dr E Wood, *Property & Building Appraisal in Uncertainty*, Liverpool Polytechnic Occasional Paper 1 – October 1977

Pilcher, *Appraisal & Control of Project Costs*, McGraw-Hill 1973

A Jaffe, *Property Management in Real Estate Investment Decision Making*, Lexington 1979

P Byrne & D Cadman, *Risk, Uncertainty & Decision Making in Property Development*, E & F N Spon 1984

D Hertz & H Thomas, *Risk Analysis and its Applications*, John Wiley 1983

C Darlow (ed), *Valuation and Investment Appraisal*, Estates Gazette 1983

CHAPTER 5

Development Construction Costs

INTRODUCTION

The implicit objective of any development is the maximisation of the potential value or income accruing from the investment. In order to achieve this goal, it is important to optimise the key factors that concern every developer whose objectives are:

1. To complete the development on time
2. Within the available budget
3. To the required quality standard

1. Completion on Time

These factors all have a direct bearing on construction costs. The developer normally requires the shortest possible construction period for the scheme in order to reduce finance charges both for the building and the site. Because speed of construction is so important, it is essential that designers take advantage, wherever practicable, of fast construction techniques such as repetitive structural solutions, dry lined partitions, off-site fabricated services, etc. The resultant design may be inherently more expensive than a slower alternative solution, but the prospect of a potentially shorter contract period may encourage keener tender prices due to reduced risk for the contractor, and to a reduction in his own finance charges.

The duration of the development period determines the finance charges on the site. This period comprises three distinct activities, design, construction and marketing, which can, to an extent, overlap. However, such a requirement should be defined at the outset if the intention is to overlap design and construction, as a cost premium could be incurred which may compromise either the available budget, or if this is fixed, the quality standard that can be achieved. Completion dates within the development period can also be critical where, for example, a pre-let has been agreed and the prospective tenant requires occupation by a key date in order to commence pre-Christmas trading, or where the resulting income is critical to the development funding.

2. Establishing the Initial Budget

During the initial appraisal stage, the developer, having established the various elements of the development cost, can determine the residual available for site purchase. As the building represents the major element of the development cost, it is essential that as accurate an assessment as possible is made, for as the scheme is developed, any cost over-run on the building budget will ultimately reduce the profit from an eventual sale, or the yield, if the development is retained as investment, will be affected.

3. Required Quality Standard

All development appraisals should be based on an investment yield and rental level which reflects the quality standard that is to be attained in the design for the building. If the threshold in terms of quality and function is not achieved, letting delays may become extended, or pre-lets may be jeopardised, with the inevitable consequence of increased finance charges. The quality and functional standards can become critical in periods of weak demand in a market of plentiful supply, when potential tenants can exercise a preference for an enhanced quality of accommodation. Therefore as the development appraisal is refined, and the brief for the design becomes more detailed, it is essential that the budget for the building is tested to ensure that it reflects the quality standard that will be necessary to achieve the required rental level and yield.

BUDGET ESTIMATES

The first estimate of building cost is invariably required prior to the preparation of drawings and specifications. As such it will be appreciated that figures prepared at this stage can only be indicative, particularly if they are calculated using average costs/m². This chapter introduces a more accurate method of preparing a budget, using quantity factors and unit costs, that can form the 'budget cost target' for the development of the scheme by the architect, engineer and quantity surveyor. However it should be stressed that even at the very earliest stage in the development process, there is no substitute for the professional advice of a quantity surveyor.

In order to establish a realistic budget, it is necessary to appreciate the major factors that influence the construction cost of a scheme. These factors include:

1. Location
2. Site characteristics
3. Design and specification criteria;

while the cost significance of these factors in terms of eventual out-turn cost will be influenced to a greater or lesser degree by:

4. The contract arrangements
5. The prevailing market conditions.

1. Location

When considering site location it is not possible to identify geographical regions that exhibit absolute variations in building prices, as there are inevitable local variations in price that result from many conflicting pressures. However, it is possible to define regional groupings of local variations in building prices as follows:

Region	*Percentage variation compared with Outer London*
Outer London	Nil
East Anglia	−12%
East Midlands	−14%
Inner London	+10%
Northern	−11%
Northern Ireland	−20%
North West	−9%
Scotland	−13%
South East	−7%
South West	−14%
Wales	−10%
West Midlands	−15%
Yorkshire and Humberside	−14%

The above percentages are indicative of price levels in metropolitan and semi-rural areas. For inner city and central area redevelopment locations outside London, a reduction of only 4–6% may be more appropriate, while particularly restricted and confined sites should be considered on an ad hoc basis. Apart from the site itself, the two main factors that contribute to localised variations in price levels are the cost of resources and the level of demand.

The basic resources as defined by labour, material and plant are affected by market conditions. Labour costs are dependent upon local availability, which will be determined by the level of activity in the area. As an example, during a period of recession for the construction industry in a particular location, building operatives may seek work elsewhere or even leave the industry, whereas enhanced wage rates will be required to attract a suitable labour force when an upturn in activity occurs. The costs of materials is dependent, among other things, upon local supply, size of load, delivery cost and the general level of construction activity. This latter factor will influence merchants' discounts and/or premiums, while cash flow, the cost of finance and contractors' credit ratings will determine the contractor's purchasing arrangements. Plant costs are influenced by the contractor's view of future workload and will determine whether plant is hired or purchased or, in the case of existing plant, whether to extend its life or replace it.

Market conditions on a localised scale can be extremely volatile. The level of building investment in an area is affected by the amount of business activity, but it is also influenced by incentives, grants, tax reliefs etc. Individual contractors are concerned about current workload, future prospects, and the need to maintain or establish a presence in a particular area.

All these factors will influence the contractor's unit costs, but decisions on tender price levels will rest at board-room level, and can involve a director's adjustment that increases or decreases the final bid price.

2. Site
The site itself has a direct bearing on the type and form of

development, and involves the consideration of such factors as soil conditions, water table and site access. In the case of redevelopment sites, it may be necessary to place an advance works contract to deal with the demolition of existing buildings or the breaking out of foundations.

In good ground conditions, base and pad foundations can represent between 4 and 7% of the total building cost of a 6–8 storey office block. If soil conditions are such that piled foundations are necessary, the proportion can be more than 10%. However, having established the need for piles, the effect on foundation costs of adding another floor is usually marginal. Basement construction is expensive, particularly in ground with a high water table, but can be economic where extensive fill exists and deep foundations are necessary to reach good load bearing soil.

When considering basement construction at the development appraisal stage, the feasibility or otherwise of underground car parking is frequently discussed. In capital cost terms, underground car parking is very difficult to justify unless severe building height and/or site restrictions exist. This is due to the high cost of forming the basement structure and the fact that, when completely underground, there is a requirement for mechanical ventilation and sprinkler installations. The following cost comparison indicates that multi-storey car parks are $7\frac{1}{2}$ times the cost of surface parking, while underground car parks can cost twice as much again.

	Index	Cost/car
		£
Surface	100	600
Multi-storey	750	4,500
Partially underground under building	1,067	6,400
Completely underground under building	1,317	7,900
Completely underground with landscaped roof	1,500	9,000

Restricted site access and storage facilities can present considerable construction phasing constraints on the contractor.

The degree to which such constraints are reflected in the contractor's tender price will be dependent upon his recent tendering performance. For example, a £5 million contract on a restricted city centre site might normally attract a premium of £100,000 (2%). However, if the contractor needs to increase his bid success rate to boost future workload, the additional cost may be discounted. Conversely, during periods of high activity, when contractors have full order books, this may be one of several reasons why such projects carry a premium of in excess of 5%.

Redevelopment sites invariably involve some form of demolition work. The preparation of reliable budget allowances for such work can prove difficult, which in itself is a product of the nature of the work, but it also reflects the estimating methods used by demolition contractors that generally place heavy reliance on subjective judgement and experience. They will be keen to deploy the most economic demolition method, which may be in conflict with the rights of adjoining owners, and to establish the salvage value of the material content that will accrue from the demolition of a building. Material credits are invariably dependent upon local demand, which may be quite stable for good quality second hand facing bricks and natural slates, but is far less certain at the most basic level when disposing of hardcore. The form of construction of the building to be demolished, and hence the ideal method of demolition, is also very significant. Load-bearing brick structures do not pose too many problems, whereas reinforced concrete framed structures can be expensive to demolish if it is not possible to deploy a ball and crane. The use of thermic lances and compressors is both time consuming and labour intensive, but are often essential, particularly where, for example, the building to be demolished abuts another building, a footpath or highway. In addition, the position of the building on the site determines the amount and type of hoardings and protection to be provided.

Where demolition prices are built-up, they are usually based on the material cubic content of the building, which is established by making a notional allowance on a percentage basis for the air space within the building, and the voids in the external envelope. The following indicative demolition pricing data will enable an order of cost for demolitions to be calculated.

Demolition Costs	Cost/m³ £
Structures	
(a) Low rise brick green field site	1·50– 2·50
(b) Brick/steel framed urban site	2·50– 7·50
(c) Reinforced concrete restricted site	8·00–17·50
(d) Reinforced concrete with limited use of ball and crane, very restricted site	11–30
Air space allowances	30–50%
Hoardings 2·4 m high	£30–£40/m
Fan protection 2·4 m wide, 6·0 m above ground	£35–£50/m

Example

As an illustration the demolition cost of an eight storey reinforced concrete framed 30 m × 30 m tower block could be calculated as follows:

	£
Building demolition and removal of debris from site	
7,200 m² (gross floor area) × 3·60 m (floor to floor height) × 50% (modern construction with over 50% glazed external envelope) × £12·50/m³ (r.c. frame urban site)	162,000
Hoardings	
150 m (site perimeter) × £35/m	5,250
Fans	
60 m (two elevations) × £45/m	2,700
say	£170,000

The demolition cost of a 2,000 m² brick built 1920 warehouse with concrete floor and timber pitched roof with welsh slates on an open site could be calculated as follows:

Building demolition and removal of debris from site 2,000 m² × 5·0 m × 30% × £2·50/m³	£7,500

3. Design and Specification Criteria

If the first estimate is to form a realistic budget, certain strategic design criteria must be considered such as construction form, height and width. These criteria also influence the available options for the building elements.

(a) *Form, Height and Width*

Generally, the fewer the number of storeys, the more economical the building in capital cost terms and the higher the proportion of net lettable floor area to gross floor area. Gross floor area, for estimating purposes, is the total area of the building measured to the internal face of the external walls across all internal partitions, voids and staircases. As the number of storeys increase, vertical ducts become larger, intermediate service zones may be required, and vertical circulation cores for lifts and stairs form a higher percentage of plan floor area. Apart from the obvious cost effect of providing additional circulation and plant area, as building height rises, constructional costs also increase. Foundation costs become progressively expensive until piled foundations are required, after which the cost associated with each additional floor can be marginal. The developer's need to maximise plot ratios on restricted city centre sites leads to the construction of tall buildings. As height increases, so do labour costs, due to the time spent by building operatives moving up and down the building and both more exposed and difficult working conditions. If these additional costs are to be minimised, it is essential that large floor plates and repetitive frame solutions are adopted.

Example

The following table summarises the effect of total building height on both the circulation/plant and net lettable areas in a speculative air conditioned office building. It also indicates the effect of height on the construction cost both in terms of gross floor area and net lettable floor area.

It can be seen from the indices how the relative cost of providing floor space progressively increases when expressed in terms of the lettable area as compared with the gross area. This is due to the rising proportion within the gross area of circulation/plant.

No of storeys	Circulation and plant	Net lettable area	Cost/m² of gross floor area		Cost/m² of mean net lettable floor area	
	%	%	£	Index	£	Index
2–4	15–18	85–82	650	100	780	100
5–9	18–24	82–76	750	115	950	122
10–14	24–28	76–72	900	138	1,220	156
15–19	28–32	72–68	975	150	1,390	178
20+	32–35	68–65	1,100	169	1,540	197

Traditionally the demand for office accommodation has concentrated on shallow buildings about 12 m wide, with a central corridor and individual offices on either side.

The movement away from shallow depth offices for owner occupiers in the UK actually started over a decade ago as deep buildings often in excess of 20 m square on plan were constructed. Such buildings enabled the occupier to arrange his office in an open plan form and so take advantage of increased layout efficiency. The philosophy behind this type of office was developed some years earlier in Germany and North America.

The lack of flexibility that existed in the traditional shallow depth office, both in terms of the functional and organisational demands of the occupier, was one of the major criticisms which deep plan buildings supposedly resolved. However, certain inherent aspects of the design of the latter that are acceptable to the owner occupier, form major shortcomings when such buildings are considered for speculative development.

Apart from the obvious disadvantage that the floor space in such buildings is difficult to sub-divide, so that the minimum letting is to a single tenant occupying a whole floor, they generally have a higher capital and occupancy cost than shallow buildings. This is despite the cost advantage of deep plan buildings in that the area of the external envelope required to enclose a given floor area reduces, the closer the plan form approaches a square. The main reason for higher capital cost is the environmental dependence of deep plan buildings on air conditioning, the cost of which more than outweighs the saving on the external walls. The higher occupancy cost results from the energy consumed not only by the air conditioning system, but also by the lighting installation which, because of building depth, is required to supplement natural daylighting for long periods of the working day.

In order to overcome the disadvantages of both shallow and deep plan offices, there has been an increasing movement towards the development of medium depth buildings around 15 m wide. Such offices have an advantage in that they can accommodate both cellular and open plan space while not necessarily requiring air conditioning.

Example

The following comparison indicates the relative costs per m² of gross floor area for two storey, shallow, medium and deep plan office buildings:

	Capital cost		Energy cost per annum	
Floor plan depth	Cost/m² £	Index	Cost/m² £	Index
Shallow with central heating	490	100	4·35	100
Medium with central heating	500	102	4·15	95
Medium with mechanical ventilation	535	109	4·90	113
Deep with air conditioning	580	118	9·25	213

(b) *Structure*

Load-bearing brick structures are generally unsuited to office buildings of more than two storeys, because of the need to provide floor space uninterrupted by structural walls. Structural steel frames can be quick to erect; however, for this saving in construction time to be exploited to the full, it is necessary to use a dry lining/paint specification for the fire protection to the steel. The cost of protection, the amount of repetition and regular plan forms, and the method of fixing the cladding generally determines the suitability of steel or concrete frames.

The significant factors when considering costs of framed superstructures, are grids and spans for columns and beams. The additional cost of the frame in non-perimeter column solutions that involve cantilevers can be 8–10%, while an increase in floor loading from 5 to 7·5 kN may increase structural costs by 5%.

(c) *Roof*

The additional cost of asphalt flat roofs on heavy slabs can be 30–50% more than felt flat roofs on lightweight decks. Mansard roofs cost more than lightweight roofs, but there can be a saving on the cost of the enclosing envelope.

(d) *External envelope*

The total range of external envelope specifications is considerable.

Example

The following costs and indices indicate the relative ranking order of the main options.

External window and wall specifications	Typical cost/m² of external window and wall area (£)	Index
Faced brick cavity walls	70	100
Exposed aggregate precast concrete panels	100	143
Brick clad precast concrete panels	120	171
Economic curtain walling	180	257
Good quality precast concrete panels	190	271
G.r.p. sandwich panels	145	207
Good quality curtain walling	255	364
High quality curtain walling	350	500
Stone or marble cladding	310	443
Single glazed steel windows	115	164
Single glazed aluminium windows	125	179
Double glazed aluminium windows	250	357
High quality double glazed windows	300	429

The major quantity-related factors that influence the cost significance of the external envelope are:

1. The area of the external envelope compared with the enclosed floor area. This is dependent upon the product

of the floor perimeter and the storey height. For a given floor area, a square is more economical in terms of perimeter length than a rectangle, with the result that the external envelope to floor area ratio ranges from 0·70 : 1·00 for shallow offices to 0·35 : 1·00 for deep offices.

2. The window to solid wall ratio within the total area of the external envelope. This ratio is generally within the range 0·45 : 1·00 to 0·25 : 1·00.

(e) *Internal Division, Finishes and Fittings*

The internal division, finishes and fittings in speculative offices are generally limited to the landlords' common areas. However, the standard of specification can still result in a wide range of costs from blockwork with plaster finishes, and screed to receive carpet, to hardwood veneered demountable partitions, louvred suspended ceilings and good quality carpet on full access raised floors. Where a budget for fitting out is to be included as an enticement to potential tenants, it is important to establish both the quality standard and the space planning options.

Example

The effect of these specifications on the cost per m² of speculative and owner occupied office blocks of similar designs is as follows:

Speculative office	*Cellular letting cost/m²*	*Cellular owner occupied cost/m²*
	£	£
(a) Block and stud walls, plastered finishes, screed to receive carpet	550	590
(b) Patent partitions, plastered walls, acoustic suspended ceiling, partial access raised floor and economic carpet	585	630
(c) Demountable partitions, good quality wall coverings, louvred suspended ceiling, full access raised floor and good quality carpet	625	705

The above costs include for partitions and finishes for the letting option to landlords' areas only, whereas the owner occupied option also includes for these elements in the office areas.

However, these costs do not include for telecoms, security, data cabling or office furniture and loose fittings, which can add a further £100–120/m² for good quality cellular offices. The equivalent figures for open plan offices can be higher due to:

1. The need to provide screens and backs to the furniture in order to create office division.
2. The cost of wire management to work stations, which is normally incorporated in the furniture in open plan offices, whereas this facility is provided by partitions in the cellular office.

(f) *Services*

The services elements can represent anything from 20 to 40% of the total cost of an office building. The services provided can range from the simplest central heating system and electrical installation incorporating light fittings to landlords' areas only, to very sophisticated air conditioning systems with zonal control and electrical installations that incorporate an energy management system and standby generator. The total budget for a building should be formulated such that the available capital resources are distributed throughout the elements in such a way as to provide overall value for money. It is not practical therefore to consider the effect of services on total building costs in isolation, as the building fabric elements should also reflect the quality and functional standards established in the services elements.

One of the basic design decisions that generally concerns developers of office buildings is whether or not a particular development warrants air conditioning in order to achieve the necessary rental or provide the required return.

Air conditioning is a term that is often applied to systems that cannot technically claim the title. The performance and capability of the systems can vary enormously depending upon the heat source, extent of humidification, refrigeration, volume of ductwork etc. The cost implications of incorporating air conditioning into an office building can be summarised as follows:

(a) An increase in electrical services.
(b) An increase in plant room and service duct areas from 3–4% of gross internal area for centrally heated buildings to 6–11%.
(c) The introduction/adaptation of suspended ceilings to obscure ductwork.
(d) An increase in storey height to accommodate ductwork.
(e) The need to reduce heat gain through glazing in order to reduce running costs.

Generally, office buildings incorporating air conditioning systems are designed to a higher overall standard of specification to that of a centrally heated office, so that it is difficult to isolate entirely the cost effects of the factors listed above. However, the differential is of the order of £120–£190/m² for a medium rise speculative office block.

Lighting installations are likely to change with the increased sophistication of the office users' demands. The trend in owner occupier offices has been to move away from the bland high illumination and energy consuming fluorescent downlighter systems. Current developments suggest that low energy uplighter and task lighting systems will become more commonplace. In capital cost terms the luminaires are still quite expensive, but economies of scale will change this position.

Speculative demand is following that of the owner occupier, albeit that the requirement is simply for suitably flexible space that will accommodate the services options.

CALCULATION OF THE INITIAL BUDGET

The initial budget is often established on the basis of overall costs/m², as at the development appraisal stage it is unlikely that anything other than schematic drawings will be available. However, these should indicate the likely number of storeys and the plan form so that the preliminary assessments can be made of the relationship between the various key elements and the gross floor area of the building.

These relationships can be expressed as Quantity factors and can be illustrated in the case of a ten storey 10,000 m² office block with 1,000 m² per floor in that the Quantity factor for the substructure would be:

$$\frac{1,000}{10,000} = 0\cdot10$$

The following table includes typical Quantity factors for a speculative office building, and otherwise describes the method of calculating the Quantity factors for the major elements:

Element	Method of calculation	Quantity factor
(a) Substructure	$\dfrac{\text{Ground floor area}}{\text{Gross floor area}}$	
(b) Superstructure		1·00
(c) Roof	$\dfrac{\text{Roof plan area}}{\text{Gross floor area}}$	
(d) External envelope (quantity factors established from analysis of actual jobs)		
— shallow (12 m–14 m)		0·85
— medium (14 m–18 m)		0·55
(e) Internal division	$\dfrac{\text{Internal wall area}}{\text{Gross floor area}}$	
Typical internal wall to floor area ratios		
— cellular/open plan offices		0·35
— cellular offices fitted out for owner occupation		1·10
(f) Finishes and fittings		1·00
(g) Mechanical and electrical services		1·00
(h) Lifts		Number

Having calculated the quantity factors from the schematic design information, the typical rates from the following Design/specification tables can be used to build up a budget cost/m²:

Design/specification tables
(a) *Substructure*   £/m² of
                                                          ground floor
                                                           plan area

good ground – shallow strip and/or bases	47 to 58
good ground – deep strips and/or bases	58 to 71
poor ground – raft foundation	76 to 104
poor ground – short bored piles	65 to 88
bad ground – piled foundations	104 to 152
bad ground – inner city redevelopment site with piled foundations	141 to 178

The above rates are for a two storey building; add £10/m² per additional storey.

(b) *Superstructure*   £/m² of gross
                                                             floor area

in situ RC slabs and staircase; no frame (load-bearing walls)	40 to 55
frame and slab up to 6 storeys	60 to 100
frame and slab 7 to 12 storeys	85 to 120
frame and slab 12+ storeys	100 to 135

(c) *Roofs*   £/m² of
                                                          roof plant area

Lightweight	
Corrugated decking on steel joists, insulation and felt	40 to 58
Heavy	
RC flat or waffle slab; insulation and asphalt	65 to 76
Mansard	
slate faced mansard and asphalt on lightweight deck	85 to 145

(d) *External Envelope*   £/m² *of external*
                                                           envelope

    Economic
      machine made facing brick and block
      with aluminium single glazed
      windows   74 to   93
      insulated coated metal cladding and
      block with aluminium single glazed
      windows   88 to 113
    Medium quality
      handmade facing brick and block
      with double glazed aluminium
      windows   119 to 148
      precast concrete cladding panels
      with double glazed windows   140 to 169
    Good quality
      stone faced precast concrete
      cladding panels with good quality
      double glazed windows   202 to 231
      good quality aluminium curtain
      walling   235 to 300
    High quality
      granite/marble cladding with high
      quality double glazed windows   286 to 343

(e) *Internal Division*   £/m² *of internal*
                                                           wall area

    Economic
      blockwork/stud partitions, plaster
      and emulsion, softwood doors   41 to   49
    Medium quality
      blockwork/stud partitions, plaster
      and vinyl, hardwood doors   46 to   55
    Good quality
      good quality solid demountable
      partitions, hardwood doors   65 to   83
    High quality
      high quality solid and glazed
      demountable partitions and doors   100 to 118

(f) *Finishes and fittings*   £/m² *of gross*
                                                            floor area

    Economic

        plaster and emulsion to walls and
        ceilings, screed and carpet tiles,
        shelves and cleaners' cupboards   27 to 36

    Medium quality

        plaster and emulsion to walls,
        exposed grid suspended ceiling,
        partial access raised floor and
        medium quality carpet, reception
        desk, shelves and cleaners' cupboards   58 to 70

    Good quality

        plaster and vinyl to walls, concealed
        grid suspended ceiling, fully

(a)   High quality

        plaster and vinyl to walls, high
        quality metal suspended ceiling,
        fully accessible computer loading
        raised floor and high quality carpet,
        high quality reception desk, shelves
        and cleaners' cupboards   121 to 178

(g) *Services*

    Sanitary, water and plumbing

        up to 12 storeys   7 to 19
        above 12 storeys   12 to 21

    Heating

        radiator/convector   30 to 52

    Ventilation and warm air heating   70 to 88

    Air conditioning

        comfort cooling   95 to 125
        fancoil/induction   100 to 160
        VAV   115 to 180

    Electrical

        supplies to floors only for letting   15 to 20
        speculative standard, lighting and
        power   50 to 72

	£/m² of gross floor area
high quality speculative standard, lighting and power	60 to 78
owner occupied standard, lighting and power	65 to 90
Lifts	£/lift
goods lift serving two levels	24,000 to 42,000
passenger lifts serving three to six levels	29,000 to 45,000
passenger lifts serving seven to eleven levels	40,000 to 86,000
passenger lifts serving twelve to fifteen levels	72,000 to 99,000
Other mechanical and electrical services	
fire fighting/hose reels	3 to 6
single level sprinkler installation	9 to 13

	% addition to building cost
(h) *External works*	
— green field	10 to 15
— restricted urban	3 to 7
— very restricted urban	2 to 4

The following calculation illustrates the build-up of the cost/m² for an eight storey medium depth office block suitable for letting, on a restricted urban site in Central London, with a ground floor area of 900 m² and a gross floor area of 7,200 m²

Element specification	QF	Rate £	Cost/m² £
(a) Foundations			
— piled foundations on poor ground	0·125	210	26
(b) Superstructure			
— frame and slab	1·00	100	100

Element specification	QF	Rate £	Cost/m² £
(c) Roof			
— RC slab and asphalt	0·125	75	9
(d) External envelope			
— stone cladding with good quality aluminium windows	0·55	340	187
(e) Internal division			
— medium quality for letting	0·35	50	18
(f) Finishes and fittings			
— medium quality with partial access raised floor	1·00	60	60
(g) Services			
— sanitary, water and plumbing	1·00	15	15
— VAV air conditioning	1·00	160	160
— lighting and power	1·00	65	65
— lifts $\dfrac{4\,\text{No @ £45,000}}{7,200}$			23
— fire fighting/hose reels			5
			645
Contingency and design reserve $+7\frac{1}{2}\%$			50
			695
Preliminaries +10%			70
			765
External works +5%			40
			805
Regional allowance for Inner London +10%			80
Total budget cost/m²			£885

The estimating technique and costs described above indicate a theoretical method of producing a budget cost. A full and detailed description of this approach to the preparation of feasibility estimates can be found in an article entitled "Offices – Initial Cost Estimating", by the author of this chapter, which appeared in the Architects' Journal dated 14 May 1986.

Office Costs per m²

The following table includes indicative costs/m² of gross floor area for various types and forms of offices

	Cost/m² £
(a) new build offices for letting	
non air conditioned	460 to 565
air conditioned	585 to 765
(b) new build offices for owner occupation	
low rise, non air conditioned	470 to 575
low rise, air conditioned	585 to 765
medium rise, non air conditioned	555 to 680
medium rise, air conditioned	775 to 900
high rise, air conditioned	1,000 to 1,500

The figures above exclude external works, drainage, external services, professional fees and VAT.

Shop Costs per m²

Where it is necessary to build up the budget cost of a mixed development that includes retail space, the developer is generally only interested in the cost of the shop shells and malls. Unlike office tenants, retailers' fitting out needs are so varied that flexible space is all that is required. Typical shop shells include landlords' supplies of services leaving the provision of finishes, shop fittings, shop fronts, mechanical services and electrical services to the retail tenant.

The cost of a shop shell is dependent upon the size and type of use, although in a pre-let, the definition of shell work, as opposed to fitting out can be the subject of negotiation with the retailer.

Moreover, the requirements of the leading retailers determine the form and layout of retail developments. The developer will be keen to optimise the distribution of the larger shop units that he hopes will attract the anchor tenants. However, it is also important, for example, that the malls are designed to an appropriate standard, any food courts are correctly positioned, and that there is adequate car parking.

The following table summarises typical costs/m² of gross floor area for shopping developments.

Shops	Cost/m²
	£
(a) shop shells	
—small	285 to 360
—large, including department stores	
and supermarkets	275 to 300
(b) retail warehouse shell	190 to 265
(c) shopping centres	
—malls comfort cooled	950 to 1,100
—retail areas, shells with capped off	
services	285 to 350
—landlords' back-up areas, plant rooms	390 to 450
(d) fitting out shell	
—small shop	325 to 600
—department store/supermarket	485 to 640
—retail warehouse	125 to 140
(e) external works (refer to earlier table for	% addition to
car parking costs)	building cost
—small infill site	4 to 6
—suburban site	7 to 10
—out of town	10 to 14

The estimating techniques described earlier in this chapter for the preparation of feasibility estimates for offices have also been developed for shopping developments. A full and detailed description of the methodology can be found in an article entitled 'Out of town shopping – Initial cost estimating' by the author of this chapter, which appeared in the Architects' Journal dated 25 February 1987.

Industrial Costs per m²

As with offices, there can be a wide difference in cost between the speculative and the owner occupied light industrial buildings.

The owner occupier will usually require a tailor made unit to meet his organisational and operational requirements. In addition, he may be keen for the building to project his corporate image. It follows, therefore, that as with shop shells, the speculative light industrial building must provide flexible space that will satisfy the needs of most tenants.

As far as cost/m² are concerned, speculative factories tend to be more expensive than warehouses. This is mainly because they are usually built as smaller units, with the result that they have more external wall to enclosed floor area. The cost/m² is also influenced by the larger provision of office and toilet accommodation in factories than is generally provided in warehouses.

The effect of size can be seen from the high cost/m² of nursery units in which the entrance doors, incoming services, toilets, etc. are apportioned over very small floor areas of between 500–1,500 square feet, as compared with in excess of 100,000 square feet for some warehouses.

The following table summarises typical costs/m² of gross floor area for various types of light industrial buildings, together with allowances for external works.

	Industrial building	*Cost/m² (£)*
(a)	low bay warehouses for letting	150 to 180
(b)	low bay warehouses for owner occupation	215 to 260
(c)	factories for letting	150 to 205
(d)	workshops and nursery units for letting	245 to 305
(e)	light industrial factories for owner occupation	250 to 345
(f)	hi-tech industrial	475 to 590
(g)	external works	% addition to building cost
	restricted site with service yard and limited car parking	10 to 15
	green field site with service yard and extensive car parking	15 to 25

BUILDING COSTS AND TENDER PRICES

The prevailing rate of building cost inflation in the construction industry is broadly in line with general inflation as measured by the retail price index. This is illustrated by the following graph which graphically plots movements in retail prices, and the Davis Belfield and Everest building cost and tender price indices over the period 1970–1986.

Valuation and Development Appraisal

In the long term building tender prices also follow the trend set by building costs, as can be seen from the same graph. However, in the short term it would be wholly misleading to refer to building cost inflation when considering movements in tender prices, as the divergence of the tender price index from the building cost index can be quite marked.

In order to appreciate the reasons for such a wide variation in inflation rates, it is necessary to understand the difference between building costs and tender prices. Building cost inflation reflects the basic costs to contractors of operatives' wages, materials and plant, while tender inflation reflects the prices charged to the client, and is influenced by the market conditions prevailing at the time of tendering. When pricing a tender, the building contractor looks at his current costs for labour, material and plant, notes how they have increased since his last tender, assesses his recent bid success rate against future workload and decides whether to pass on the full effect of past inflation or absorb the increases. During periods when work is short, he may adopt the latter course in an effort to boost orders for his firm. Clearly there is a limit to the extent to which the contractor can do this, particularly during periods of recession when the compound effect of several unprofitable contracts can result in the contractor's bankruptcy. However, he will certainly endeavour to pass on the consequences of aggressive tender prices to his employees, sub-contractors and suppliers of materials and plant.

When work is plentiful, contrary pressures will apply. Competitors will be bidding for the limited labour force and material supplies and will be paying a premium for them in the process. Basic costs are therefore linked to, but not the same as, tender prices. The former are the basis of the latter, but the estimator's judgement of the market determines the precise relationship.

Examination of tender price movements relative to building costs on the graph between 1972 and 1973 provides a good example of the effects of a boom during which property investment was expanding rapidly and the demand for construction capacity was far greater than the supply. The supposed profit taking, as expressed by the shortfall between building costs and tender prices at this time, was far more apparent than

Movements in Building Costs   Tender Prices and Retail Prices

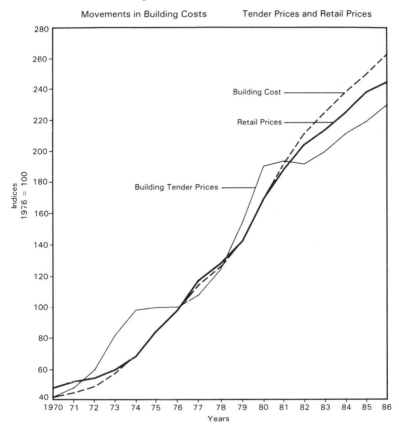

Years

real, to the extent that contractors were paying premiums on materials and attracting operatives by paying over and above the basic wage rates. The culmination of this period occurred on 13 November 1973 when a state of emergency was announced and the minimum lending rate increased from $11\frac{1}{4}$ to 13%. Following on from this period, building cost inflation outstripped tender prices, the latter remaining quite stable until mid 1978.

Examination of the relative movements of tenders and costs illustrates the need for careful consideration of the correct measure of inflation when calculating the first estimate in a development appraisal. There are several tender price and building cost indices in existence, including those prepared by the Building Cost Information Service for the RICS and the Directorate of Quantity Surveying Services for the PSA. In addition, building cost and tender price indices are prepared quarterly by Davis Belfield and Everest, and published in "Cost Forecast" articles in the Architects', Journal.

The following table includes a time series of these two indices, together with year on year inflation percentages.

Davis Belfield and Everest building cost and tender price indices

| | | Building costs | | Building tender prices | |
| | | Index | Year on Year | Index | Year on Year |
Year	Quarter	(1976 = 100)	increase %	(1976 = 100)	increase %
1970	1	40		41	
	2	41		41	
	3	42		43	
	4	43		43	
1971	1	44	10	45	10
	2	45	10	46	12
	3	46	10	48	12
	4	46	7	50	16
1972	1	46	5	55	22
	2	47	4	57	24
	3	49	7	61	27
	4	55	20	67	34
1973	1	56	22	73	33
	2	56	19	79	39
	3	59	20	86	41
	4	61	11	92	37
1974	1	63	13	97	33
	2	68	21	100	27
	3	71	20	99	15
	4	73	20	97	5
1975	1	78	24	101	4
	2	82	21	103	3
	3	89	25	98	−1
	4	90	23	100	3

Year	Quarter	Building costs		Building tender prices	
		Index (1976 = 100)	Year on Year increase %	Index (1976 = 100)	Year on Year increase %
1976	1	93	19	97	−4
	2	97	18	98	−5
	3	104	17	102	4
	4	107	19	103	3
1977	1	109	17	105	8
	2	112	15	105	7
	3	116	12	109	7
	4	117	9	110	7
1978	1	118	8	113	8
	2	120	7	116	10
	3	127	9	126	16
	4	129	10	139	26
1979	1	131	11	142	26
	2	135	13	146	26
	3	149	17	160	27
	4	153	19	167	20
1980	1	157	20	179	26
	2	161	19	200	37
	3	180	21	192	20
	4	181	18	188	13
1981	1	182	16	199	11
	2	185	15	193	−3
	3	195	8	190	−1
	4	199	10	195	4
1982	1	203	12	191	−4
	2	206	11	188	−3
	3	214	10	195	3
	4	216	9	195	0
1983	1	217	7	198	4
	2	219	6	200	6
	3	227	6	198	2
	4	229	6	200	3
1984	1	230	6	205	4
	2	232	6	206	3
	3	239	5	214	8
	4	241	5	215	8

Year	Quarter	Building costs		Building tender prices	
		Index (1976 = 100)	Year on Year increase %	Index (1976 = 100)	Year on Year increase %
1985	1	243	6	215	5
	2	245	6	219	6
	3	252	5	219	2
	4	254	5	220	2
1986	1	256	5	221	3
	2	258	5	226	2
	3	266	6	234	7
	4	268	6	236	7

As can be seen from the above table, there is no discernible relationship in percentage terms between building cost and tender price inflation. It is therefore important when carrying out development appraisals that forecasts of tender inflation take account of contemporary and future prospects for the construction industry, rather than being prepared from simple extrapolation of historic indices.

The quarterly "Cost Forecast" article mentioned above, regularly discusses the market conditions that influence both costs and prices, and incorporates a twenty four month forecast of inflation.

The tender price indices listed above can be used to update the estimating data in this chapter from January 1987 to the projected date of the tender. This will establish the estimated tender price excluding increased costs recoverable by the contractor during the construction contract. The assessment of the increased costs recoverable during this period should be carried out using building cost indices, which, as has already been explained, do not reflect the vagaries of market forces in a direct way.

CONTRACT ARRANGEMENTS

Having established a realistic budget estimate for a particular project, the method of procurement must involve a programme

Davis Belfield and Everest forecast of building costs and tender indices as published in the Architects' Journal 1 July 1987

Year	Quarter	Building cost indices (1976 = 100)	Building tender price indices (1976 = 100)	
1986	3	266	234	
	4	267	234	
1987	1	270	242	
			min	max
	2	271	244	250
	3	280	253	259
	4	285	255	263
1988	1	284	264	272
	2	286	272	281
	3	297	280	291
	4	299	281	295
1989	1	301	291	305
	2	303	300	315

of tendering procedures and contractural arrangements that will satisfy the developer's main objectives.

As far as the contract arrangements are concerned, the developer's objectives can be safeguarded by the following:

(a) The selection of a competent contractor to complete the development within the programme.

(b) The introduction of the contractor into the design/build team at the most appropriate time in the development programme.

(c) By securing value for money in terms of time, cost and quality.

(d) By ensuring that genuine competition exists and that it is on the basis of equal information for each tenderer.

(e) By distributing the risk between the contractor and the employer in such a way that the employer obtains the greatest possible commitment to the maximum price, without paying an unacceptable price for ridding himself of the risk.

(f) By providing a basis for valuing works in progress and variations.

The degree to which the objectives are satisfied is dependent upon the tendering procedure used and the contractual arrangements subsequently entered into. The two main methods of obtaining a tender are:

(1) selection either by the client or by interview followed by negotiation.
(2) selected competition.

Both methods of tender can result in the selection of a suitable contractor. However, only selected competition can ensure that the contractor seeks out the best price, in that he has a cost discipline imposed upon him that should encourage efficiency. During negotiation the contractor will naturally tend towards the maximum figure that will be remotely reasonable in negotiating every rate. Even after tough negotiation, the cost premium can be of the order of 5–10%. The only sanction open to the client is to withdraw from the negotiation and go elsewhere. This course may cause disruption and delay, but may also be financially beneficial.

The contract arrangements that are used within the construction industry for medium and large development projects fall broadly into four categories. These are lump sum, remeasurement, cost reimbursement and management contracts.

(a) *Management Contracts and Cost Reimbursement Contracts*
Management contracts involve the execution of the work by sub-contractors under the supervision and co-ordination of a Management Contractor who does not actually carry out any building work. Cost reimbursement contracts involve the reimbursement of the contractor's actual costs for materials, plant and labour with the addition of a fee for profit and overheads. One of the supposed advantages of both of these methods is the early introduction of the contractor into the design/build team. However, the developer's objectives are only satisfied if this early involvement is at the appropriate time and the contractor has a positive contribution to make. This is not always the case as the contractor's advice on construction may not contribute anything that a competent design team would not have considered.

Each contractor will have a different view of the best method of construction and he will inevitably favour that which suits his own organisation, but this may not reconcile with the need to satisfy the development brief.

The purported advantages of both these methods of procurement can form something of a smokescreen to enable the contractor to become involved in the project prior to there being enough detailed information available on the design to allow genuine price competition.

In the case of management contracts, it is also argued that each of the sub-contracts is subject to competition, but it is often impossible to satisfy this objective for every package of work. Moreover, the terms for the appointment of sub-contractors under some management contractors' own standard forms pass full responsibility from the management contractor to the sub-contractor. The burden of such a requirement can be extremely onerous for a small firm and the only way in which this increased responsibility can be covered by the sub-contractor is by reflecting it in higher prices, which in turn transfers the cost of this risk to the client in full. Another area in which lack of competition exists is in the absence of a lead building contractor who can benefit from the discounts and purchasing arrangements available to a bulk purchaser of materials.

Cost reimbursement contracts appear to relieve the client of the premium involved in transferring abnormal risks to the contractor, but in return the client is obliged to meet all costs with limited price commitment on the part of the contractor. This can result in the subsidy of inefficiency. There is a sanction within the agreed fee which may be fixed or calculated on a percentage basis, but this provides little incentive to the contractor to minimise costs. As the contractor is almost indemnified against loss, cost reimbursement contracts have little to recommend them, expect in the case of work that is incapable of definition at the start and therefore realistic estimation.

Typical fees are 2–5% for management contracts and 4–7$\frac{1}{2}$% for cost reimbursement contracts.

(b) *Lump Sum and Remeasurement Contracts*
Lump sum and remeasurement contracts are generally based on bills of quantities. In the case of the former, firm bills are used, while the latter involves bills which are approximate

at tender stage, but which reflect the character of the work by way of accurately weighted quantities. As construction proceeds, the work is remeasured and priced using the rate in the approximate bills of quantities.

Lump sum tenders based on selected competition introduce competition to the highest proportion of the contract value and ensure a cost and time commitment by the contractor with the consequent acceptance of risk. The desire to make a profit in a competitive market, while at the same time mitigate the effects of any risk, encourages efficiency. At the same time it provides a method of gauging the value of an offer, which is impossible under those contracts where price competition does not exist.

Remeasurement contracts have an advantage in that an early start on site can be made, as all the design information does not have to be available for the preparation of tender documentation. However, the cost commitment is not as good in that the contractor will not be able to quote a firm price for undefined aspects of the design.

Both methods exploit the advantage of a lead building contractor, albeit that he may employ domestic sub-contractors. The main contractor, in addition to controlling the price of his own work, can exert considerable purchasing power over sub-contractors and material suppliers in order to arrive at his most competitive price within the current market conditions. Thus these two methods of building procurement successfully satisfy most of the main objects listed above.

Comparison of Contract Arrangements

It is impossible to evaluate the success of the above contract arrangements in absolute terms; however, the following table provides an indicative assessment against four criteria, with four stars indicating a good rating.

From the above, it is apparent that the lump sum tender, based on firm bills of quantities, provides the most effective method of satisfying the key criteria. The other options may result in improved time economy, but cost reimbursement and management contracts involve greater risks in terms of cost economy, financial commitment and post contract cost control.

Evaluation of contractual arrangements against key development
criteria

Criteria	Lump sum contract based on bills of quantities	Remeasurement contract based on bills of approx. quantities	Cost Reimbursement contract based on cost plus	based on target cost	Management contracts
1. Time economy	**	****	****	****	****
2. Cost economy	****	***	*	**	**
3. Financial commitment	****	**	*	**	**
4. Post contract cost control	****	***	*	**	**

FIXED PRICE TENDERS AND CONSTRUCTION CASH FLOW FORECASTS

One element of risk that it may not be realistic for the developer to pass on to the contractor at the tender stage is the effect on his bid of inflation during the construction period. During the 1960's and up until the early 1970's, contractors were quite readily prepared to submit fixed price bids. However, having experienced a period of high inflation contractors were, until the mid 1980's, reticent about accepting the risk involved in assessing future cost increases. Currently the maximum construction period upon which it can be anticipated that a contractor will put a realistic assessment of increased costs, is between 15 and 18 months. Bids for contracts of greater duration will generally be on a fluctuating basis with the contractor recovering increases in labour and material by one of two methods:

1. The traditional method, which involves the calculation of material increased costs from the actual invoices for the purchase of materials by the contractor, compared with a basic list of prices submitted with his tender, while labour increased costs are calculated from increases in the natio-

nally agreed wage rates, taxes and expenses using actual time sheets for the operatives employed on site.
2. The formula adjustment method, which involves the calculation of increased costs by applying published indices to the contract value.

The decision as to the method of dealing with increased costs that is to be included in the contract documentation lies with the client. Of the two methods, the traditional approach is preferable to most developers, as the higher recovery that is achieved with formula adjustment is generally not reflected in keener prices at the tender stage.

For budget estimating purposes, an estimate of increased costs can be made using building cost indices:

Contract	*Date*	*Building Cost Index*
		1976 = 100
Tender date	November 1986	268
Completion date	February 1988	286

The total increase during the construction period = 6·7%.

However it would be inappropriate to apply, for the total increase during the construction period at the start of the contract the contractor's prices will be current, while only at the end of the contract will the total increase apply.

For early budgetary calculations, an allowance of a half of the total increase ensures an appropriate assessment of increased costs.

Having established the budget estimate together with the calculation of the increased costs, it is then necessary to arrive at the expenditure cash flow during the construction period. Building contracts generally operate on a system of monthly payments to the contractor based on the valuation of the work done by the client's quantity surveyor. Under the Joint Contract Tribunal Standard Form of Building Contract, which is the form most commonly used for large and medium sized projects, a retention of 3% is deducted from the gross value of work done until the works are completed, when half the retention is released. The balance of the retention is released on the making good of any defects, which is generally six months after the works are completed.

The value of the work done under a building contract, when plotted over the contract period, generally takes the form of an "S" curve in that there is a slow build-up in spend rate during the early part of the contract whilst the contractor becomes established on site. The spend rate increases to a peak after the mid-point of the construction period and then slows once more as the contractor enters the run down period to completion. The profile of cash flow is related to both contract value and type of building, so that given sufficient data, it is possible to develop an "S" curve to suit a particular project. However, a typical cash flow for a medium size project is represented in the following graph with percentages for both contract period and value.

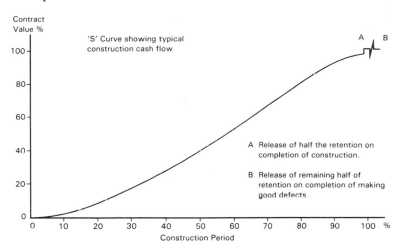

PROFESSIONAL FEES

Architects', quantity surveyors' and consulting engineers' professsional services and charges are defined in scales of fees that are produced by the professional bodies that represent each discipline. The fees for architects are based on percentage scales, while quantity surveyors' fees are generally calculated on the basis of lump sums and percentage scales that relate to ranges of total construction costs and types of work. Structural, mechanical and electrical engineers' fees are calculated in a similar way, except that the lump sums and percentage scales relate to the value of the work in their particular discipline, rather than the total construction cost. The timing for the payment of fees is related to the design and construction periods, but the actual fee cash flow is dependent upon the fee agreements between the professionals and the client. In order to assess the total cost of professional fees, it is necessary to define the services to be provided, and the construction cost. The professional fees for an office development, for example, can range from 11 to over 15% with as much as 60% of the fees being expended during the design period and the balance spread over the construction period.

For budgetary purposes, the following table summarises a typical example of the professional fees incurred on a medium sized office development with an indication of the proportion expended during the design and construction periods.

Profession	Fee as a % of total construction cost	Proportion expended during:	
		Design period %	Construction period %
Architect	$5\frac{3}{4}$	75	25
Quantity surveyor	$3\frac{1}{2}$	50	50
Structural engineer	$2\frac{1}{4}$	50	50
Mechanical and electrical engineer	2	50	50
Total	$13\frac{1}{2}$	60	40

The total of professional fees and charges for the services of the design team is subject to value added tax at the appropriate rate, which is currently 15%. Clients who are taxable persons under the Finance Act will of course be able to recover such input tax from Customs and Excise.

CONCLUSION

The developer's objective is to maximise the potential value or income from a development; it is therefore of paramount importance that the strategic planning at the development appraisal stage is based on the optimum amount of information.

In order to satisfy this objective, it is essential that the feasibility estimate is based on a sound appreciation of the influence of location and site characteristics on the outturn cost. In addition the likely market conditions for the development period should be considered.

The development appraisal itself will involve an anticipated rental level and yield which will define an assumed quality standard for the building. Against this background it can be appreciated that a developer increases his risk if he relies upon average building costs/m² that do not reflect the influence of the design and specification characteristics that will be necessary to achieve the desired quality standard.

The establishment of a realistic budget is therefore fundamental to the success of a development. However, as well as being realistic the budget must be attainable to the extent that the contract arrangements must not jeopardise the development viability. In order to satisfy this requirement, it is necessary for the building design to be developed to the point where selective competition will ensure that the contractor's commitment is such that the developer is not incurring unnecessary risk with regard to the cost of the development. Having established a financial commitment by a contractor, the contract arrangements must also involve a control procedure that safeguards the developer's interests with regard to the final cost.

It should therefore be apparent from this chapter that to produce the initial construction cost budget to the required level of accuracy requires a considerable amount of knowledge and expertise. Moreover, it is essential that sound advice is sought at an early stage as to the procurement procedures that are most likely to ensure that the development proposals are implemented within the parameters that were established in the initial appraisal.

R. SMITH

BIBLIOGRAPHY

Initial Cost Estimating Offices, *Architects' Journal* 14, May 1986.

Initial Cost Estimating Out of Town Retailing, *Architects' Journal* 25, February 1987.

Initial Cost Estimating Office/Industrial Buildings, *Architects' Journal* 3, June 1987.

Cost Forecast, *Architects' Journal* 1, July 1987.

Spon's Architects' and Builders' Price Book, 113th Edition, 1988.

CHAPTER 6

Market Analysis and Project Evaluation

Most major markets today are already quite well satisfied and, as a result, new projects, that must effectively compete with, and complement existing developments rather than merely duplicate them, require the benefits of a thorough and detailed understanding of the market place, if they are to be successful.

MARKET ANALYSIS

Market analysis is a four stage study of the relative social and economic characteristics of a cohesive area, in order to determine the demand for the product analysed. The process of analysis can be broken down in the following manner:

(a) Data collection which, in the case of a development project, is oriented primarily towards study of the site and the quality of access routes to it; past, present and future population levels within the market area; the social characteristics of its population; per capita income levels and expenditure patterns by retail store type, and most importantly, the quality and size of existing and proposed competition to the project under study.

(b) Data analysis in order to understand fully the current and likely future conditions in the market.

(c) Analysis of the effect of introducing the new project into the market, thus modifying the existing competitive structure.

(d) The development of conclusions and recommendations based on the preceding analysis.

MARKET RESEARCH AND PROJECT CONCEPT

Up to the mid-1970's, most markets were so badly underserved that it was often possible for the developer, with flair, to take a quick look at the existing competition and then move ahead with the construction of his development, safe in the knowledge that as the market was so badly underserved his project was bound to succeed. In any event, the rapidly rising suburban population provided an additional safety net and time would cure any slight over-building problem.

Today the picture has overwhelmingly changed. Population in many major metropolitan areas is static if not declining; almost every identifiable market area is already well served by modern facilities. Thus market research is essential in order to define market segments that are not being served adequately, so that new projects can be planned to complement or compete effectively against existing projects rather merely duplicate existing facilities.

For shopping centres, in particular, market research should be a continuing process. It permits a clear definition of the market to be served, and accurate design of the project to suit that particular market. Market research data substantiates, for future tenants, financial institutions and local authorities the potential values to be created and can determine the probable future impact of new developments upon the existing local facilities. Continuing market research permits the developer to monitor changes in the behaviour of trade area residents, the strength of local competition and the impact of his own project.

Thus, to be effective, market research should be a continuing process and the consultant responsible for preparing such research should form an integral part of the development and management team. For example, most successful shopping centre developments are created by a working team consisting of at least three permanent members: the developer as the initiating force, the consultant to establish the economic base and operational methods and the architect to create the planning concept which gives the project physical shape, style and form. The team, if created at the inception of the project, should operate continuously throughout the planning and construction period until the project is completed. Thereafter, in a major development scheme, the team should meet at regular intervals to review changes that have occured, as evidenced by the on-going market research programme, to ensure that

the project is managed effectively, is kept up-to-date and anti-
cipates the changing demands of both tenants and customers,
so that it maintains its dominance in the market it serves.

The detailed techniques of market research generally fall into
two categories:

1. Area research,
2. Consumer research.

(1) *Area research* is the analysis of the characteristics of the
market, in order to determine the size and nature of project
which should be built. It is a quantitative analysis and
should, thus, determine the optimum size of project, providing the basis for the preliminary financial analysis, and
architectural design. Area research is also necessary to provide information for phasing the project, together with
expansion opportunities at a later date; to provide data
used for obtaining planning permission and for studies of
the impact of the new product upon the environment and
existing competition; to provide information to financial
institutions regarding the economic feasibility of the product, and to provide information to potential tenants,
enabling them to decide whether or not to rent space in
the project.

Thus, area research should be a continuing process starting at the initial planning stage of a new project and continuing during its development, supplying a continuous flow
of information to the developer for use in negotiations with
third parties and continuing after completion of the project, enabling the owner to expand, modify or renovate the
project to keep pace with the changing demands of the
market.

(2) *Consumer research* is a qualitative analysis determining
the attitudes of consumers in the area, with regard to existing facilities, their preferences, life styles and the most
effective types of advertising. Consumer research may be
conducted among all the residents of the market or among
those specific groups of residents likely to be most
attracted to the project. Such research is useful in determining consumer reactions to existing facilities, whether
their requirements have been adequately satisfied or not,

identifies facilities required by consumers and not currently available and by identifying media habits, assists in preparing advertising campaigns.

Both forms of market research are essential tools in decision making at all stages of a development, both before and after opening. Market research provides the facts which through competent analysis furnish a true picture of the market. Such information is essential to successful developers.

These two techniques are now discussed in detail in the following pages.

AREA RESEARCH

The essence of property is the fact that every single piece of land is unique in its location and in its inability to adapt its locational advantages or disadvantages to changing conditions. Almost every other tangible with which we deal in ordinary business terms can be duplicated, but each parcel of land differs from every other parcel by reason of its specific location.

There are two basic approaches which may be made in measuring the influence of present conditions and probable changes on the value of any particular location: namely statistical measurement and the use of property based judgements.

Statistical Measurement

Since Professor Reilly developed his law of retail gravitation in 1931, there have been innumerable attempts to develop arithmetical expressions which would permit trouble free and repetitive determination of the opportunity for development at specific locations. The use of statistical models, generally for purposes of evaluating retail sales potential or square metres of retail space justified for development, reached a high peak of acceptance in the United Kingdom in the late 1960's but the proven inaccuracies of such forecasting techniques for specific sites has led to a considerable decrease in their popularity. On the Continent and in North America, property developers and financing institutions have generally preferred to stay with analyses based on real estate judgement.

Among the many models and theories put forward to explain

the workings of various aspects of retailing, three basic lines of approach can be identified:

(a) Central place theory – this relates to the purpose, frequency and length of shopping trips to a hierarchy of centres.
(b) Spatial interaction or gravity models which are basically refinements of Reilly's 1931 law of retail gravitation.
(c) Rent models – seeking to describe the way land-use is determined by way of the land market.

One of the major problems with all models is that their high input of technicalities tends to conceal the judgements made about the content of the model. Judgements occur especially in the choice of model, the collection of data and their interpretation, the procedure used to fit the data to the model and the way in which the model is used to forecast. Obviously, the quality of these judgements is vital to a satisfactory analysis based on the use of a mathematical model. This factor is precisely the one which is least questioned when examining the reliability of models.

The great number of different models used – without any clear concensus as to their reliability, or the substantial differences in the types of data used as proxies for the model's variables, and the different procedures used to calibrate models – are all factors which create doubts as to the suitability of mathematical models for micro-economic analysis. For a more detailed examination of the reliability of urban shopping models, the reader is referred to "An Investigation into the Estimation and Reliability of Urban Shopping Models" by R. Turner & H. S. D. Cole published in Urban Studies 1980.

Mathematical models undoubtedly have their uses at a regional or county level where the collection of specific data by in-the-field surveys becomes prohibitively expensive or in the preparation of a large number of repetitive analyses for relatively small projects where budgets may not stretch to individual site analyses based on real estate judgement, and where a certain proportion of error is acceptable. For individual sites, where the quality of analysis is important, the use of such techniques is not recommended. Those seeking more detailed information about the use of mathematical models should refer to specialist publications, since this chapter is devoted entirely to techniques of analysis based upon the use of judgement and experience.

Real Estate Judgement

This is predicated on a thorough knowledge of development and on experience in considering the effects of the various factors on a particular site; it enables the analyst to compensate for variations in the different factors used in area analysis. The very real lack of adequate base statistical material in countries other than the United States and Canada, relating to such factors as average per capita income levels in market areas, retail sales by store type, per capita expenditures, etc., forces the analyst to rely even more heavily on his own judgement than in North America. The acquisition of critical judgement can only be developed through experience over a number of years, but it is the most vital ingredient of any market analysis.

Analyses

The most frequently employed forms of area research are the "residual" and "share of the market" analyses. The two approaches may be used independently, in combination or as a cross-check, the one upon the other. The residual analysis tends to be more conservative than the share of the market approach, since only the residue or remaining potential (after subtraction of the effect of existing and probable future competition) is considered to be available to the project. In contrast, the share of the market analysis is predicated on the assumption that a strong and well conceived project is likely to be capable of achieving a certain percentage share of the market in its own category, almost regardless of competition.

Because the data collection process for a residual analysis is likely to be more lengthy, and therefore more costly, there is an increasing tendency to rely on share of the market approaches. It will be clear however, that a share of the market analysis relies even more heavily than a residual analysis upon the use of experienced subjective judgement and, for this reason, it is generally recommended that the residual approach be followed.

As will be demonstrated, market analyses are prepared for various types of developments. It is recognised that increasingly, developments are of a multi-use nature and thus a typical demand analysis may include two or more of the various types which are discussed later.

EXAMPLE OF RETAIL ANALYSIS

The single or multi-shop shopping centre retail analysis is now generally accepted as a basic requirement for public enquiries, presentation to financial institutions, presentation to eventual tenants and as a basis for the decision as to whether to undertake the development, or not.

Such an analysis will be based upon the following considerations:

1. Background.
2. Site.
3. Access.
4. Trade (or catchment) area.
5. Population.
6. Income and buying power.
7. Competition.
8. Sales potential.

Based on the above considerations, the consultant will make recommendations as to the size and scope of the project justified for development, indicating by store type and on a store by store basis, the nature of the warranted project. These recommendations, after approval by the developer, then serve as the first part of the developer's instructions to the architect, enabling him to develop a coherent concept which will satisfy trade area requirements. The second part of these instructions is of course the preliminary financial analysis which indicates permissible budgets, bearing in mind anticipated rents that can be achieved from the project, cost of financing, construction, etc.

1. *Background Analysis*

The background analysis is designed to provide a framework for the subsequent site analysis and enables the analyst to develop an understanding of the broader market area within which the project will operate. This will enable him to take into account specific factors relating to the metropolitan area as a whole which will have an influence on the project but which cannot readily be determined on the basis of the trade area analysis alone. The background analysis is particularly important when the analyst is working in a new area and must inevitably first discipline himself to an understanding of how the metropolitan area functions and its strengths and weaknesses before venturing into the more familiar territory of the site itself.

This part of the study will include, but will not necessarily be limited to, an examination of the following factors:

(a) Geographic extent of the metropolitan area – the area tributary to the city centre for shopping trips, work trips and for other regular visits, whether for purposes of education, visiting government offices, recreation or leisure activities.

(b) Public Transportation and Road Patterns – existing and proposed public transportation network and major road patterns in the metropolitan area and any major changes likely to modify shopper access patterns in the area.

(c) Population levels by sector of the metropolitan area in order to determine growth areas.

(d) Employment levels by sector of the metropolitan area. Is employment well diversified, do a major proportion of local companies act as sub-contractor to the major employer, does the region have a strong and effective programme to attract new industry, etc.?

(e) Retail sales patterns by store type. This is particularly necessary if the researcher is not conversant with local retail trading levels and as a cross-check on per capita expenditure patterns.

(f) Per capita income levels by sector. This is used to determine distribution of wealth within the metropolitan area.

2. Trade (or Catchment) Area Analysis

Provided that the metropolitan area analysis or economic base study has shown potential for growth in the area generally, or in specific sections of that area, then a detailed market analysis of the trade or catchment area is undertaken, in order to determine the potential available to the site for development purposes.

As an introduction to the trade area analysis, the analyst must first list the basic assumptions that he has made in preparing his study; specific assumptions relating to particular points discussed during the course of the analysis will be identified at those points. Typically, the basic assumptions will relate to such factors as:

(a) The general economic level of the community over the study forecast period.
(b) The planned opening dates of new public transportation routes, motorways and interchanges to the extent that these may modify area shopping habits.
(c) The type of centre to be developed and the size and nature of the major tenants to be included in the project.
(d) Other major assumptions which may include the projected rate of population growth within the trade area; the level of competence in management of the planned centre, the architectural design; leasing and promotion techniques; future income and expenditure increases of trade area residents, etc.

Any major changes in the basic assumptions that might occur during the life of the study would require that the report be reexamined as the conclusions and recommendations might then have to be changed.

(i) Site Analysis

The site analysis examines the suitability of the site for the development envisaged in the light of its size (particularly if this is a limiting factor), its configuration and environment, and its location in relation to the surrounding residential and commercial developments.

(ii) Access Analysis

This includes a detailed examination of the roads currently servicing the site and any proposed road improvements which might modify access conditions; an understanding of the orientation of major access patterns will of course be an essential element in the trade area delineation. The problems associated with entering and leaving the site must also be anticipated and any limiting factors clearly identified. In addition to the problems of traffic, the study should, when necessary, take into account conditions of access for shoppers coming by public transportation, noting the location of bus, tram and underground railway stops, the frequency of service and the area served and the ease of entering or leaving the site from such stops.

(iii) Trade (or Catchment) Area

A sound understanding of access pattern to the site will assist in delineating the trade area limits. These should be so defined as to include between 80% and 90% of the project's future customers, the remaining 10% to 20% being derived from people working within the area, but residing outside it, occasional visitors to the area, tourists and others.

The extent of the trade area will depend upon the following considerations:

(a) The size and nature of the retail development envisaged.
(b) Natural or man-made barriers such as rivers, mountains and railroad lines which may create physical or psychological barriers to shopping customers.
(c) Existing and proposed access conditions which control travelling times to the site.
(d) The size and location of existing and proposed competitive shopping facilities serving the same trade area.

Once the extent of the trade area has been defined, the total area is subdivided into zones, in order to reflect the variations in the impact of the proposed development upon the expenditure of trade area residents. The secondary, and possibly tertiary, zones may be further subdivided in order to reflect more clearly the competitive impact of the nearby city centre or other major shopping developments.

Population

Historic population trends within the different zones of the trade area will be determined on the basis of published census data – further subdivision of urban areas can usually be obtained by application to the relevant census or planning authority. Care is, however, needed to ensure that changes in boundary limits between census dates are fully understood.

Care should also be taken to exclude persons residing in institutions, etc. This is important since such residents may not ordinarily shop to any great extent in conventional shopping areas.

Example:

Historic Population of the Trade Area

Trade area zone	1961	1971	1981	Annual Change 1961–71 Persons	Percent	Annual Change 1971–81 Persons	Percent
Primary	111,000	115,000	117,000	400	0·36%	200	0·17%

Present and future population levels within the trade area must be determined through projection of past data. New residential construction figures and official projections will be of assistance but the analyst must necessarily depend upon his own judgement in interpreting past trends in the light of present and anticipated future conditions. It must be borne in mind, that new residential construction is often accompanied by a decline in the number of persons per housing unit in the existing residential stock. Thus, although the total population may not increase, there may be an increase in the number of family formations.

Example:

Present and Future Trade Area Population

Trade area zone	1986*	1989**	1991***	Annual Change 1986–1991 Persons	Percent
Primary	118,000	118,500	118,800	160	0·14%

* Present date.
** Planned year of opening of new project.
*** Year by which project should have reached full trade area penetration.

(v) *Income and Buying Power*

Per capita income levels within specific metropolitan areas, or within sectors of them, cannot be obtained in the United Kingdom directly from official data. Per capita income levels are, however, of utmost importance in determining current expenditure patterns of trade area residents.

National per capita income levels are obtained from the personal income table of the U.K. National Accounts and up-dated to the present time on the basis of the national income growth rates. In adjusting from the national to the regional level, the analyst must rely heavily on his own judgement, using such index relationships as can be determined from:

(a) The regional tables published in the Family Expenditure Survey. This assumes that there is a fairly constant relationship between per capita expenditures and per capita income levels in different parts of the country in any one year.

(b) The Survey of Personal Incomes published by the Board of the Inland Revenue, which provides an estimate of total personal income over the effective exemption limit, for the nation and by region.

(c) The New Earnings Survey published by the Department of Employment, which provides average gross weekly earnings for the nation and by region. Such data may be used in conjunction with S.I.C. employment figures to provide weighted averages and adjusted by unemployment rates.

Regional per capita income figures must then be adjusted to the trade area and its various sectors, on the basis of field examination using such data as average house prices, etc.

Example:

Estimated 1985 per Capita Incomes

		Index
Primary Zone	£5,245	97·5
United Kingdom	£5,380	100·0

National per capita expenditure patterns by merchandise type can be determined from the Family Expenditure Survey published by the Department of Employment. The declared expenditures can be adjusted for under-reporting on the basis of the consumer expenditure patterns published in the personal expenditure table of the U.K. National Accounts. Adjusted merchandise type expenditures can then be regrouped into store type expenditures, on the basis of experience and the

Business Statistics Office publication "Retailing". It should also be noted that the Unit for Retail Planning Information Ltd in Reading, publishes information briefs on per capita retail expenditures by type of business for Great Britain and can provide such estimates by merchandise line for user defined areas.

Past expenditure elasticity coefficients can be developed on the basis of Family Expenditure Survey results over a number of years, adjusted on the basis of experience to reflect the current situation. These can then be applied to the national per capita store type expenditure patterns to adjust them to the per capita income levels determined for each zone of the trade area. Finally, the large area store expenditures must be adjusted to reflect the state of the competition currently affecting the expenditure habits of trade area residents and to reflect the likely future evolution of such competition. It may be noted that for convenience of analysis, food and non-food sales are often separated for large area stores (which include department stores, variety chain stores, superstores and hypermarkets).

The sales volume currently achieved by large area shops and stores in the area can be determined on the basis of a field survey, pacing out each store's sales area, noting its apparent level of activity, and applying standard sales turnover levels. Some cross-check can be obtained by analysing the annual reports of prominent retailers and the national turnover figures quoted in the Business Statistics publication "Retailing".

Example:

Trade Area per Capita Expenditures 1985

Expenditure Category	Primary Zone
Food	£ 710 p.a.
Ironmongery	35
Chemist	45
Large Area Stores*	165
Clothing	145
Furniture and Appliances	120
Other Comparison Goods	170
Total	£1,390 p.a.

* Excluding supermarket expenditures made in these stores, which are grouped with other food expenditures under the heading "Food".

(vi) *Competition*

Sufficient time must be spent in the field to survey thoroughly each retail district or shopping area which may affect trade area residents' expenditure patterns. As a minimum, all large area stores must be visited, their size paced out and the probable operating level (sales per square metre of selling floor area) determined. For a residual analysis, it is necessary to measure all the stores affecting trade area expenditures and any proposals for new retail development must also be included. Competition is grouped by store type as used in the expenditure patterns and the overall level of competition determined by store type and by retail cluster.

As a cross-check on the data obtained through fieldwork, it should be noted that a number of local authorities maintain surveys of retail floorspace but the qualitative analysis can only be undertaken in the field.

The Goads plans (published by Charles Goads) cover many shopping areas in the United Kingdom and can be helpful in determining the approximate gross ground floor area of individual shops and stores.

The analysis of competition is a vital part of the analysis, since it will reveal that either the trade area's existing facilities are insufficient to satisfy the market demand and thus additional demand for new facilities does exist, or that existing facilities in the trade area are sufficient.

(vii) *Sales Potential*

Total expenditures of the trade area residents are derived by multiplying the projected population for each zone for the applicable year by the expenditures in each store type.

If the project is located in a suburban area, then a suburban share of total expenditures is determined by store type; if located in the centre of the urban area, then a city centre share is determined also by sectors of the trade area. Depending upon the evolution of retail trade in the town under analysis, the 1971 Census of Distribution may provide some useful historic data in this regard, reinforced by fieldwork to determine these shares. With competent data gathering in the field the large area stores' suburban or city centre share can quite readily be determined. Again, proposals for new stores must be included in this calculation. Generally, suburban shares in convenience shops such as food and chemist shops will be higher than for comparison shops. However, the large size of building required for new furniture and do-it-yourself stores and their low rent paying ability means that such units are now usually located in suburban areas and thus the city centre share of these store types is usually quite low.

In a residual analysis, the effective competition is then subtracted from the suburban, or city centre potential. Effective competition is obtained by calculating the proportion of total sales capacity* for each retail cluster which is likely to be accounted for in the future by trade area residents. These competitive facilities are appraised during the fieldwork, by store type and by trade area zone. The project share is then determined by store type and by zone of the trade area.

As a check on the residual analysis, a share of the market analysis is frequently developed, particularly for the prospective major tenant. Such an analysis assumes that a major department store, superstore, or hypermarket, is able to attract a certain share of the total market within an area, almost regardless of the strength of the competition. If the major tenant is known, its market share in other developments can be calculated and applied to the project under study. Failing that information, an average market share may be taken, or a share determined on the basis of the relationship between the floor area planned for that store in the new project and the total floor areas of that store type existing in the locality and which have an influence on trade area residents, adjusted by the analysts estimate of the relative market strength of each competitive cluster.

Thus, if the market area contains 50,000 square metres of large area store space of which 30,000 square metres has effective drawing power on the project trade area and the large area store in the project should be 10,000 square metres in

---

* The estimated sales volume that existing shops and stores are capable of obtaining and holding under normal competitive conditions, when adequate facilities with competent management are available to customers. It is an estimate of the amount of business that would be retained by existing shops from trade area residents in the face of new competition, including the development project under analysis.

Example:

Large Area Store Sales Potential
(£000's – 1985 Constant Value)

	Total Expenditures		*Town Centre Share*	*Town Centre Potential*	
	1989	1991		1989	1991
(Population)	(118,500)	(118,800)			
Per Capita Large Area Store Expenditures £165	£19,552	£19,602	50%	£9,776	£9,801

	Unsatisfied Potential		*Project Share*	*Project Potential*	
Less Effective	1989	1991		1989	1991
*Competition** £1,786	£7,990	£8,015	40%	£3,196	£3,206

* This term refers to that portion of the total sales capacity of a competitive unit or retail cluster which will be obtained from within the trade area after the proposed project is completed and has established itself in the market.

size, then it would represent about 25% of the total effective large area store space in the trade area. This represents the basic market share of the large area store in the project. It must be recognised, however, that sales per square metre of individual retailers in the same retail category, vary quite considerably from each other and that even sales per square metre of the same retailer in different localities, also vary. Thus experience in the field is important to make the necessary adjustments.

Usually, a new development is not able to capture its full market share in its first year of operation and two or three years must elapse before it is fully established and influential on trade area residents' shopping patterns.

(viii) Recommended Size of Development

In the final stage of the analysis, the project potential is translated into warranted floor area using store type operating levels as used in the sales capacity calculations described previously. In the example above, where the appropriate large area store operating level is £1,000 per square metre of total area (sales, storage and administrative areas combined), a new development of about 3,196 square metres of large area store space would be justified by 1989.

The mathematical results of the sales potential may provide some imbalance between store types. The mathematical results should therefore be adjusted on the basis of experience, to provide a balanced recommended project. Restaurants and other eating facilities, and service trades, banks, hairdressers, etc., which are not ordinarily included in the retail analysis will be integrated into the recommended project area schedule, on the following page.

It is desirable to add a detailed area schedule – subdividing the areas by retail category into individual shops and stores. This further subdivision is completed on the basis of experience in the letting market with recognition of any particular local requirements as noted during the competition survey conducted in the field. This detailed area schedule is essential to enable the architect to develop a realistic concept and to permit preparation of the detailed financial analysis and valuations.

Example:

Recommended Area Schedule

	Area (m²)	% of Total
Superstore		
Food	4,000	26·7
Non Food	3,000	20·0
Total	7,000	46·7
Shopping Gallery		
D.I.Y.	3,000	20·0
Chemist	150	1·0
Clothing	650	4·3
Furniture and Appliances	1,200	8·0
Other Comparison Shops	1,500	10·0
Eating and Drinking	1,000	6·7
Services and Institutions	500	3·3
Total	8,000	53·3
Total Project	15,000	100·0

3. Impact Studies

Increasingly, local planning authorities at public inquiries require an assessment of the likely future impact of the proposed retail development.

Such studies may be limited to the effect of the development upon the retail sales achieved by existing retail facilities in the area to be served by the new development, or be extended to cover all types of environmental impact: traffic, parking, public facilities, urban landscape, etc.

The following matters are appropriate to a study of the project's impact on existing retail facilities:

(a) The first stage in the impact study is to determine the potential for the new store or project to be obtained from each sector of the defined trade area in the manner described previously under the heading "trade area analysis". It may be noted that some analysts use travel time isochrones, plotted at five minute intervals instead of a zonal division of the trade area, as the basis for determining the sales potential of the project under study. However, customer residence analysis of existing shopping centres shows clearly that the penetration of a shopping centre or retail store (number of customers per "x" residents or sales achieved per "y" of total retail expenditures in the appropriate categories) is more accurately defined in terms of sectors of the trade area than in terms of travel time isochrones.

(b) If budgets permit, a survey should be made, by sector, of the future trade area residents to determine their current expenditure patterns by store type and by existing retail facility. Generally 500 to 1,000 surveys will suffice, completed on a pre-determined grid to ensure even distribution throughout the different sectors of the trade area. The turnover of each existing centre must be obtained from existing data or calculated analysis on the basis of its trade area.

The results of the customer survey by existing retail facility must be compared with the known or calculated sales of the existing facility to ensure an exact "fit".

(c) The potential to be captured by the new facility from each sector of its trade area is then related to the expenditure of the residents of that sector by existing retail facility. Similarly the transfer, or diversion, from each existing centre is evaluated on the basis of judgement. It should be noted that the loss of sales in existing facilities through transfer is similar to the concept of "effective competition" referred to under sales potential in the trade area analysis section above.

Thus as may be seen from the table on page 190, the Primary sector of the new project will transfer or divert £200 from Centre A and £100 from Centre B. If Centre A achieves sales of £1,000 and Centre B £2,000 then the diversion from Centre A will be 20% and from Centre B 5%. Similar calculations can be made for the other sectors of the new project's trade area. Obviously, the total diversion should reasonably equal projected sales for the new project, although there is some evidence that retail stores compete not only with other retail stores but also with other beneficiaries of residents' earning power such as savings, holidays, restaurants, etc., not to mention consumer credit.

Example:

Primary Sector

Total resident expenditures is £1,500
of which the distribution is as
follows:

	Present Conditions		Future Situation	
Centre A	£1,000	Potential new centre	£300
Centre B	500	Will be spent in Centre A	800
		Will be spent in Centre B	400
Total	£1,500	Total	£1,500

Where budgets do not permit running the expenditure survey among area residents then a market analysis must be prepared for each competing centre and the amount of sales generated by each competing centre in each sector of the future project's trade area determined. Thereafter the calculations proceed as above.

MARKET STRATEGY

When preparing market analyses for retailers, it is necessary first to define the objectives of the client as a pre-requisite for any market analysis. Whereas the developer's objective is usually to develop the largest profitable shopping centre compatible with the site area and the sales potential available, the retailer's objectives are normally somewhat more complicated. These may be grouped under three main headings.

(i) *Market Coverage* – Historically, many major retailers have developed in the central areas, but frequently have not followed the growth in suburban population by opening branch stores in such locations. Thus, their share of metropolitan area expenditures has declined as suburban population has grown.

One controlling factor in a retail expansion policy is the size of the market share which is set as a goal. Three degrees of this goal may be stated, simply, as follows:

(a) Dominance – A dominant store group may seek to develop an aggressive expansion programme for maintaining or increasing its market dominance. A non-dominant group may attempt to reach the dominant position by aggressive expansion into any area where a reasonable sales volume and profit can be anticipated.

(b) Maintenance of Share – Such a policy of market coverage will also require an expansion programme as the retail company seeks to maintain its current market share in the face of future expansion of the market.

(c) Protection of Profits – The least aggressive of these goals might best be achieved simply by improved management within the existing shops in the group.

The retailer's market coverage policy must thus first be

determined and then research can be undertaken into the areas most likely to provide the required results.

(ii) *Store Image* – This requires a clear idea as to the image which the parent store seeks to give to the proposed branch stores. Some retailers are prepared to adjust their store image and merchandising policies to the particular requirements of specific trade areas whereas others wish to maintain a constant image throughout the metropolitan area. In the latter case, it is probable that the expansion programme will be much more limited than in the former.

(iii) *Sales Turnover Objectives* – The minimum sales volume requirement and the proposed merchandise mix for new branch stores are also basic requirements before undertaking any market strategy study.

The preparation of a market analysis for a specific retailer also requires an in-depth understanding of the client's current operation. Wherever possible customer surveys should first be conducted in existing stores to determine the current extent of that retailer's trade areas and the current market shares achieved by the existing stores. Customers are asked to indicate exact place of residence and these are plotted on a large-scale map. The current trade area is then delineated, the number of people resident within the trade area determined, their total expenditures in the relevant store type calculated and compared with current sales achieved by the store. The result of these calculations provides the current market share achieved by the retailer in question. This furnishes a sound basis for evaluating the likely future market share.

TRAFFIC AND PARKING STUDIES FOR SHOPPING DEVELOPMENTS

Although traffic generation and parking requirements studies are best prepared by qualified traffic experts, they are closely related to the economic demand analysis for retail facilities and thus the basic procedures are indicated below.

In the context of a shopping centre development, it is necessary to use the techniques of traffic analysis to resolve two major issues. These are:

- Firstly, how many parking spaces will be necessary to satisfy shopper's requirements?
- Secondly, what road construction and improvements should be undertaken to provide an acceptable level of access, in view of the additional traffic that the shopping centre will generate?

Such traffic analysis is particularly important in relation to larger shopping centre projects (10,000 square metres or more), whose trade area extends beyond local neighbourhoods and where a significant proportion of the sales potential will be derived from car-borne shoppers. Also, it is evident that such centres will achieve their anticipated sales potential, only if access conditions and parking facilities are compatible with shoppers requirements.

The traffic study process involves seven distinct stages which examine successively the following aspects:

(a) How many shopping trips will the centre attract?
(b) What proportion of clients will use a private car, as opposed to public transport or travel on foot, to visit the centre?
(c) What proportion of shopping trips will occur on each day of the week; how many clients will arrive during the peak hour?
(d) What proportion of traffic to and from the centre use each of the possible approach routes? What road improvements will be necessary to handle such additional traffic?
(e) How many parking spaces will be required?
   Parking requirements are dependent upon daily traffic flows generated by the shopping centre and the expected maximum accumulation of vehicles in the car park, this being related to the average duration of visit.

Example:

Anytown Shopping Centre

Cars per Day	Maximum Accumulation	Parking Requirements
Monday to Thursday: 1,300 cars	15%	195 spaces
Friday : 2,000 cars	17%	340 spaces
Saturday : 2,800 cars	18%	504 spaces

In practice, sufficient spaces are normally provided to satisfy peak requirements during the average week. In the present example, the car park should contain about 500 spaces. Parking requirements during the end of year exceed those of the average week by about 20%. Nevertheless, for reasons of economy, car parks are rarely dimensioned to satisfy fully such peak requirements.

(f) What size of parking space is required?

The figure below shows parking bay space requirements in relation to parking angle. The free bay width "w" should be at least 2·3 metres and can be increased to 2·4 metres to facilitate door opening. The parking depth "d" is sometimes taken at 4·75 metres in more recent car parks, reflecting the trend toward smaller, shorter cars. 90° angle parking is generally the most economical solution in terms of space per car and also provides for the most flexible car park operation since flows in the adjacent alley can be two-way. However, where the parking alley is one-way, its width "a" can be reduced to 5·0 metres with a parking angle of less than 90°.

However, should flows be one-way in a 90° angle parking arrangement, the alley width "a" may be reduced to 5·0

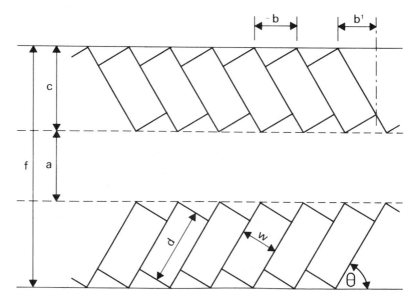

metres. Where the parking angle is less than 90°, one-way circulation in the alleys is obligatory.

Example:

Angle θ	d	w	a	b	b1	c	f
90°	5·00 m	2·30 m	6·00 m	2·30 m	0·00 m	5·00 m	16·00 m
80°	5·00	2·30	5·00	2·34	0·83	5·34	15·68
70°	5·00	2·30	4·80	2·45	1·64	5·51	15·82
60°	5·00	2·30	4·50	2·65	1·89	5·45	15·40
45°	5·00	2·30	3·50	3·25	3·40	5·23	13·96

Where "d" is the bay depth, "w" is the free bay width, "a" is the alley width and "θ" is the parking angle.

(g) What is the total parking area required?
In general, the area required per parking space is of the order of 24–26 square metres in large open-air car parks and 26–30 square metres in multi-storey or underground car park structures. This area includes entrances and exits, main traffic alleys, pedestrian facilities, pay booth areas, etc. Thus, a parking area of 1,000 square metres should normally accommodate approximately 40 cars at grade, and at least 33 cars in a covered structure. If these norms cannot be met, parking layouts and, where appropriate, the design of the structure should be reviewed, since it is likely that there is room for improvement in the basic concept of the car park.

THE FINANCIAL FEASIBILITY STUDY
The economic analysis, after approval by the client, provides the basic area information enabling the architect to develop a preliminary concept. A preliminary financial feasibility study is then prepared to provide a construction cost budget (after consideration of probable rental income, and the required return on investment, etc.). The study will also assist the architect to develop a design concept. It should be emphasised that the construction cost budget included in the financial study is not the quantity surveyor's costing of the architectural plans, but rather a guideline for the architect and quantity surveyor as to the level of investment that can be supported

by the rental income to be generated by the proposed development.

(i) *Rent Appraisal* – Starting with the detailed area schedule included at the end of the economic analysis, the anticipated rental income or sales price is appraised. Although "percentage rents" (i.e. rents calculated as a percentage of sales volume achieved) are as yet rare in the United Kingdom, they are commonly used in many other developed countries. It is therefore recommended that these might also be calculated, if only to cross-check the conventional rack rental values that have been applied. A detailed rent schedule is as follows:

Example:

Store type	Gross area	Guaranteed rent per m²	Guaranteed rent Total	Projected sales turnover per m²	Projected sales turnover Total	Percentage rent per m²	Percentage rent Total	Stabilised rent
Family shoes	150 m₂	£75	£11,250	£1,300	£195,000	6%	£11,700	£11,700 p.a.

In the above example, the anticipated rent is £75 per square metre of gross lettable area and the anticipated sales per square metre £1,300. Such a store might be able to pay rent equivalent to 6% on sales, or in total, £11,700. The stabilised rent is thus the highest of the guaranteed and percentage rents. It represents, in constant money terms, the rent level which the store should be able to pay some two or three years after opening, when it has reached its normal operating level. Percentage rents currently applied in the United States are published by the Urban Land Institute in Washington D.C. in the publication entitled "Dollars and Cents of Shopping Centres" and will serve as a basis, to be adjusted to local conditions.

In countries where long term finance for project development is difficult to obtain, due to high levels of inflation, government policies, etc., it is frequently necessary to capitalize part of the rental income by selling some of the major stores to potential tenants. Of course this practice, if not properly controlled, can lead to great difficulties in the management of the centre after opening.

(ii) *Management Expenses* – In most instances today, almost all of the traditional management expenses are passed on to tenants, either directly or in the form of service charges. Thus for purposes of the preliminary financial analysis, such expenses can well be eliminated.

(iii) *Development Cost Budget* – In the light of his experience with other similar projects and general discussions with the architect and quantity surveyor, the analyst will be able to determine the development cost budget for his project. The concept as to what items should be included in the budget varies between developers in accordance with their own philosophy on the matter.

For purposes of this preliminary financial study both rents and costs can be determined on the basis of current rates, without regard to the date of opening since it is assumed that rents will at least increase in line with future construction cost increases. More refined calculations can be developed at a later date, once the construction cost budget has been accepted.

CONSUMER RESEARCH

Consumer research is concerned with people's attitudes towards shopping centres and in this context, is of major importance once the shopping centre has been opened, and re-letting or up-dating the tenant mix is required. It is also sometimes undertaken before the centre is constructed. Such information provides a profile of customers in the trade area, and their particular requirements and is vital information to retailers planning to open a store in the development, enabling them to orient their merchandise mix towards customers' needs and aspirations.

(i) *Pre-Opening Research*

A considerable amount of data can be derived from the Census of Population, including:

(a) Population by age, sex and marital condition. This may indicate opportunities for maternity shops, teenager shops, record and toy shops, etc.

(b) Economically active population by sex and age; economically active housewives suggest higher average income levels.
(c) Country of birth. The proportion of foreign born trade area residents may be important in establishing an appropriate mix of retail tenants, and in ensuring that ethnic requirements are catered for.
(d) Housing data, including whether the home is owned or rented, vacant dwellings, etc.

Since, however, census data is generally compiled every ten years, it is frequently necessary to up-date that information through consumer surveys undertaken in the home of trade area residents. Generally, 300 or 500 surveys will suffice, completed on a predetermined grid to ensure even distribution throughout the trade area. Telephone and postal interviews are also used, primarily for cost reasons, but undoubtedly home interviews produce the better result.

(ii) *Consumer Surveys*
These may be used to obtain information on the following points:

(a) Household size and occupation of employed persons in the family.
(b) Median age and sex of the shopper.
(c) Educational level attained.
(d) Family size and composition.
(e) Preferred shopping districts and favourite shops.
(f) Favourite newspapers, radio stations and TV channel.
(g) Family income level.

(iii) *Post-Opening Research*
After the shopping centre has opened, a continuing consumer research programme will enable the owner to remain aware of changes in the trade area and he can react to them by changing his tenant mix, up-grading the centre, etc. Such programmes are particularly necessary if a centre fails to reach planned operating levels upon opening or when extensions, additional facilities or major remodelling are planned. Continuing consumer research may include:

(a) Consumer home surveys.
(b) In-centre consumer surveys.
(c) Visitor and car counts.
(d) Cheque/credit card surveys.
(e) Vehicle registration surveys.

ANALYSES FOR OTHER LAND USES

1. *Residential Development Projects*

The basic procedure for undertaking a residential demand analysis follows that described in the introduction to this chapter and in the preceding section on retail analysis. (In fact, this basic skeleton is applicable to all forms of market analysis).

(i) *Site and Access*

This subject has been discussed previously and will present no fresh or unusual problem to the analyst.

(ii) *Market Area*

The geographical area from which the proposed residential development could expect to attract the major portion of its clientele, usually between 80% and 90%, is defined as its market area. The delineation of this area will depend primarily upon the interdependence of the general site area and the nearby major generators of employment, the city centre, and particularly the relationship between residence and workplace. The Work-Place table of the Census of Population will be of assistance in this regard. Consideration will also be given to acceptable modes and times of travel and the other factors mentioned in the trade area delineation. The market area may be subdivided into two or more zones to facilitate determination of the varying impact of the project upon different parts of the overall market area.

(iii) *Population*

Past and present population within the market area will be determined and projections made for the planned completion year and at intervals thereafter. The market area population must be carefully reviewed on the basis of census data to determine such characteristics as family size (growing families require larger homes), employment levels and changes in the type of employment locally (additional female employment permits higher incomes for families with two wage earners), rate of family formation and age of the head of family (young families usually rent first and buy later), car ownership, etc. Income levels will also be determined as this is a limiting factor on the sales (or rent) price of the new units.

(iv) Competition

An examination of the current housing stock should be under-taken on the basis of census data and local research. Such information should include dwelling type, age, condition and size, vacancy and rental/sales value. Existing sub-standard housing should be noted and local plans for its demolition or rehabilitation. Current developments should be inventoried to determine rate of sale, selling/rental price, type of construction, facilities offered, etc. Popular areas for residential construction will be noted, agents interviewed, etc.

(v) Single Family Home Analysis

The total market demand will be determined by dividing the anticipated future market area population by the projected number of persons per dwelling unit. Of this total, a share will be taken for single family homes, as opposed to multiple family dwellings.

In the following example, the proposed selling price range is known and, thus, on the basis of the foregoing local research, it is possible to evaluate the development share of that particular market segment.

Example:

Estimated Market Share of Single Family Homes
under normal, competitive market conditions

	1987–1989	1990–1993
Primary zone		
Total average yearly demand	285	313
In price group £75,000–£90,000	8%	10%
Total number in this price group	23	31

	1987–1989	1990–1993
Estimated development share		
Low 30%	7	9
Medium 35%	8	
High 40%	9	12
Total estimated development share		
Primary zone (medium share)	8	11
Rest of market area (low-medium share)	4	5
Sub-total	12	16
Probable demand from outside market		
area (at 10 to 15% of total)	2	2
Demand from second-hand market	9	9
Total annual	23	27
Cumulative	46	181

2. Office Development Projects

(i) Site and Access

The preparation of office demand analyses is quite difficult owing to a lack of reliable and current base data regarding the evolution of office employment. In such studies, the initial steps are site and access analysis and delineation of the market area, which is often identical to the metropolitan area referred to previously, census data with regard to place of residence and place of work coupled with travel times will all be of assistance in defining the market area.

(ii) Population

The population analysis will include evaluation of past, present and future population within the market area; past, present and future employed population trends, and identification of the numbers of office workers in the past with projection to the present time and in the future. In the absence of more precise data, the analyst will have to rely on his judgement in interpreting S.I.C. classifications to determine the probable number of office workers.

(iii) Competition

Research in the field includes an inventory of existing office space if possible, determination of trends in average floor space per worker, inventory of major new office buildings – number of floors, area of floors, facilities offered, price/rental range, etc. In addition, vacancies, average rental rates of older office space, existing substandard space, etc., should be surveyed and recorded in much the same way as for a housing analysis, but related to office premises.

Example:

The following table shows a simplified presentation of historic data for a provincial city with no recent office developments.

Existing General Office Space Evolution
Metropolitan Area

	1975	1985	1986
Metropolitan area population	795,280	1,175,000	1,210,000
Total office workers	46,000	100,000	113,000
Percentage (2:1)	5·8%	8·5%	9·3%
Office space available	427,340 m²	1,207,700 m²	1,364,700 m²
Average floor space per office worker (3:2)	9·3 m²	12·1 m²	12·1 m²
Existing first class office space	55,740 m²	557,400 m²	678,200 m²
Percentage (4:3)	13·0%	46·2%	49·7%
Existing first class office space in city core	N.A.	N.A.	271,270 m²
City core share	—	—	40%

On the basis of the above presentation of the office accommodation position, it is possible to determine the proposed office development's share.

Example:

Existing General Office Space Evolution
Metropolitan Area

	1986	1989	1992
Metropolitan area population	1,210,000	1,420,000	1,540,000
Percentage	9·3%	10·6%	11·0%
Total office workers	113,000	150,000	170,000
Average floor space per office worker in square metres	12·1	13·0	13·2
Office space required	1,365,000	1,951,000	2,251,000

	1986	1989	1992
Percentage	49·7%	55·0%	58·0%
First class office space	678,000	975,000	1,307,000
Central business district share	40·0%	45·0%	47·5%
CBD office space	271,000	439,000	621,000
Less existing	271,000	271,000	271,000
Cumulative demand forecast	—	168,000	350,000
Project share in square metres at:			
10·0%		16,800	35,000
12·5		21,000	43,750
15·0		25,200	52,500

Where reliable data exists regarding the age and quality of the existing office stock, additional refinements can be added to include, for example, an allowance for replacement of aged and obsolescent office stock.

3. Hotel and Motel Developments

A hotel or motel demand analysis, if the project is located in an established metropolitan area, is based on the demand generated by metropolitan area residents. In a tourist resort, the problem is frequently much more complicated since the local residents may generate almost no demand for hotel facilities. Any forecast for such facilities will depend to a much greater extend on the projected tourist arrivals to the country and particular area in question, with consideration of other factors such as fashion in holiday areas, political stability, currency exchange rates, airline routes, etc.

In developed metropolitan areas, the study follows the standard pattern described previously. The site and access analysis is of considerable importance recognising that quality hotel visitors are likely to be out late at night visiting theatres, nightclubs, etc., and thus security of environment, taxi availability, etc., are most important.

In-the-field research is of great importance and, normally, local tourist boards publish a considerable amount of data by size or quality of hotel relating to average stay, domestic and foreign visitors, number of rooms available by size or quality of hotel, vacancy levels, price ranges, facilities offered, etc. Such data should be assembled for past years and analysed to determine trends.

A simplified table illustrating quality hotel demand in the central city and the proposed project's share is given below:

Example:

Quality Hotel Room Demand
Metropolitan Area

Total Demand		1986	1989	1982
Projected population		1,210,000	1,420,000	1,540,000
Quality hotel rooms per				
1,000 inhabitants		3·95	4·60	5·0
Total rooms required		4,780	6,532	7,700
Rooms constructed		4,502	—	—

Period Demand		1986/1989	1989/1992
Period demand		2,030	1,168 rooms
Replacement demand*		555	333 rooms
Total period demand		2,585	1,501 rooms

Central city share	32·5%	840	488 rooms
of period demand:	35·0%	905	525 rooms
	37·5%	969	563 rooms

	35·0%	317	184 rooms
Site share at:	40·0%	362	210 rooms
	45·0%	407	236 rooms

* 50% of annual replacement demand – Total replacement demand calculated annually on the basis of 3% of the total inventory of 7,400 rooms.

4. Marina Demand

The catchment area for a marina development will be developed in a manner similar to the shopping centre trade area. The extent of such a service area may be quite large, ranging from 30 kilometres up to as much as 150 kilometres from the site for a major project.

Where compulsory registration for boats is in force quite detailed data usually exists with regard to the composition of the boat park existing in past years, by length and type of motive power. In the United Kingdom, the Ship and Boat

Builders National Federation have conducted enquiries into boat ownership throughout the country. Existing marinas should be inventoried to determine size, vacancies, if any, facilities offered and berthing rates.

Historic trends in boat ownership, if possible by length and type of motive power will be determined and projections of increasing boat ownership per 1,000 residents in the service area developed against future population projections, if possible again by size and type of motive power.

It will be recognised, that not all boats require wet berths, since the major proportion of boats owned in the United Kingdom are too small for wet berthing. For example, over 60% of pleasure boats owned in the United Kingdom were in the small boat dihghy and other categories, motor cruisers and sailing yachts accounted for only 11·4% of all pleasure boats and class sailing 18·5%. This factor must be taken into account in any wet berth demand analysis.

A market share will be taken of the period demand for wet berths, as applicable to the project. Generally such market share is developed in a range with the mid-point considered realistic for the project being selected. It must be remembered that a new project cannot compete for its full market share in the first year or so of opening. A certain lapse of time, often two or three years, is necessary for the project to reach its full impact upon area residents.

5. *Miscellaneous Uses*

The basic technique of site and access analysis, trade area delineation, population projections, competition analysis and site share can be used for a large number of other land uses – pleasure and theme parks, dry ski-slopes, golf courses, cinemas, holiday homes, branch banks, and leisure centres etc.

MARK NORTON

BIBLIOGRAPHY
Most methodologies used in market research have been designed by the individual companies and organisations who use them, for their own particular purposes. Thus there are no relevant published reference books.

CHAPTER 7

The Supply and Sources of Development Finance

INTRODUCTION

Property development finance is but a small area of the financial sector of the economy as a whole. It has its place within the overall structure of the investment market but cannot be viewed in isolation from structural movements and longer term trends that are taking place within the market as a whole. However, property investment and permanent development finance is relatively unaffected by short term fluctuations in interest rates and other more volatile movements in the wider investment markets. This resistance is partly due to the relative scarcity of prime quality property investments, the long term nature of the property medium and the large funds potentially available for development and investment opportunities. However, the cost and availability of development finance is influenced by major movements in interest rates and investment yields, and also by the current attitudes and opinions of investors on the state of the economy and their expectations of the future. In particular the prospect of the property development industry must be judged against not only interest rates, but also inflation, politically motivated discrimination, rental growth, property investment yields, availability of institutional funds, letting prospects, the supply of suitable development sites, building costs, the advent of new technology and its influence on future location and design of commercial developments, a volatile stock market, complex and property exclusive taxation, levels of unemployment and structural changes in the economy; all are producing a complicated and unsettled scenario within which development decisions have to be made.

THE DIFFERENT TYPES OF DEVELOPERS

By the very nature of their activity, developers will have different objectives. But they are all concerned with future projections and expectations. It is also worth remembering that so far as UK commercial property development is concerned the rationale rests largely on the assumption that consumers will continue to have an overwhelming preference to rent the resultant floor space, rather than as in a number of other countries, where the practice is to purchase the project with vacant possession for owner occupation. Without this expectation of a rental income a radical change in the industry would be inevitable. There is now increasing production of developments for sale, on completion, to intending occupiers and this could become a mainstream activity for some developers.

Property developers are essentially no different from many other manufacturing businesses. They work on margins between cost and sale price whether it be in capital terms or income flow. Without that margin, from whence the developer's profit is made, there is no motivation or financial incentive and thus there would be few, if any developments. It is of course the developments of today that are the property investments of the future. Investors are attracted by the prospect of a (hopefully) secure and growing rental stream of income supported by a tangible, physical, asset base.

Decisions on the period for which the funding is required will be influenced by the developer's own objectives (as well as the availability of the type of finance required and its cost). Developers fall into two main categories:

(i) *The Merchant Developer*
Here the raison d'être is akin to that of a manufacturer. A project is physically developed, let and then sold as a completed investment. In times of restricted and expensive long term finance this may well be the only modus operandi that a developer can adopt if he is to maintain an active business. Hence the more aggressive and entreprenurial developers who specialise in this type of activity are in the nature of traders, seeking to "add value" to projects. This brings with it tax consequences, as will be seen later, as the developer's profits are regarded as being trading income and thus subject to income or corporation tax. This can be at a higher rate than capital gains tax although tax reliefs can change the balance in certain circumstances.

The developer will therefore be interested in short to medium term loans, i.e. typically 2 to 5 years to cover the development period. The skill in devising and arranging suitable funding is now an important aspect of his expertise.

(ii) *The Investor Developer*

Here the intention will be to retain ownership of the project, or an interest therein, indefinitely. Thus the developer requires short term bridging finance during the actual construction and development period and then permanent long term funds. If he is planning to undertake the scheme in association with an investor who will be supplying most if not all of the long term funding, then arrangements are often made for that same investor to provide the bridging finance as well.

THE SOURCE OF FUNDS

A very substantial percentage of the nation's personal sector savings is now professionally managed, through "collective" schemes. Pension and Insurance funds and Unit Trusts are typical examples. The growth in "collectivisation" has been considerable and the following table shows the distribution of the financial assets of the personal sector.

Financial Assets of the Personal Sector in 1985

	£million	%
British Government Securities	22·9	3·7
National Savings	30·6	4·9
Stocks and Shares (UK)	66·7	10·7
Bank Deposits	63·7	10·2
Building Society Deposits	103·8	16·6
Equity in Life Assurance and Pension Funds	272·5	43·5
Overseas Assets	9·2	1·5
Notes and Coins	10·4	1·7
Unit Trusts	9·9	1·6
Overseas Assets	36·3	5·8
Total	£626·0	100·0

Source: Financial Statistics

For developers, most of the different vehicles used by investors as a medium, or intermediary, for their investments are potential sources for funding. Until recently however there were restrictions on some of these institutions investing in property; it was not considered "safe". The ebb and flow of funds from the three principal sources is illustrated by the following graph. However as a result of the "Big Bang" and the accompanying deregulation of the financial markets of the City of London, the situation is rapidly changing. The Financial

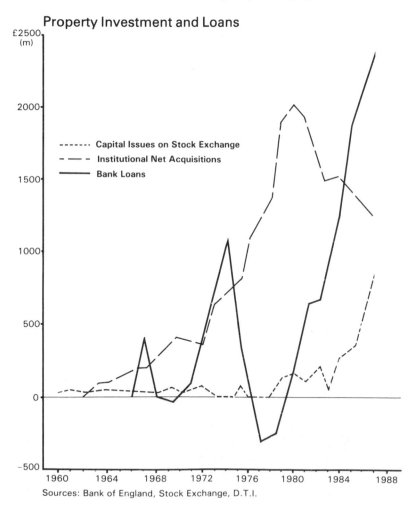

Property Investment and Loans

Sources: Bank of England, Stock Exchange, D.T.I.

Services Act and the Building Societies Act, both enacted in 1986 have very considerably loosened the restrictions, and widened the scope for investment in property.

APPLICATION OF FUNDS

The wide and ever changing list of the suppliers and the different types of financing techniques that are available at any one time depend upon individual circumstances. The list is only limited by the ingenuity of those who operate in this specialised market. The system is flexible but diverse and innovative, yet competitive but secretive. Every project will tend to attract its own individual management structure and funding technique. There are few absolutes in the source, nature and application of funds. Frequently the documented final agreement will be lengthy, bulky and complicated. In the final analysis it will be a test of the negotiating skills of the parties to the agreement that will determine its contents. Statistics are scarce, but the following give an indication of the enormous size of the property development and investment market:

Market capitalisation of listed property companies mid-1987	£11,000 million
Outstanding commercial loans to property companies mid-1987	£10,000 million
Institutional direct and indirect purchase of property in 1986 (including Building Society mortgages)	£25,480 million

Within this large and dynamic market the financing of property development basically takes two forms, namely through corporate finance and/or direct project funding.

Tax and legal considerations usually determine the particular legal vehicle that is used by a lender/investor of development finance, and this tends to cloud the distinction between funding a company (i.e. corporate finance) and funding the project through the intermediary of a company, or other suitable vehicle, established for that express purpose. Because of the exempt or partially relieved tax status of the principal financial institutions and the well established landlord and tenant system the long term funding of most commercial developments has, historically been partly project based and partly through the stock market/company share medium. The property development financier has however developed his techniques from the much older and well tested methods of the investment banker and his use of the stock market. William Zeckendorf tells of his envy at the ease in which a banker could structure the finances for the purchase of a $10 million company compared to the then very limited alternatives available with which to finance a $10 million freehold office block. It was whilst fishing in Hawaii and daydreaming of adapting the corporate finance methods to property development that he made one of the first innovative conversions of corporate to property techniques of financing which he called the "Hawaiian Technique". This was the forerunner of many adaptations based on conventional corporate finance methods. Zeckendorf summarised the situation thus:

> The investment banker can divide and sell the ownership and rights in a corporation in a great many ways, a piece at a time. For instance, he can sell first-mortgage bonds to an insurance company, at the prime rate of interest. He could also offer debentures, which, though they take a second position to the bonds, offer a higher rate of interest, in compensation. For investors interested in a speculative fillip (in case the company does very well), there are convertible debentures that can be turned into common stock. He can issue preferred shares (convertible or straight), which tend to be especially attractive to corporate investors, because preferred dividends passing from one corporation to another are taxed lightly. Finally, there is the common stock, the basic equity of a corporation, but the availability of capital does not stop there; there are also bank loans, accounts receivable (which may be financed with a factor), warrants to buy stock, and various other ways to draw investment capital into a corporation. In fact, investment bankers have over the generations invented as many ways of catering to investors as there are investors with particular personal needs, whims, or tax requirements. (The autobiography of W. Zeckendorf.)

As will be seen many of these techniques have been modified and reapplied to the particular requirements of property development funding operations.

The pace of change and the ingenuity that is being applied to designing and improving funding techniques, received a significant impetus as part of the "Big Bang" in the City of London. In 1986 the financial and investment markets were deregulated in order to increase competitiveness and broaden the range of services that individual financial companies could provide. The "revolution" in the City of London, was dubbed the "Big Bang" by the press media and the principal legislation which accompanied this, freer and competitive business philosophy, to provide investor protection were the Financial Services and the Building Societies Acts. One of the many upheavals that took place in the wake of the "Big Bang" was a significant increase in the number of very large institutional financial groups – particularly from North America – who became represented in the City's financial and investment markets. Because Wall Street in New York, had experienced their own "Big Bang", some years earlier on 1 May 1975, they were therefore able to bring with them their experience of operating in a more liberated environment as well as their knowledge of "packaging" development funding techniques in a variety of ways which, for a number of reasons, had not been possible, or appropriate, here in the UK. This invasion of foreign banks and investment houses added yet further stimulus to the independent endeavours that had been taking place by British companies to develop and expand the range and capacity of development funding techniques. The result of this potent fusion of financial forces and entrepreneurial skills has been the introduction of some radical new approaches to the problems of finding long term capital for the development industry. These will be discussed in the appropriate context later, but in the meantime it is necessary to distinguish between funding through a company and direct financing of the project.

(i) *Corporate Finance*
Traditionally companies provided the funds for new projects from retained earnings (out to profits), the issue of new shares and borrowings. In the early post-war era fixed interest debentures, bank loans and mortgages were commonplace for all property development companies. Nowadays, however, they have devised a corporate finance strategy which encompasses a new range of corporate debt and equity funding techniques.

These corporate funds may well be applied to a particular development project (through the medium of a limited liability company, or occasionally a partnership) or to the holding company or its principal subsidiary. The choice between, and the mixture of corporate fincancing and/or direct project funding will be determined by individual circumstances viewed against a wide spectrum of factors.

(ii) Project Finance

This approach is usually determined by the fact that the principal, indeed often the only security for the finance to be provided, is the property itself, although supporting guarantees and additional, collateral, assets may also be requested by the lender/investor. Although a special "off the shelf" company may be utilised as the legal vehicle through which the transaction is effected, the essential characteristic of project finance is its direct relationship with the actual development: Mortgages, Non Recourse loans, and Sale and Leasebacks are typical examples of direct funding, as the principal security for the finance is the project itself.

DURATION OF FUNDING

An early decision of the developer will be the duration of the period of the funding.

(i) Short Term Finance

The conventional City definition of short term finance is usually regarded as being for up to 3 years. Although this usually covers most property development situations, more complex or larger projects require greater flexibility to enable finance to cover a development period of up to 4, or even 6 years to be provided by means of a bridging loan. The main sources for short term borrowings traditionally have been the clearing and merchant banks. The cost of such loans usually being by reference to the bank's own base rate, or the London Interbank Offered Rate (LIBOR) on a fixed or floating rate basis.

(ii) Medium Term

This covers the 3 to 10 years spectrum which is appropriate for larger developments and gives developers adequate time to make permanent arrangements for those projects which they intend to keep as long term investments themselves, or alternatively sell, so as to repay the loan. Sources include the banks and syndicated term loans.

(iii) *Long Term*

For periods over 10 years this implies long term loans such as debentures and mortgages for 20 to 25 years (and longer), or for freehold and very long leasehold interests, i.e. 99 to 125 years, through a sale and leaseback. The principal suppliers of long term capital include the insurance companies, the pension funds property unit trusts, some larger property companies and other long term investors. More recently, various forms of syndicated long term loans have been designed for property companies. For example the "drop-lock option" gives the developer the right to borrow, in agreed tranches within a specified period, development and investment funds for periods of up to 40 years. The "option" is triggered if interest rates fall below a stipulated level and the rate once "locked" remains constant for the remainder of the period.

SUPPLY OF FINANCE

There is no definitive list of the different categories of sources of funds, let alone the individual potential suppliers. It is an ever changing market in which it is impossible to record individual transactions. Sources come and go and have included, "hot money" from foreign crime syndicates and dictators which is "laundered" through respectable city sources; the ill-fated excursions into property funding by the Crown Agents; the omnipresent Vatican, and the one time seemingly endless supply of Middle East petro-currency. These and many others are of course independent agencies carrying out property funding transactions alongside, but overshadowed by, the established major financial conglomerates, banks and UK investment institutions who dominate the market. Many of these institutions establish a comfortable relationship with their own "stable" of property development companies and entrepreneurs to whom they supply finance, project by project. Developers who have a good track record with an institution enjoy a high degree of mutual respect and trust to the extent that commitments are sometimes made, over the telephone, based on the essential project information given by the developer. On the principle of "my word is my bond" a developer often relies on this promise of finance from a trusted funding source and enters into major financial obligations, for example by signing a contract to purchase a site, in the confident expectation that both the finance and mutually acceptable legal documentation will follow in due course.

Following the property crash in 1973/74 funding techniques began a radical change as institutional investors reappraised their views on property. This process of evolution quickened noticeably as "Big Bang" approached in 1986. The revolution in the City's business practices which was engendered by the sweeping deregulation and liberalisation also dramatically increased competition. Major new international financial conglomerates were formed, often initiated by incoming large and powerful American based banks, finance houses and financial service companies. They also brought with them very substantial financial "fire power" with which to market and underwrite the "new" funding techniques, developed back home in North America.

(i) Factors influencing supply of finance

All suppliers of potential finance for development operations will take into account the following considerations:

(a) The general economic climate and political stability of the nation; its fiscal, legal and property framework.
(b) The need to achieve a balanced spread of their loans and investments which will also match anticipated liabilities with assets.
(c) The comparative performance and anticipated trends of alternative investment opportunities, in addition to real estate.
(d) The tax structure and its effects on the attractiveness, in terms of net profitability to the individual investor, of the various alternative opportunities.
(e) The anticipated returns and risk associated with the particular investment under consideration; its location, quality and letting potential.

(f) The duration of the investment, its "liquidity" and size.

(g) The availability of alternative property funding/investment "on offer" within the same time frame.

(ii) *Choice of Supplier*

The developer will be influenced in his initial choice of the supplier of the funds he requires by such factors as:

(a) The size and type of the loan/investment and its duration.

(b) The characteristics of the project itself and any special project tax considerations which would attract or deter a particular funding source.

(c) The terms on which the funding is available.

(d) Knowledge of which source is "in the market" for the type of project on offer.

(e) Personal relationships and direct introductions.

(f) The reputation and experience of the potential source.

If a developer does not have personal knowledge of funding sources he will often turn to the larger firms of commercial surveyors and estate agents who will act for either the developer, or the funding source, in negotiating the requisite finance. Merchant bankers, solicitors, stockbrokers, are also knowledgeable and useful intermediaries. Post "Big Bang", the trend is for the international financial conglomerates to establish specialist departments to deal with property funding.

THE PRINCIPAL SUPPLIERS

As indicated earlier in this chapter the suppliers of development finance are many and varied. Nevertheless the largest single class of long term suppliers are the financial conglomerates and the investment institutions; in particular, the insurance companies, banks and the gross fund* especially the superannuation funds, and the property unit trusts. Although of major importance to the urban property market as a whole, Building Societies were not directly involved with the provi-

---

* *The Gross Funds* include those investors who are exempt from income, corporation and capital gains tax such as charities, local authorities, approved pension funds, friendly societies and registered trade unions. Others, such as the life insurance companies, enjoy partial relief by being assessed at a special rate of tax.

sion of development funds although this may soon change as a result of the freedom they have recently been given to widen very considerably their operations, through the Building Societies Act 1986.

Over past decades the volume of net new money poured into the financial institutions has been very substantial. However the direct and indirect net investment by the gross funds into property and development has been declining, since its peak in 1981, as shown in the graph.

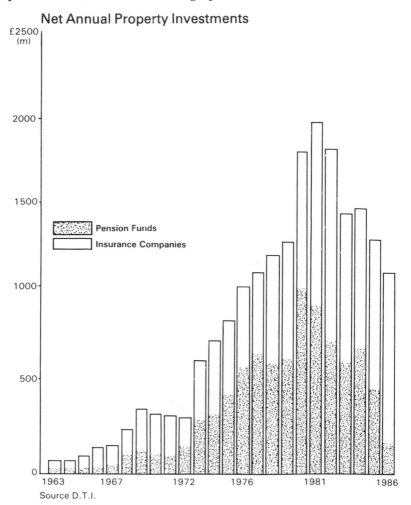

Net Annual Property Investments

Source D.T.I.

In 1986, the total financial institutional investment in property (including residential loans) was as follows:

House purchase loans	(Million)	
Building Society net new loans	£19,062	
Misc. Financials	736	
Other institutions	132	£19,930
Direct investment in property		
Insurance companies	877	
Pension funds	306	
Property unit trust	55	
Other institutions (e.g. property		
bonds and charities)	59	£ 1,133

In addition to the institutional investment there are:

Property loans by the banking sector		
Advances to property companies	2,303	
Advances for house purchase	4,417	£ 6,720
Total direct and indirect involve-		
ment in property		£27,783

(Money into Property by Debenham Tewson & Chinnocks)

Although these annual figures of involvement are impressive they understate the pictures for a variety of technical reasons in the way in which the statistics are returned. In addition, there are the very substantial indirect property investments via shareholding and other securities in quoted property companies purchased by the financial institutions during the year.

(i) *The Insurance Companies*

British life offices derive a substantial proportion of their income from investment of the life funds which finance a wide range of projects. At the same time, subject to the statutory requirement to match liabilities with assets, life offices are under an obligation to seek the best real long-term returns for their policyholders and (where applicable) their shareholders.

During the 1950s and 1960s the most important suppliers of long term finance for property development were the life funds and pension schemes of the insurance companies. But by 1985 their net acquisition of land, property and ground rents amounted to £803 m or 14% of their total annual investment (whereas in 1981 it was £1·1 Bn).

The accumulated funds of insurance companies as illustrated in the chart below which shows the market value of the total invested assets of UK insurance companies and their overseas subsidiaries, and the UK branches of overseas companies. (The totals do not include cash and other short term assets.)

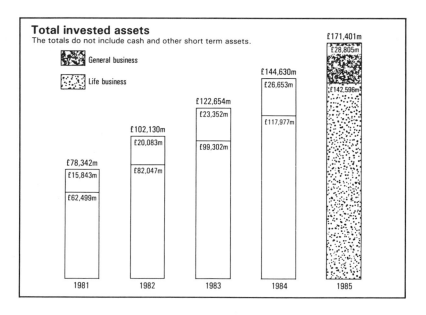

Total invested assets
The totals do not include cash and other short term assets.

General business

Life business

£171,401m
£28,805m
£142,596m

£144,630m
£26,653m
£117,977m

£122,654m
£23,352m
£99,302m

£102,130m
£20,083m
£82,047m

£78,342m
£15,843m
£62,499m

1981 1982 1983 1984 1985

(a) *General Funds*

These are the non-life insurance business (fire, theft, motor and marine) and the fund represents the unexpired part of current premiums and a contingency fund to meet exceptional losses. General funds, because of the nature of their business are not significant suppliers of development finance and only invested some 8% of their funds into property in 1985 amounting to £2·3 m.

(b) *The Life Funds*

These are built up from the returns on investments and the premiums paid by the members and participants of the wide variety of schemes offered by or under the management of insurance companies, ranging from whole life insurance, pension plans and endowment policies. One of the specialised forms of investment are " Property Bonds", which were started in 1966 and provided the individual investor of modest means with the only direct way to invest in prime commercial property. (Authorised unit trusts could only invest in property company shares and unauthorised property unit trusts have been limited to tax exempt institutions and charities). Essentially, a property bond is a unit linked life assurance policy which used the insurance company as a vehicle to get around the prohibition on unit trusts investing in property. The premium is used principally to buy a capital "unit" which is invested through a pooled fund, into property. The small balance of the premium provided life assurance cover which brought some tax advantages to the bond holder. Bonds also pay tax at life assurance rates on their investment income, but unlike unit trusts they are liable for capital gains tax.

There are over 90 Property funds on offer although the sector is dominated by two giants, Abbey and Allied Dunbar valued at £420 and £280 million respectively. Although these two are substantially larger than any of the others – the nearest is Barclays Life at £57 million, many of them are potential sources for development funds. Abbey was quoted as saying "if you want a good quality property investment, you often have to create it yourself", and had some 10% earmarked for development ventures.

Also, most bond funds have a high degree of liquidity, 20% being fairly representative, which is indicative of the volume of cash available at any one moment of time.

The percentages shown below (previous year's figures are in parentheses) give a breakdown of their investments by sectors.

By the end of 1985 property development and investment represented 14% of the life funds total investment. However to give an indication of the change in the investment portfolio of these funds, the insurance companies held property investments with a market value in excess of £15 Bn, in 1980,

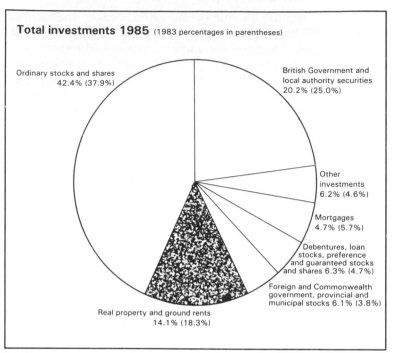

Total investments 1985 (1983 percentages in parentheses)

Ordinary stocks and shares
42.4% (37.9%)

British Government and
local authority securities
20.2% (25.0%)

Other
investments
6.2% (4.6%)

Mortgages
4.7% (5.7%)

Debentures, loan
stocks, preference
and guaranteed stocks
and shares 6.3% (4.7%)

Foreign and Commonwealth
government, provincial and
municipal stocks 6.1% (3.8%)

Real property and ground rents
14.1% (18.3%)

Note: These percentages are based on the market value of assets at the end of the year.

accounting for almost one quarter of their total assets. By 1985 the situation had changed and their property assets had dropped to under 15%, although the value of their property portfolio was approximately £20 Bn.

(ii) *The Pension Funds*

Having their origins in Victorian times the traditional funds grew through regular contributions, usually by employers and employees, and profits and interest thereon, to make provision for the future payment of pensions to their members. Their investment strategy has been essentially long term and as they are "funded" by contributions and accumulations they have continued to expand in size, and in influence in the main investment markets.

Principally as a result of successive tax reliefs and government encouragement of savings, a wide range of "pension" investment vehicles have been designed and marketed. This in turn has led to many more pension schemes and funds, particularly through the insurance companies, having substantial sums to invest. Not only are there the company and occupational pension schemes, providing for both private and public sector employees, but there are also the pooled, self-administered, managed and self-employed varieties. Pension contributions are therefore pouring into the wider investment markets through many different sources, using various vehicles or channels. Their complete tax exemption is a powerful attraction to investors.

This "collectivisation" of savings, through the insurance companies and pension funds involved the investment of nearly £18 Bn during 1985, pushing the total market-value of their collective investments to over £274 Bn.

Of the top 12 pension funds, each with assets in excess of £2 Bn, the first 6 are (or were) nationalised industries, namely the National Coal Board with £7 Bn, British Telecommunications with over £6 Bn, followed by the Electricity Supply Industry, the Post Office, British Rail and British Gas, at £3 Bn. Trailing behind, private enterprise is represented by Barclays Bank at £2·9 Bn and I.C.I., Shell and B.P., none of which make the top 6, by size of fund. All of the major funds, and indeed very many smaller ones have significant property investments and frequently carry out developments in association with development companies and local authorities. They also become involved in direct development on their own account, without a partner. Because of their significant tax advantages they are powerful and effective competitors in the property development market.

(iii) *Unit Trusts*

There are two basic classifications for this particular investment medium, namely (Investment) Unit Trusts and Property Unit Trusts, although as a consequence of the Financial Services Act the species is likely to be extended.

(a) (Investment) Unit trusts provide an indirect route into stock market investment. Private investors' subscriptions are pooled in a trust fund which is then invested in selected stocks and shares in accordance with the provisions of the trust deed, managed by professional managers and supervised by trustees. Generally investments have been limited to securities quoted on a recognised Stock Exchange. The trust fund is divided into units which represent equal portions of the total value of the fund. The price at which units in a particular fund can be purchased – the "offer" price, and the price at which they can be sold – the "bid" price, are published daily. These prices are based on the current asset value of the fund which comprises the underlying investments, cash and accumulated income. At the end of 1986 there were over 900 authorised UK unit trusts having more than £27 billion of funds under the management of some 120 professional managers who are members of the Unit Trust Association. Five unit trusts specialise in investing in property company shares.

(b) Property Unit Trusts (PUTs) are a far more specialised medium of investment into property and are restricted to pension funds and charities. Partly as a result of the Finance Act 1965, special unit trusts were introduced for tax exempt and partially exempt funds who could obtain higher rates of return (because of their tax status) by investing directly into property, rather than indirectly through property company equity shares. "Exempt" property Unit Trusts also appeal especially to smaller funds who do not have the requisite expertise in property and for whom an individual property investment would cause a severe imbalance to their portfolio spread because of the typically large value of any single transaction. The steady and impressive growth of these trusts provided them with the confidence and experience to expand into direct development, both with and without a developer/partner, normally through a sale and leaseback. There are now some 17 such trusts. The original pioneer, the Pension Fund Property Unit Trust was the first to successfully navigate a way through the then governing legislation for unit trusts, in particular the Prevention of Fraud (Investment) Act 1958. Property unit trusts were not "authorised" and thus required individual consent to operate from the Department of Trade. However, it is anticipated that as a result of the Financial Services Act, by the end of 1987, the controls on promoting and marketing property unit trusts will have been relaxed. This in turn could lead to a more active secondary market in which units are traded between buyers and sellers, rather than being bought by the trust managers. Property unit trusts in particular suffer from periodic investor disenchantment which causes a "run" of withdrawals. Any improvement in the "liquidity" of PUTs is likely to increase their appeal to investors and thus attract more inward investment. PUTs are potential suppliers of funds for developers as well as being purchasers of completed developments.

(iv) *Investment Trusts*

Unlike Unit Trusts which are in fact technically "trusts", in the conventional sense, with trustees, Investment Trusts are merely limited companies who invest in other companies' shares. (Unit trusts are "open ended" in the sense that new investors can always buy into the trusts by purchasing units at the underlying asset value and which they can sell back to the trust). Investment Trusts however are "closed ended" and their shares are traded on the Stock Exchange although at a price which usually carries a discount of around 25% of the asset value of the company. As Investment Trusts are permitted to borrow money they can achieve a measure of gearing.

There are nearly 200 Investment Trusts "approved" by the Inland Revenue with assets of £22 Bn. Provided they do not distribute any capital gains by way of dividends, they are exempt from capital gains tax. Investors suffer standard rate tax which is deducted before the dividend is paid, by the company.

(v) *Building Societies*

Although an important member of the group of financial institutions, Building Societies had no direct involvement in commercial property (other than their own premises), until the passing of the Building Societies Act 1986. As part of the movement in favour of deregulation of financial institutions ("Big Bang") the situation has now changed and Building Societies have been given far greater freedom than before. It is therefore possible, indeed probable, that they will "spread their wings" and become much more active in the development sector.

Their potential importance can be judged by their very large, collective, size. With total assets of £135 Bn, they made loans to nearly 7 million borrowers of whom 937,000 received loans of about £27 Bn in 1986. It is therefore tempting for the developer to look forward to the day when he might be able to tap this very significant potential source of funding, especially as the Building Societies can now raise "wholesale" funds in the money markets, for onward lending. The securitisation of mortgages is also likely to improve their general liquidity.

(vi) The Banks

For many decades prior to World War II this was the principal, often the only, source of external short term development funding. Projects were usually sold to owner occupiers or, when let and income producing, sold to investors. A small number were retained as investments by developers. Until comparatively recently bank lending to developers was essentially short term, to provide a "bridge" between the commencement of the development and its sale, or refinanced on a long term basis through a debenture or mortgage. The market has until recently, prior to the "Big Bang", been dominated by the six members of the London Clearing House which is best known by the big four, i.e. Barclays, National Westminster, Midland and Lloyds, with a 12,000 branch network. The explosive growth in bank lending, leading up to the property crash in 1973, and the even greater, more recent expansion are clearly shown in the following graph.

For the property developer these are often the first choice for short and medium term bridging finance. For many years Barclays and National Westminister Banks had been regarded as the property developer's friend. This was because of their receptive attitude to, and significant loans for, property development. Much however, depends on a variety of factors as to whether a particular branch of a clearing bank might be willing to provide the development loan required. These include:

(a) Directives and "advice" from the Bank of England. Develop-

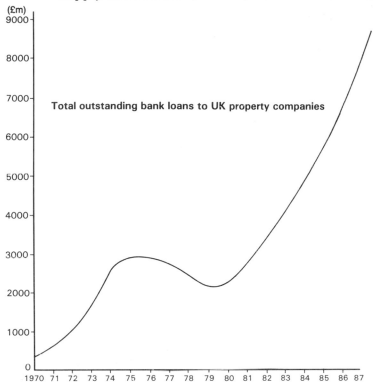

Total outstanding bank loans to UK property companies

ment and consumer credit loans are invariably the first
to be restricted in times of national economic difficulty.
(b) The Bank's own head office policy.
(c) The manager's interpretation of (a) and (b) and his own
branch's relationship with the developer client.
(d) The developer's track record and the details of the project.
(e) The arrangements for repaying the loan.

An alternative banking source was the Merchant Banks who
of all the financial institutions probably are the most enterprising, sophisticated (and expensive!). A merchant banker will
give a superficial distinction between clearing banks and his
own bank by reference to the former living on their deposits
whilst the latter lives on its wits. The accolade of success for
a merchant bank is to become a member of the prestigious

"Accepting House Committee". Unlike the clearers, merchant banks prefer to limit their property loans to a short term basis but can be ingenious and productive in arranging an attractive funding package for a particular development, using other people's money. (It is significant that a number of the newly formed financial conglomerates have recently opened up specialist property investment and development funding departments, principally to bridge the gap between potential investors and the growing and lucrative market of development finance and investment.) Of the merchant banker's many skills, it is his ability to "package" a project into an acceptable form and his extensive range of investment clients, that justified his fee and frequent "equity participation" in the transaction. This latter inducement was also an acknowledgement of his willingness to be responsible for, or to skilfully eliminate, that extra element of risk or uncertainty which prevented the developer from funding his scheme through more conventional sources, in the first place.

The list of foreign banks establishing branches, subsidiary banking companies and joining financial conglomerates has been growing at an impressive rate. Many of these are part of the major international investment sector, particularly from North America. They bring with them a familiarity with, and an interest in, development funding. In addition they are also well placed to arrange foreign currency loan facilities for any developer brave (or foolish) enough to take on this added dimension of risk in the development process. The graph opposite shows the amount of funding provided by Retail and Overseas Banks to property companies over the past 15 years.

(vii) *Trusts and Charities, The Crown Estate, The Church Commissioners, The Great Estates, The Oxbridge Colleges' Estates*

Although these organisations have substantial funds available for investment they are limited and controlled by their own Trust Deeds and also by the relevant statute law as to their investment strategies. Nevertheless they are a potential source of funding. Many of the largest aristocratic landed estates, particularly in London, are major developers in their own right but have also undertaken a wide variety of partnership devel-

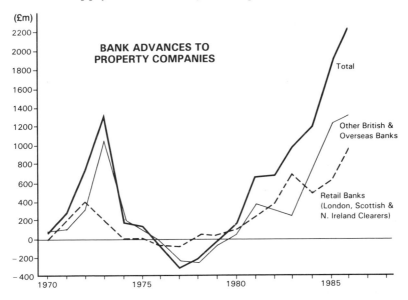

opments both on and off their own freehold estates. These experiences gave confidence to extend into the mainstream of commercial development both in partnership with others and solo. They usually enjoy borrowing facilities which together with their own funds can provide a significant contribution to a joint venture. They may also introduce their own site or finance, or both, for a redevelopment project.

(viii) *Public Property Companies*

Since 1957 property companies have enjoyed their own individual section on the Stock Exchange list and now number some 135 separate companies with over 280 different, listed, securities with a collective market capitalisation of over £11,000 million. The Land Securities Investment Trust Co. Ltd. is one of the largest in the world, with a market capitalisation of about £1,700 million. Another eight companies have market values of over £200 million.

At first sight it may seem strange for one property developer to turn to another for assistance with funding. However, a publicly quoted company will almost certainly be able to raise finance at a lower cost than his fledgling cousin. This is because of his established relationship with the prime lenders, the strength of his own covenant and balance sheet, and the ability to access into the wide range of corporate funding techniques. He also brings an extra degree of confidence through his involvement with the project to the funding institution. He may also have liquid cash available.

Finance is usually provided on the basis of a base rate of interest and an equity split of the profits. The larger company may require a sufficient shareholding of the joint company formed to undertake the development to be regarded as a subsidiary (i.e. over 50% of the shareholding) even though he must consolidate the joint company's accounts into his own statutory annual accounts. The cost of the loan is charged direct to the project with the profit being taken through the equity share capital of the joint venture company, or a partnership. Increasingly, however, many developers prefer to keep their financial arrangements "off balance sheet". This means that because they have a minority interest (though not necessarily minority effective control) they do not have to disclose their financial commitment in their formal accounts.

The choice between the two legal vehicles used will depend on the particular circumstances of the case; partnerships are often preferred as the rights and obligations of each party are clearly defined without restricting control over their own affairs. They can also enable each party to maximise its own tax advantage without prejudicing the other's position, which is more difficult with a joint venture company.

(ix) Other Companies

There are a variety of reasons why non-property companies, both public and private, provide development funds. Sometimes they will own the property which is to be developed and will allow the developer/partner to use this as security for a loan; they may have surplus liquid funds and are attracted by the returns offered by property developers (including the bait of "equity participation"); alternatively they may be seeking opportunities for diversification. The need to maximise their returns on any cash surpluses are also pressing. Hence short term development funding with a share in the profits, is appealing.

Building contractors in particular are always eager for lucrative building orders and will often agree to "roll-up" the stage payments due under a building contract between themselves and a developer. Indeed a number of such specialist building companies have been launched under Business Expansion Schemes. The total cost, plus accrued interest thereon, is not paid until the development is completed and sold. The danger to the developer, of course, is to keep sufficient control over the building costs charged by his partner (whose main interest is the building contract itself) so as to be sure that there is sufficient equity left at the end of the day for him!

(x) *European, Central and Local Government*
Such has been the growth in the availability of grants, loans, financial incentives, tax reliefs and other forms of assistance from government sources to industry and business that a number of specialist guides and directories to this particular maze have been published. Some of the large firms of accountants have "on-line" computer data banks which are updated weekly so as to keep abreast of the frequent changes taking place. It is typically a condition precedent to any government offer of assistance that the recipient is actually running the business which is to benefit, e.g. manufacturing and service industries. Increasingly new commercial development projects may qualify for assistance under the enlarged programme of inner city, derelict land, and urban development grant regimes. Because of the expanding range of government sponsored initiatives to encourage employment and improve the physical environment (especially of inner cities and other depressed areas) the scope of the programme is continually changing. It should therefore be kept under regular review by developers, as well as such innovations as "Enterprise Zones", "Urban Development Corporations" and "Free-Ports".

Within the Enterprise Zones so far announced and the seven Urban Development Corporations, the thrust of the government's programme has been more towards reducing red tape and increasing tax incentives rather than providing direct financial assistance to developers. Many of the grant schemes are modelled on the original Regional Development Areas aid programme but are now refocused on those areas with the most serious unemployment levels and structural economic weakness. It should be noted, however, that there is often an extensive time lag before the grant is actually paid and this can cause a strain on the developer's cashflow. It is also invariably a basic condition of all such schemes that the "project" must be approved before any work commences and needless to remark the paperwork can be formidable.

Appendix I contains a list, together with an explanation, of all those grants and initiatives which are available in 1987, and which have a direct relevance to property and development.

The EEC is another important source of grants and financial aid packages. For example an industrial developer found that his estate was unsuccessful because there were no public transport facilities. The bus company were willing to extend the nearest route into the development but part of the intervening access road was a substandard country lane. The widening of the lane, including the purchase of the necessary land was funded through an EEC grant.

(xi) *Private Investors*

As in the case of Trusts there are sufficient very wealthy individuals interested in funding operations to include them for consideration. One of the practical problems of course is to know who they are. Seclusion and anonymity are increasingly symptomatic of the species. Nevertheless they do operate through their merchant bankers, investment advisers, managers and agents. As is so often the case in finding/selecting suitable financial partners it is a question of "horses for courses". The oil sheiks, third world politicians, Swiss gnomes, international financiers, rich widows, sporting superstars and pop singers are all obvious examples.

Traditionally banks, especially the merchant banks, acted in the roles of intermediaries between sources of capital and borrowers. One of the many changes taking place in the major financial and investment markets is a process of "disintermediation". This means that intermediaries are becoming somewhat less essential to the funding process as borrowers are finding more direct routes to lenders. The by-passing of intermediaries is being achieved through the evolution and development of a new generation of tradeable "financial paper"; Eurobonds were one of the earlier examples and which have grown very significantly in both the amount issued and the volume traded.

(xii) The Stock Exchange

Although not the oldest in the world, London is in the top three, internationally, and provides one of the major international forums in which capital is raised, new shares issued and existing ones traded. The Stock Exchange was the very centre of the "revolution" in the City's financial markets, that took place in 1986. This was the culmination of nearly twenty one years of reaction to, and negotiation with, the government and its campaign against cartels, monopolies and artificially restricted markets.

In 1951 the Restrictive Trade Practices Act was passed and eventually the Stock Exchange was forced to register its rules and code of conduct with the Office of Fair Trading. Notwithstanding that the Stock Exchange Council argued that its practices were not *against* but *in* the public interest, it was not until 1983 that it agreed to abandon its minimum commission requirement and a deal was struck with the Government that it would withdraw the reference to the Restrictive Practices Court in July of that year. In the meantime, across the Atlantic back in May 1975 Wall Street had reorganised and deregulated its financial market. (At that time here in London, there were then some 350 foreign banks directly or indirectly represented. By 1986 the figure was about 460, an increase of one third.) The "second stage" was initiated on 27 October 1986 when the market was formally deregulated. As a consequence of "Big Bang" minimum commission rates for stockbrokers were abolished and the introduction of "dual capacity" market makers has taken place. The prohibition against outside ownership of trading firms was removed and the establishment of a screen based system of buying and selling introduced. This has all been accompanied by, indeed could not have been accomplished without, the huge advance in the new generation of computer technology.

An indication of the main sectors, and volume by market values, of financial securities dealt with on the Stock Exchange (at the start of 1987) can be gained from the following:

	£bn
Public Sector Securities	147
Eurobonds	124
Company Securities	1,176
Total	1,447

Shares are formally admitted to a Stock Exchange listing by "going public" through a "prospectus issue" or inviting a "tender offer" for the shares. Other routes available to companies who wish to see a market develop for their shares include a formal "offer for sale" or a "placing" direct with investors. If no new funds are required a company's existing shares can be "introduced"; typically this covers the case where its shares are already traded on some other foreign exchange.

Currently the Stock Exchange embraces three separate but related markets for shares in companies. There is, as discussed previously, the main market where the shares in mature companies (which meet the strict criteria imposed by the Exchange for full listing) are traded. Then there is the USM or junior market for less mature companies with as yet a not fully proven track record. This "Unlisted Securities Market" was officially started at the end of 1980 and has continued to expand ever since. It has also attracted a steady flow of property companies as it enables younger companies to obtain a "quote" for their shares. At the end of 1986 there were over 500 companies listed on the USM (including a dozen property development companies) with a market capitalisation approaching £5 Bn. Lastly there is the recently launched (1987), third tier market for companies who only have to show a one year trading record. (It is anticipated that many new entrants will be transfers under the Exchange's rule 535, which permitted the matching of bargains in the shares of these fledgling companies.) The Third Market will be attractive to development companies seeking to raise up to £1 m of new funds as it permits a company to gain a measure of access to the major captial market by relaxing the more stringent regulations normally applied and contained in the "Yellow Book"*. The RICS has also become

---

* "Admission of Securities to Listing".

closely involved in certain aspects of the Stock Exchange's regulatory role through its Assets Standards Valuation Committee and the advice and guidance it gives on the valuation of property assets, for Stock Exchange and accounting purposes, in its own "Red Book".

There are some 135 public property companies with their own separate section within the Stock Exchange classifications. The total market capitalisation for the sector exceeds £11 Bn and property development companies have over the decades found the Stock Exchange a useful vehicle for raising new and additional capital, especially in 1985 and 1986.

CLIVE DARLOW

BIBLIOGRAPHY

"Structure and activity of the development industry," Property Advisory Group (DOE) [HMSO 1980].

"Money into Property," Debenham, Tewson & Chinnocks annually.

"Report of the committee to review the functioning of financial institutions" [HMSO 1980].

"That's the way the money goes," Plender J. [André Deutsch 1982].

"A guide to institutional property investment," McIntosh A. & Sykes S. [Macmillan 1985].

"The dynamics of urban property development," Rose J. [Spon 1985].

"The property boom," Marriot O. [Pan 1969].

"Finance in property" [RICS 1979].

"International dictionary of the securities industry," Valentine S. [Macmillan 1987]

"Commercial Property Development" DOE (Pilcher Report) [HMSO 1976].

"Partners in Property," Whitehouse B. [Birn Shaw 1963].

"The Property Boom and its Collapse" [RICS 1978].

"Secondary Banking Crisis 1973–75," Reid M. [Macmillan 1982].

CHAPTER 8

Corporate and Share Capital Funding

INTRODUCTION

Successful property development companies are frequently a product of the combination of financial expertise and property skills. Many a poor property venture has been transformed by clever financing. While the property man will frequently be obsessed with the physical aspects of a project, the finance director will be concentrating on the "bottom line" figure. He is indifferent to the emotional satisfaction and pride that a developer may derive from a particular pet scheme. The financier's expertise is well tested in the fields of debt and corporate finance, as opposed to project financing; (where the funding arrangements are exclusively directed to, and secured by, the physical development). Corporate finance involves the financial structure of the company itself and the "paper" securities it issues. Although a field for other experts and somewhat beyond the scope of this book it is nevertheless appropriate to indicate, in general terms, how corporate finance can be, and increasingly is, an essential ingredient of overall development finance strategy. Indeed major funding arrangements are often a mixture of both property and corporate funding techniques.

There are a variety of ways in which a development company can raise capital for new projects. This will involve debt and, or equity capital.

DEBT CAPITAL

(i) Debenture Stock

This is secured on specific assets of the company with interest on the loan being paid, normally half yearly. Not only are debentures a first priority claim on assets but debenture stock often have trustees to look after the holder's interests. Debentures can be irredeemable or redeemable (with or without a sinking fund). Convertible debentures carry the right to convert part or all of the stock into equity (or other) shares at a previously determined price, at stated future date(s).

(ii) *Loan Stock*

By contrast this is unsecured and carries interest payments twice yearly. As with debentures, convertible loan stock enables the company to raise capital at a slightly lower rate of interest but, in return it gives the holder a right to switch his holding into equity shares at a stated date in the future at a fixed price. If this right of subscription is detachable from the loan stock itself then this is known as a warrant and can be separately bought and sold.

SHARE CAPITAL

(i) *Preference Shares*

These rank after debentures and loan stock, but before ordinary shares. They are however not company liabilities but part of its share capital. If there are insufficient profits available to pay the fixed rate dividend, then if they are "cumulative" preference shares, the arrears are carried forward for payment in future profitable trading years. Conversion rights may also be included in the same way as for debentures and loan stock. Another variation is for preference shares to be redeemable at a stated date in the future. Generally, preference shareholders have little if any voice in the management of the company as few have voting rights.

(ii) *Ordinary Shares*

Being the "equity" in the company they participate in its true profit once the demands of priority interests have been met. However, this does not necessarily mean all the profits are distributed through dividends to the equity shareholders as part are usually ploughed back to finance further expansion and development. Voting rights will be restricted, if they exist at all, for holders of any "A" ordinary shares which the company might have issued.

(iii) *Scrip Issues*

Property (and indeed other) companies sometimes find that the total of accumulated and retained profits in the company's reserves have grown disproportionately large in size in relation to the issued equity share capital. This imbalance is adjusted by a "scrip" or "capitalisation" or "free" issue of new additional shares on a previously determined ratio to reduce the reserve and increase the issued equity capital. This technical adjustment does not increase the value of the shares held by the existing shareholders.

(iv) *Rights Issues*

A company can use this method of raising additional capital by offering existing shareholders the right to purchase a stated number of additional shares usually at a special, favourable, price.

The following table shows how, over the past quarter of a century quoted property companies have raised substantial funds, through both share issues and debt instruments on the Stock Exchange. Of particular interest is the upsurge in 1972 (before the crash of 1973) and the significant boom in 1986.

The capital structure of a development company will typically be a mixture of loan capital (i.e. debenture, loan stock and preference shares), and equity capital (i.e. ordinary shares). The ratio between loan capital and equity capital is referred to as "gearing". This means that a movement at one level will cause a much larger, or "geared" movement at another level. A company with high gearing indicates that loan and prior charge capital is large in relation to the equity capital; this requires a large percentage of the company's income to service its loan capital. Whilst high gearing is attractive to shareholders in times of rapid expansion and income growth it can be calamitous in reverse circumstances.

SECURITISATION AND MODERN DEBT INSTRUMENTS

There has been a strong movement since the end of the 1970s for corporate borrowers to raise capital direct from the prime lenders rather, as in the past, through the agency or "intermediation" of third parties such as banks. This movement has

Valuation and Development Appraisal

Property companies – new issues 1960–86 (£m.)

	Shares		Debt		Total issues
	Ordinary	Preference	Convertible	Other	
1960	18·6	—	—	14·4	33·0
61	27·6	—	20·4	7·8	55·8
62	18·9	—	6·6	19·4	44·9
63	4·8	—	4·5	43·4	52·7
64	6·7	0·5	4·2	23·3	34·7
65	0·7	—	—	29·4	30·1
66	0·3	—	2·6	26.5	29·4
67	0·7	—	3·6	20·1	24·4
68	2·0	—	9·9	8·9	20·8
69	1·5	—	52·6	7·9	62·0
70	0·1	—	37·5	1·0	38·6
71	4·4	0·5	2·4	42·4	49·7
72	29·4	—	2·0	68·8	100·2
73	1·4	—	1·3	—	2·7
74	5·1	—	—	—	5·1
75	3·9	—	79·2	—	83·1
76	3.2	—	4·2	—	7·4
77	0·4	—	—	7·5	7·9
78	2·6	—	—	—	2·6
79	100·8	—	24·9	4·9	130·6
80	142·2	—	16·8	—	159·0
81	50·8	—	58·1	—	108·9
82	146·7	—	—	41·7	188·4
83	36·5	—	10·2	3·0	49·7
84	61·6	—	32·2	135·4	229·2
85	41·2	15·4	7·0	225·1	288·7
86	305·7	13·0	19·1	589·4	927·2

Source: Midland Bank

been facilitated by the recent deregulation of the investment markets and the greater flexibility that has resulted enabling more innovative design and marketing of a new range of "debt instruments". Thus the variety of instruments that can now be issued and subsequently traded in the financial markets has been increased. Borrowers are therefore more inclined to by-pass banks as they can now often raise funding more cheaply by borrowing direct from prime lenders; this process is known

as disintermediation. Essentially major corporate borrowers
are replacing bank loans with various types of "paper" securities which they issue and which can then be subsequently
brought and sold "second hand" in the recognised exchange
markets, by investors. In this way the essential liquidity is
introduced for investors so that they do not have to wait until
the maturity date of their loan before being able to realise their
investment for cash. In addition to the even more recent movement towards securitisation and unitisation of single property
investments, which is dealt with in a following section, the
various forms of securitised corporate debt include:

(i) Commercial Paper

These are generally short term i.e. for less than one year unsecured promissory notes (or capital IOUs) issued by major companies in return for loans from investors. Typically they are
issued at a discount to their par value and therefore pay no
interest prior to maturity, but the investor receives back more
than he has loaned by way of compensation for the absence
of any receipt of interest in the intervening period. The UK
market in sterling commercial paper only started in 1986
(although it has been well established in the USA where it
now accounts for almost one quarter of the total business debt).
Already a growing number of the UK property developers have
arranged commercial paper programmes with which to raise
funding for their developments. Examples include Peachey
Property Company who have arranged a £50 m programme;
Hammersons £100 m; Stockley £100 m; MEPC £200 m; Property
Security Investment Trust £50 m and by the end of 1986 the
property and insurance sector companies accounted for nearly
25% of the commercial paper programmes announced by the
year end.

(ii) Bonds

These are certificates which witness the liability of a borrower
to repay a debt of a fixed amount at a future stated date. Interest is paid on pre-arranged, regular, dates without deduction
of tax. However, an important characteristic of a bond is that
it is issued on an unsecured basis i.e. the lender/investor in

a bond relies on the credit worthiness, and ability to pay, of the borrower rather than the security provided by a specific underlying asset owned by the borrower.

(iii) *Eurobonds*

Another well established and much larger market than commercial paper for raising external funds, is the Eurobond Investment Market. Eurobonds are usually sold outside the country of the borrower and are underwritten by an international syndicate of banks. They are a useful vehicle for major "triple A borrowers" to raise large capital sums and are attractive to investors because of the quality of the borrower, the wide range of currencies in which they are issued with a good choice of medium to long term maturities. They too, like bonds, are unsecured and therefore there is no charge over the borrower's assets as security for the loan. There is a strong secondary market in Eurobonds and the property sector has been increasingly active in the market raising finance for development including Wates City of London Properties with a 9½% £25 m issue, and Securities 9½% £100 m issue, MEPC 10½% £12.5 m issue and somewhat more innovatively Hammersons recently launched a DM150 m 6% bearer bond.

INTERNAL FUNDING

This is the use of funds generated from within the company itself, principally from retained profits i.e. profits which are not distributed to share-holders in the form of dividends or used for sinking funds and provisions which have been made for depreciation. On the international scene Japanese and American companies have been employing significantly higher percentage of external funds (as a percentage of total sources of finance) than have British and German companies. UK property companies according to an analysis by the Economist Intelligence Unit of some of the larger organisations were only able to retain just under 20% of their net pre-tax income. Having regard to the fact that tax took approximately one third and dividends approximately one half, the scope for property companies to fund major large scale projects without the use of external finance is obviously limited.

CONTROL AND ACQUISITION THROUGH COMPANY SHARES

(i) *Control*

Until comparatively recently, de facto control of a development company could be achieved through separate but interlocking shareholdings. For example, family dynasties could be perpetuated through a series of adroit share transfers whereby the founding developer transfered his shares to a charitable foundation of which near relations are trustees (in addition to being directors of the operational development company). This transfer was exempt from the then relevant Capital Transfer Tax, so long as the donor survived for one year thereafter. After this, more shares can be purchased from the income accumulated within the charitable foundation, funded by the receipt of dividends on its existing holdings. Furthermore the trustees often invested in a tax efficient life policy secured on the founder's life, which when it matures provides further capital with which to buy (his own) retained and remaining shares. Thus the family control remains undiluted and the dynasty is perpetuated.

(ii) *Acquisitions*

Not only can the stock market be an efficient medium for raising capital finance and for subsequently buying and selling the resultant stocks and shares, but it also enables control to be gained of an existing company by adept and skilful manipulations of its issued securities. This periodically reached such excesses over the years that it attracted much adverse publicity and entered the political arena as a consequence. This in turn has led to controversy and debate over the degree of control and statutory supervision that is needed for company takeovers and merger. "Predators", "asset strippers", "manipulators" are less attractive terms used to describe some of the more conspicuous exponents of the art of company takeovers.

Typically a property developer will be searching for a company which has unnoticed or undervalued property assets which he can exploit by redevelopment, or by sales, or by refinancing. Neglected underlying assets are also symptomatic of sleepy management. The characteristics of these circumstances are reflected in a lack-lustre share performance, a low price earnings ratio and a share price standing at a discount on the underlying true asset value of the company's properties.

Recent concern over investor protection was responsible for the Financial Services Act 1986 which, together with the subsequent Regulations, introduced a new set of rules. This took the form of a small army of new "Regulatory" Associations, stricter codes of conduct, disclosure requirements and proper supervision of the activities of members. Public concern has also been heightened by "insider dealing" where members of the financial community have improperly used privileged information so as to make large personal gains by trading in the relevant shares, typically in connection with company takeovers.

(iii) *Property Company Shares*

Over the decades the financial institutions and other investors have been attracted to property company shares by:

(a) The quality of the underlying assets.
(b) The expertise of the management.
(c) The benefits to be derived from gearing.
(d) The discount on assets, i.e. the share price was less than the value of the underlying assets.
(e) The expectation of a steady growth in rental income and or in capital values which would be reflected in share prices and dividend growth.

However, the attractions waned somewhat following the introduction of corporation tax and capital gains tax in 1965. Many financial institutions are "gross funds", i.e. they receive income gross, without deduction of tax. Property companies are subject to corporation tax on their profits and capital gains tax on any property investment disposals. Thus they pay dividends out of net, after tax, profits. Furthermore dividends are subject to standard rate income tax which the company pays by way of Advance Corporation Tax. Although the gross funds can recover the "imputed" tax on their dividend, the original rental income from which the dividend stems, has suffered corporation tax and this is irrecoverable. Similarly with any capital gains tax paid by the company on the sale of any of its investment properties.

While the above applies to all share investment portfolios held by the institutions, property is almost unique in one respect. The alternative to investing indirectly in property through a shareholding in the company, is to own, develop and manage property directly. Although direct property involvement requires specialist knowledge it does not involve investment in manufacturing plant and equipment, a large labour force, stocks of raw material etc. which would be required if direct management took place of most other types of business activities.

But of even greater significance is the fact that by owning and developing property themselves, for many institutions, the resultant income is not subject to tax. Hence the attraction to the institutions of property both by direct purchases of individual buildings and sites for development, and also on the company takeover front. Each year sees property companies being taken over by institutions through the acquisition of shares capital in order to gain full direct control over, and ownership of, the properties held by the company.

(iv) *Takeover Activity*

The battlefield of company takeovers during the past decade or so has not only reduced the number of quoted property companies but in the process some of the victors themselves have since died of financial indigestion as a result of their earlier conquests. Starting in 1969 the list was soon reduced by thirteen companies being absorbed by others (although new companies coming to the market helped redress the balance). Of the 118 public property companies which were listed in 1970 some 40 had been taken over by 1980, including 9 which have fallen into the bottomless financial pits of the institutions and are no longer a separate publicily quoted entity. The turnover has escalated significantly since then. Between December 1985 and June 1986 some 23 new companies came to the market and 19 had been taken over. At the end of 1986 many of the 135 quoted property companies had an identifiable percentage of their shares held by the institutions. In some cases these single shareholdings were as high as 65%.

The exact mixture of cash, shares and, or convertible loan stock, etc. offered to the shareholders of the "victim" company will of course vary significantly from case to case. Both the motivation for, and the advantages resulting from, a company takeover by a developer can include:

(a) Acquisition of skilled, entrepreneurial and/or technical management.
(b) A ready supply of development sites and projects, perhaps with the benefit of current planning permission.
(c) The potential to exploit the "marriage value" of different but interlocking property interests in the same or adjoining properties, separately owned by the two companies involved. The possibility of "adding value" to the properties.
(d) The opportunity to use more dynamically the benefits of any existing mortgages and long term debentures at historically low coupons. This can be achieved by substituting a new property as security for the loan thereby releasing the original property which by now may be worth much more than the "cover" needed for the loan.
(e) An immediate geographical or sector diversification.
(f) Where the shares of the company to be taken over are at a discount on net asset value then effectively the underlying properties in the portfolio can be acquired at below their individual open market value (the reverse of course applies if the shares are at a premium).
(g) Loan stock, which if quoted at below par, can be "bought-in" by the acquiring company, after the takeover, at its discounted stock market value thereby improving the net asset position of the balance sheet.
(h) Depending on the relative strength of the two companies' share prices and overall financial positions, the acquiring company may well be able to accomplish the take-over through a judicious mix of "paper", i.e. shares and loan stock, thereby avoiding the need to pay for its purchase with hard cash. Take-overs are often sparked by a strong, even over-valued, price of the shares of the acquiring company which may be trading at a healthy premium whereas the victim's shares stand at a discount.
(i) While probably not of sufficient justification for the take-over in itself, the availability of tax advantages to be

unlocked by the acquisition can also be an influencing factor. This was well demonstrated by the take-over of Cunard Steamships by developers Trafalgar House Ltd. who shrewdly foresaw the opportunity of utilising the tax relief on a substantial fleet modernisation programme, throughout the entire Trafalgar group.

(j) Access to any liquid funds within the subject company and the utilisation of advantageous loan facilities which may have been arranged prior to its purchase.

TECHNIQUES OF ANALYSIS

The ability to identify and evaluate suitable development motivated company takeovers is a unique synthesis of art and science. Clearly the objective is to arrive at a meaningful financial and property appraisal of a potential "victim" company. This will involve an investigation into many factors, including:

(a) The company's property assets; their existing and projected income, value and trading potential.

(b) The overall state of the company's financial position, its borrowings, liabilities, earnings, etc.

(c) The price and performance of the issued shares, dividend history and market capitalisation.

(d) Whether or not it will fit comfortably into the portfolio and management philosophy of the acquiring company or group.

The problem lies in assembling and analysing the pertinent data. Few companies, if they suspect a takeover threat, will "open their books' for full inspection. Hence there is often an element of "hunch" and subjective judgement needed in carrying out the analyses. There are, however, a series of financial tests, measurements and techniques that can be applied, although such recently developed techniques as "off balance sheet" finance complicates the task of producing an accurate financial picture.

Having identified, as best one can, the salient basic financial data, this is then expressed in a form that enables inter-company comparisons to be made and also to provide a common basis of financial/investment measurement. The techniques used include balance sheet ratios, profit and loss statement ratios and share performance analysis and measurement.

The following is an illustration of the more common techniques of analysis which incorporates various financial characteristics of the shares themselves:

(i) Price Earnings Ratio and Earnings Yield

A popular analytical tool is the Price Earnings ratio. This measures the relationship between the market price of a company's share and the annual earnings attributable to that share. It is very similar to the Year's Purchase multiplier, used by the valuer in capitalising rental income. For example if a company's earnings were £225,000 and there were one million shares in issue the earnings per share are

$$\frac{£225,000}{1,000,000} = £0·225p$$

Assuming that the current price of the share is £2·475, the P/E ratio is £2·475/£0·225 = 11·0; or to express it another way the Price Earnings equals the number of years it will take for current annual earnings to equal the share price, i.e. £0·225 × 11 = £2·475. The P/E ratio is the reciprocal of the "earnings yield", which is arrived at by dividing the earnings per share by its price, i.e.

$$\frac{£0·225p}{£2·475} \times 100 = 9·09\%; \text{ (and } \frac{100}{9·09} = 11·0, \text{ the P/E ratio)}$$

The significance to the property sector of a high P/E ratio (or low earnings yield) is that it indicates a strong expectation of growth and confidence by the market. This is analogous to using a high YP (or low yield) in valuing a property with strong rental growth prospects. Property companies as a whole, at the start of 1987 had a P/E ratio (net) of 24, which was $1\frac{1}{2}$ times higher than that of the P/E for the FTA 500 share index.

(ii) Net Asset Value per Share

The difficulty with this calculation is often caused by the lack of information on up-to-date values of the property portfolio.

The property assets of a property company as shown in its

annual accounts can have changed significantly since the last published report because of new projects, acquisitions and disposals, etc. Also care must be exercised to confirm whether any individual figures are based on:

(a) Valuation; or
(b) Cost; or
(c) Net realisable value, or
(d) A combination of the above.

It will be recalled that the distinction between properties held for investment, or dealing, or development can have important tax consequences which will also influence the takeover evaluation.

(iii) Share Price Discount

A property company with a premium on its assets, as expressed by the share price, may be well placed to make an offer to the existing shareholders of the "victim" company to acquire their shares, in exchange for an issue of its own shares. Here it is acquiring undervalued assets with a relatively more valuable "paper" currency. In simple terms if the shares of the company to be taken over are selling at a price of say 20% below their asset value but the shares of the acquiring company are valued by the market at a 10% premium, then the acquisition through a share issue would take place on the basis of unequal discounts as far as the relative share prices are concerned. The discount on the estimated assets in the quoted property sector ranges from 50% to premiums of up to 20%. Some of the more popular dynamic "Merchant Developer" companies have been consistently experiencing premiums above their asset values. As mentioned earlier, the difficulty with the above calculations is often due to the lack of information on the value of properties in the portfolio, to say nothing of the detective work needed to identify them!

Valuers have made very considerable progress in standardising their approach to property company valuations, for a wide variety of different purposes, and this is well documented by the RICS Assets Standards Valuation Committee's publications which follow the detailed requirements of the Stock Exchange. The approach to valuing development properties, recommended by the RICS is of obvious interest to both valuers and analysts but there are still circumstances where a true indication of current property asset values is difficult to ascertain. It is the ability to identify "hidden" values of properties within a portfolio which have unrealised potential, that often sparks a takeover bid.

(iv) Share Dividend

The company will usually declare a half-year, interim, and then a year-end, final, dividend on the issued shares. This can be expressed as a percentage rate of return on the original par, or face, value of the shares. The yield is, of course, the dividend expressed as a percentage return on the current market price of the shares. Thus a share originally issued at £1·10 in respect of which a dividend of 10% has been declared, and which is now priced at £2·30 will yield:

$$\frac{£1·10}{£2·30} \times \frac{10}{100} \times 100 = 4·78\%$$

Early in 1987 property company shares were averaging a 3·3% gross dividend yield (with ACT at 29%) compared to the 10·6% for Oil and Gas and 18·5% for Banks. In contemplating a takeover, the ability to maintain or improve recent dividend performance will be another important consideration by the acquiring company and shareholders.

(v) Dividend Cover

This is simply the number of times that the current dividends are covered by the profits available for distribution, and is arrived at by dividing the earnings of the company by the amount of the dividend payments.

(vi) Off Balance Sheet Finance

This is a comparatively recent accounting technique which has been adopted with considerable enthusiasm by property companies over recent years. The consequence of using this method is to "keep off" the balance sheet the company's involvement in property developments through joint ventures or partnerships with others. Providing that the company's shareholding in such a joint venture is less than 50% and providing no guarantee as to the repayment of the debt is given by the parent company, or its subsidiary, then it need not show the extent of its involvement in these joint ventures. Because of the very substantial sums of money now involved in off balance sheet financing it is a cause of some considerable concern to the Accounts Standards Committee of the Chartered Accountants Institute of England and Wales and has been the subject of a number of recent briefing papers from the Bank of England.

PROPERTY SECURITISATION AND UNITISATION

The movement towards corporate securitisation of conventional debt, discussed earlier, has during the past year or so gathered considerable momentum and significantly together with unitisation it has been applied to property investment and development with some vigor. The cause for this heightened interest and current excitement over securitisation and unitisation can be attributed to the following:

(a) Property investment has become extremely "lumpy" and "illiquid" due to the large value of each investment and the time it takes to liquidate an individual investment for a cash receipt.

(b) The tax disadvantages of holding property indirectly, for example through an investment in a property company share, has discriminated in favour of direct ownership.

(c) The comparative lack of recent interest by the major financial institutions in investing in property, due to its lacklustre performance and the much higher returns available from alternative forms of investment has restricted the funding market.

(d) The opportunity which fortuitously presented itself by the general shake-up of the City's financial and investments markets and in particular through the regulations embodied in the Financial Services Act 1986 presented the chance to persuade the legislators to remove a number of comparatively minor but nevertheless formidable historical impediments which had prevented widening the ways in which property investments could take place.

(e) With steadily rising values, the size of projects and the

threshold of investments, has increased significantly thereby often putting it out of reach of all but the very largest
major investing institutions.

(f) The problems with (e) above bring with them difficulties
to the valuer in trying to assess open market values of large
property assets for which their exists only a very restricted
market.

(g) The desire to widen the spread of potential investors by
significantly reducing the "unit" price of each investment
will in turn improve the prospects of raising the very large
sums of funding now needed for new projects. It will also,
it is hoped, open the way to a large number of new, small,
investors being encouraged to provide the funds for new
property developments.

The net result of the above is that two principal routes are
being actively pursued. The first is a corporate approach whereby the debt and equity finance for a single property asset would
be securitised and traded on a recognised investment exchange.
The alternative is to work within existing UK trust law and
introduce a new legal, acceptable and marketable method of
dividing the ownership of, and benefit from, a single property
among a (very) large number of individual investors. As with
the corporate approach, this unitisation route will have as an
essential sine qua non the requirement that there is an active,
regulated and recognised secondary market in which the property units can be bought and sold by individual investors. The
trust route is however dependent upon some changes being
successfully completed to the historical, legal impediments
which have effectively frustrated its launch.

One of the first recent examples of corporate property securitisation in 1986 was the so called "Billingsgate" model. This
involved the raising of some £60 m of funding to reimburse
the developers with long term funding for the recently completed high quality London office development which had been
let, in its entirety, to a major international tenant. The details
of the transaction were as follows and were achieved through
segmenting or layering the rental income of the project into
three different classes of securities:

(a) A first mortgage debenture of £52·5m nominal at $6\frac{5}{8}\%$

issued at a deep discount of 67·302%, and which raised £35·3 m.

(b) Preferred equity shares raised a further £25·8m at an annual yield of 5·9%.

(c) The ordinary shares (which have not yet actually been floated) had a value of nearly £18m and these are being held by the developers as they are to benefit from 67·56% of all increases in rents and capital values after the first rent review.

Another major initiative which is at a very advanced stage of preparation and is expected to be officially launched during 1987 is the Property Income Certificate (PINCs). This, like the "Billingsgate" model, operates within the existing body of relevant laws and is not dependent upon any legislative changes. In essence it proposes to give investors both a share in the rental income of a single property asset as well as a share in the company which owns and manages the building.

All of these new investment vehicles hold attractive prospects for raising finance for new developments after they gain operational experience and investor acceptance with existing, standing, single properties. The following table provides a comparative summary of the characteristics of the various alternatives currently under active discussion, although it is anticipated that variations and further alternatives will be introduced as and when the new market of "property unitisation" is launched and becomes operational.

As a precursor to what is likely to develop within the commercial mortgage market it is appropriate to make brief reference to yet another variation of securitisation techniques and that is "mortgage securitisation". This too is an import from the United States' property investment markets where for many years now it has been the established practice, principally through a government sponsored agency, to "securitise" mortgages. In its simple form what this means is that the agency collects up a portfolio of mortgages and it then securitises or translates the portfolio into tradeable financial securities of small denominations which it then issues and which can be traded in the secondary market. The security behind these investments is of course the mortgaged property itself,

Comparison of Multiple Ownership Investment Vehicles of Single Properties

	PINCs (Property Income Certificates)	SPOTs (Single Property Ownership Trust)	Billingsgate (Securitisation)	SAPCos (Single Asset Property Company)
1. Availability	No change in law.	Required changes to Financial Services Bill and Taxes Acts.	No change in law.	No change in law.
2. Tax transparency	Fully transparent – vehicle not subject to Corporation Tax or CGT.	Intended to be tax transparent (if appropriate legislation passed).	Intermediate company subject to both Corporation Tax and CGT.	Intermediate company subject to both Corporation Tax and CGT.
3. Applicability to a variety of properties	No restrictions.	No restrictions.	Not applicable to multi-let buildings without substantially changing the investor's risk profile.	No restrictions.
4. Management	Direct control by investors through appointment of Directors of Management Company.	Manager appointed by the trustee (independent of the investors).	Investors have theoretical control but subject to vendor's reserved rights	Direct control by investors through appointment of Directors.
5. Funds for Refurbishment	Vehicle has power to borrow and can also make rights issue or be subject to takeover.	Not clear whether trusts will have borrowing rights or on what terms they can issue further units or be taken over.	Not addressed in the Billingsgate structure.	As PINCs.

6. Method of Valuation of Shares	Market pricing by supply and demand.	Market pricing by supply and demand.	Market to be made by sponsors of the issue but price at end of arrangement will be subject to a conventional valuation.	Market pricing by supply and demand.
7. Potential Investors	Open to all – listed on London Stock Exchange.	Open to all from the outset.	Open to all – quoted on Luxembourg Stock Exchange.	Open to all.
8. Establishing an Active Market	Listed on established and prestigious market. Concerned effort by PINCs sponsors especially with professional investors. Professional market research undertaken.	SPCT sponsors seeking wide industry support and aiming for substantial interest from investors.	Issue marketed on a conventional basis.	As SPOTs.
9. Vendor's Capital Gains Tax Position	Liability only for that portion of building actually sold to investors.	Full CGT liability on building realised even if vendor retains an interest.	Liability deferred until and unless vehicle company ceases to be a 75% subsidiary whereupon full liability is incurred.	Full CGT liability on building realised unless vendor retains 75% or more interest.

Source: PINCs Newsletter 1987

reinforced by the guarantee of repayment both of interest and of principal by the issuing agency. Already in the UK a limited number of securitised residential mortgage portfolios have been launched and it is anticipated that is it is now only a matter of time before the market follows the USA pattern of securitising commercial property mortgages. This too, when it comes about, will bring with it a much greater liquidity and a wider investor net for property development funding.

CLIVE DARLOW

BIBLIOGRAPHY

"Admissions of securities to listing" ('yellow book') [Stock Exchange].

"Growth and Impact of Institutional Investors," Bristow R. J. & Dobbins R. [Inst. Chartered Accountants 1980].

"Inside the City," Clarke W. M. [Allen & Unwin 1979].

"Property Company Accounts," Phillips S. [CALUS 1984].

"Investment in Land and Structure of Property Companies," Barras R. & Catalano A. [CES 1982].

"Investors Guide to the Stock Market," Cumming G. [Investors Chronicle 1984].

CHAPTER 9
Direct Project Funding

THE HISTORY OF FUNDING

Development funding has evolved remarkably over the years, in response to ever changing circumstances. The principal phases of its evolution can be identified as follows:

1900 to 1950 – Half a Century of Fixed Interest Finance

Property development during this period was quite different from that which was to follow, as the economy was generally depressed for most of the first half of the century and in any event was severely interrupted by World Wars I and II. Even with central London offices, the supply of accommodation generally exceeded demand. Development was principally undertaken by builders, who sold the property when completed, to either owner occupiers or occasionally, if fully let, to the comparatively few long term property investors in the market. In 1920, for example, there were twenty five public property investment companies quoted on the Stock Exchange and even by 1939 this number had only increased to thirty five. In addition, less than six of the major insurance companies had any noticeable property investments in their portfolios. Development funding was principally provided by the banks on a short term loan basis, with mortgages being available for long term investors; property companies were able to raise capital through share issues and debentures at fixed rates of interest.

1950 to 1960 – The Move Towards Equity Participation

During this period the post-war reconstruction and building boom started with a strong boost in 1955 after building controls and licences were removed. Initially, institutional investors were prepared to provide long term development finance on the historical basis of fixed interest loans through mortgages and debentures. However as escalating and permanent inflation began to cause concern, investors became disillusioned with fixed interest type of securities and therefore sought alternatives with real growth potential. Thus the cult of the equity was born and while appreciating the tangible assets that property offered as security for a loan, the institutions demanded, in addition, a share in its future profit. This they did by acquiring equity shares in the development company and/or by insisting on share options and particularly on convertible debenture rights. A number of jointly owned ventures were also established on a profit sharing basis with funds provided by the institutions.

1960 to 1970 – Growth of the Sale and Leaseback

Just as the development boom was reaching its peak in the mid 60s tough credit control restrictions were imposed on the raising of new capital and on bank lending. However, the developer by this time had forged close links with the insurance companies; these had long term funds available and were still attracted to property as an investment medium. However, on seeing the high level of profits then being made by developers – on the back of their (i.e. institutional) money – the institutions' earlier moves away from fixed interest funding was reinforced by the trend to sale and leaseback finance. Surprisingly this method did not fall foul of the Capital Issues Committee and was further encouraged by the introduction in 1965 of Capital Gains Tax and Corporation Tax a year earlier, which made investing in property through the medium of an intermediary, less effective. Furthermore, the pension funds were experiencing a rapid build up of cash available for investment and they too were attracted to property, increasingly through the sale and leaseback funding route. During this decade the sale and leaseback technique continued to grow in popularity and has continued to be refined and modified ever since; first with the "top slice" arrangement and then with the "vertical slice" method of sharing project income.

1970 to 1974 – Stoking the Fires with Bank Loans

With the economy dangerously overheating as a result of Chancellor of the Exchequer Barber's "dash for growth" the removal of credit restrictions and the introduction of low interest rates but high inflation, all combined to attract very large sums of bank loans (especially from the "secondary banks") to the property sector. Bank lending leapt from £430 m in 1971 to £2·74 Bn in 1974; Corporate funding through share issues also reached new heights with over £100 m raised in 1972 alone (which was then an all time high) and which was used to further fuel take-overs and acquisitions. In addition, many developers were borrowing short term with a view to selling their projects, as investments, when completed, or intending to arrange long term finance when rates had fallen. Fierce competition between developers had forced yields downwards and because of the reverse yield gap between property yields and interest rates the dangerous technique of "deficit financing" was increasingly practised. As history now testifies the property market crashed in 1974, inflation soared (up 20% in 1974) and the whole of the western world went into economic trauma after the overnight massive increase in the oil producers' price and their accompanying restrictions on supply.

1975 to 1985 – Innovation, Tax Driven Funding and Massive Bank Lending

The world's economies entered a period of severe depression and investor confidence disappeared (by the end of 1974 the stock market had fallen by over 50%) and property development and investment virtually dried up. A massive amount of bank debt was outstanding as the market crashed, to such an extent that the Bank of England was forced to mastermind a major rescue strategy as many developers, like lemmings, fell over the cliff and into liquidation. Many projects ground to a halt, half built through lack of funds. Other projects, if built, remained unoccupied through lack of tenant demand, and if let, were virtually unsaleable as there were no long term investors in the market.

Life gradually returned to the market, initially through the investment institutions acquiring substantial portfolios of properties from beleaguered property companies who were, as a consequence, able to reduce their gearing and with the proceeds complete their unfinished developments. However institutional property investments averaged only 15% of their total annual acquisitions for the five years following the crash whereas for the two previous years it has averaged over 21%. And as the economy gradually began to improve and activity returned to the property sector, developments restarted. But by this time the institutions had learnt an expensive lesson and they were therefore much more cautious and demanding in their attitude towards development funding. Mortgage finance was effectively ruled out because of the prevailing high rates of interest and the comparatively low yields on property investments. Sale and leasebacks became selectively available for prime projects from proven developers, with forward sales and project management arrangements proving to be a more popular alternative. By 1980 the banks had finally managed to sort out the consequences of their earlier profligate lending which led up to the crash in 1974 and were once again beginning to fill the funding gap left by the absent and reticent financial institutions. Developers for their part were having to react to, and in some cases anticipate, the rapid changes which were taking place in consumers' requirements as well as changing patterns of living: hypermarkets and superstores; out of town shopping and retail parks; high tech buildings and campus offices; "intelligent" offices and leisure oriented developments were all coming on stream at the same time as important changes in the tax regime were taking place. Innovative funding and property investment schemes were therefore pioneered, particularly those which could use the new tax allowances to attract the high paying, "tax driven" investor. Thus Business Expansion Schemes; Enterprise Zones and Finance Leases were refined and directed at procuring funding for new developments. The need to devise alternative sources and methods of long term funding was considerably accentuated by the significant downturn in the institutional property investment and direct funding activities.

Because of the inherent poor performance of property during the 1980s (thus far) and the much more spectacular returns available from Gilts and Equities, institutions' property investment has declined steadily from its peak in 1980/81. By 1987 their net purchases of property had declined to only 5% of their total annual investment, a percentage share not seen for over 25 years. This is represented a continual decrease in the amount invested from over £2 Bn in 1981 to just over £1 Bn in 1986. However, in stark contrast, bank lending has soared, filling much of the void left by the disinclined long term investing institutions and by the middle of 1987 UK property companies owed the banks over £11 Bn of debt (or over 7 years' supply of institutional investment on current levels of their property acquisitions). The following graph shows how the down turn in institutional investment has been compensated by the increase in bank loans and capital raised in the Stock Exchange.

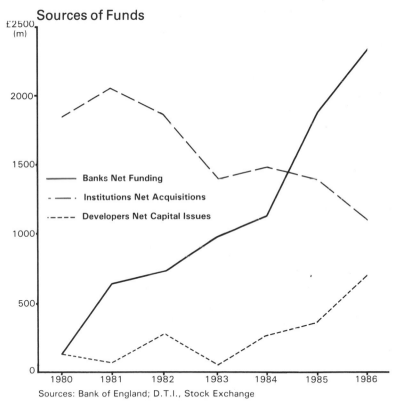

Sources of Funds

Banks Net Funding
Institutions Net Acquisitions
Developers Net Capital Issues

Sources: Bank of England; D.T.I., Stock Exchange

1985 Onwards – The Dawn of Unitisation, Securitisation and Americanisation of Funding Techniques

Just as investors' sophistication has developed appreciably over recent years and investment markets have become increasingly internationalised and deregulated, so the new generation of merchant developers has emerged. Not only have these modern property entrepreneurs brought new creativity and advance techniques of design, management and marketing to the actual project but, together with the new generation of merchant bankers and investment experts, they have, during the post property crash era, designed, adapted and pioneered a seemingly endless range of new funding techniques. These include the continuing development of Business Expansion Schemes, Finance Leases and Enterprise Zone Investment Trusts. Additionally, conventional bank lending has been made much more sophisticated. Thus we have seen the introduction of "drop-lock" and "non recourse" bank loans as well as "tender panels". The use of techniques employed in the mainstream of the financial markets, particularly those which have been pioneered in America following the earlier deregulation of Wall Street in May 1975, have been adapted and applied to the UK funding market. These include the use of various investment and banking instruments such as Eurobonds, Commercial Paper and Multiple Option Tender Panel Facilities, yet further refined by the use of "Exchange Rate Swaps", "Caps", "Collars" and "Floors". A typical "tombstone" advertisement is that recording the £50 million facility arranged for the British Land Company PLC. The securitisation of various types of corporate debt, particularly mortgages has also started. In 1986 a particularly interesting milestone in the evolution of development funding was reached with the "Billingsgate" package of loan stock, preference shares and equity shares being unveiled and listed on the Luxembourg Stock Exchange.

In addition to the continuation of the strong upward surge in bank lending, the enlargement of the range of more specialised "specific to the project" funding vehicles has been energetically pursued. The choice is likely to be expanded still further following the impending introduction of property unitisation. It is argued by supporters of unitisation that this will introduce the essential liquidity into the market and will hopefully fill the void left by the considerably reduced involvement of the institutions, by attracting a large number of small investors, who for the first time, will be able to have direct shared ownership of a single building. In the meantime the institutions

THE BRITISH LAND COMPANY PLC

£50,000,000

TEN YEAR UNSECURED REVOLVING UNDERWRITTEN MULTI-CURRENCY CASH ADVANCE AND STERLING COMMERCIAL PAPER FACILITY VIA TENDER PANEL

Arranged and managed by

Guinness Mahon & Co. Limited

Underwriters:

Crédit Lyonnais, London Branch
Den Danske Bank
National Westminster Bank PLC
The Royal Bank of Canada Group

The Sanwa Bank, Limited
TSB England & Wales plc
Union Bank of Switzerland, London Branch

Tender Panel Members:

Banca Nazionale del Lavoro London Branch
Banco de Bilbao S.A.
The Bank of Tokyo, Ltd.
The Bank of Yokohama, Ltd
Banque Belge Limited
Banque Nationale de Paris London Branch
Banque Paribas (London)
Bayerische Vereinsbank Aktiengesellschaft London Branch
CIC-Union Européenne, International et Cie London Branch
Commerzbank Aktiengesellschaft (London Branch)
Commonwealth Bank of Australia
County NatWest Capital Markets Limited
Crédit Commercial de France, London Branch
Crédit Lyonnais, London Branch
Credit Suisse
Den Danske Bank
Dresdner Bank Aktiengesellschaft London Branch
First Chicago Limited
The First National Bank of Chicago
Guinness Mahon & Co. Limited
Hill Samuel & Co. Limited

Lloyds Merchant Bank Limited
Manufacturers Hanover Limited
Morgan Grenfell & Co. Limited
National Australia Bank Limited
National Bank of Canada
National Westminster Bank PLC
Orion Royal Bank Limited
Phillips & Drew
The Royal Bank of Canada Group
Samuel Montagu & Co. Limited
The Sanwa Bank, Limited
Security Pacific Hoare Govett Limited
Shearson Lehman Brothers International
The Sumitomo Bank, Limited
Sumitomo Finance International
The Tokai Bank, Ltd
The Toyo Trust and Banking Company, Limited
TSB England & Wales plc
Union Bank of Switzerland, London Branch
S. G. Warburg & Co. Ltd.

Agent

Guinness Mahon & Co. Limited

November 1986

remain largely engaged elsewhere, attracted by the much higher returns available from Gilts and Equities; this is further accentuated by the poor intrinsic investment performance of property itself. For example during the period 1980 to 1986 the total return on property was approximately 60% whereas the Financial Times All Share Index had risen by nearly 200%.

THE SCENARIO

Direct property development funding represents an ever changing kaleidoscope of financial ingenuity responding to a wide variety of different circumstances. There are comparatively few, if any, absolutes in the methods used. New techniques and refinements to existing formulae are constantly being promoted. Unfortunately, inadequate authoritative detailed information is published on either the amount of funding that takes place, by whom, or the methods used.

The bare bones of some transactions can occasionally be gleaned from companies' annual reports and from press reporting of the occasional funding operation. Like the property market itself development funding shares many of the same characteristics. For example:

(a) There is no central agency or institution to co-ordinate the business of property funding, as exists for insurance through Lloyds.

(b) There is no physical focal point where the business can be transacted as is the case with the Stock Exchange for shares.

(c) The "market" is in fact an abstract aggregation of separate, individual, unrelated and unco-ordinated funding transactions. However with the advent of the proposed property "Unitisation" a central trading market for the various new forms of property investment "paper" is expected to be established as part of the Stock Exchange.

(d) It is diverse and complex, increasingly involving international funds.

(e) The market is imperfect with fragmented knowledge and little published data; there is no central listing of formulae, yields and other essential information, as with the daily reports and analyses of Stock Exchange transactions.

(f) There is limited freedom of entry and exit from the funding market because of the large financial size of each investment and the considerable legal, taxation and time constraints. And the risks!

The essentially confidential (some would say secretive) nature of funding makes it extremely difficult for those who are not regularly involved in such transactions to obtain a detailed understanding as to what alternative methods might be available at any time, from whom, and just as importantly, at what cost. Even for those who participate frequently in arranging development finance, it is almost impossible to keep abreast fully on a day to day basis as to which suppliers of finance are in the market, and for what type and size of investment and the forms of funding they are currently offering. This market intelligence is of major importance in securing the very best terms available.

The majority of property investment managers are given an annual, or more frequent, budget allocation of funds earmarked for investment into property development ventures. Their supervising Boards of Directors, or Trustees, will frequently express changing preferences and goals as to their ideal type of investment. For example shop development might be favoured, or provincial offices instead of City of London offices, or an industrial project. Depending on how urgent are these requirements and how close is their financial year end, their need in times of limited selection is often expressed in an extra competitive edge to the terms upon which they will enter into a funding agreement. Thus the problem is how to bring both developer and investor together at an opportune time for both parties. Property funding operates in a very dynamic market and lenders therefore have to be competitive, not only in the financial terms offered but also in the speed with which they can respond to individual propositions.

Most small developers try and observe the following rules when formulating their funding strategy:

(a) Never to use all of their own money in a development; always striving to arrange optimum external funding.

(b) Never to give a personal guarantee or personal collateral for any loan.

(c) Always to roll-up the interest during the development period.
(d) To keep as much of the equity as possible.
(e) To restrict the funding to the currency of the country in which the project is based.
(f) To avoid 50–50 relationships; someone has got to be in control.
(g) To be ever watchful of the tax liabilities.
(h) To realise that the bigger the project is, the more likely it is to stir up a political hornet's nest and thus disrupt the cashflow, escalate the costs, and so require additional finance.
(i) To read the funding agreement personally very carefully, especially the "fine print" and to rehearse the consequences of the project not turning out as anticipated. This is especially important in the context of cost overruns, major fluctuations in the projected rental income, and unexpected taxes.
(j) To secure all the necessary funding commitments from the outset.

THE DIFFERENT FUNDING METHODS

There is no definitive list, as such, of funding methods; new and innovative techniques respond to the underlying dynamics of the market. Investment fashions change and politically motivated taxation directed at property development periodically hangs above the market like the Sword of Damocles. The gyrations of the overall structure of interest rates and levels of inflation also have significant effects; for example, the cyclical hibernation of commercial mortgages in the United Kingdom.

Although funding seldom presents a static scenario the principal methods are discussed and illustrated notwithstanding the fact that little new business may be currently carried out with some of the methods reviewed at a particular point in time. It will be appreciated, that there are many funding arrangements still in operational use, even though they were written on terms not countenanced in today's market. They will therefore run their course until the lease or loan expires; sale and lease backs and mortages are classical examples. Nevertheless it is possible that some or all these will return to favour in years to come as others recede in use; new methods will certainly be introduced. In summary, the methods of direct funding may include one or more of the following:

1. Bank loans
2. Project management
3. Forward sale
4. Mortgage and other fixed interest finance
5. Sale (or lease) and leaseback
6. Reverse leaseback
7. Sale and leaseback coupled with a mortgage
8. Tax driven techniques
9. Government grants, loans and subsidies

Basic Example: The Clivesville District Centre

The principal methods (1 to 7) are illustrated and compared by reference to the same basic development project. For the purpose of this simulation the proposed development involved the purchase of a freehold site on which was constructed a district shopping centre and which was then offered for sale in the open market, as a fully let investment, in 1973 (i.e. before the crash of 1974). This is a convenient date for demonstration purposes as most of the principal methods were, uniquely, all available concurrently at that time. Furthermore, many projects funded at the peak of the boom era are now experiencing the need for modernisation and refurbishment. This in turn is giving rise to resurrecting, reviewing and frequently renegotiating the terms on which they were originally funded, back in the early 1970s. (In the intervening years, probably the most significant change that has taken place has been the downward trend in Corporation and Income Tax rates, although Capital Gains Tax remains largely unaltered.)

The development feasibility studies indicate the following:

(a) Anticipated net rents when fully let   £60,000 p.a.
     (net rents actually achieved   £66,000 p.a.)

(b) Total development cost including site
    purchase and interest costs   £640,000
(c) Legal interest to be sold   Freehold
(d) Current investment yield for the
    completed scheme fully let $5\frac{1}{2}\%$
(e) "Yield" for forward commitment to
    purchase when fully let   6%
(f) "Special yield" for joint venture,
    development unlet, with bridging finance $6\frac{1}{2}\%$
(g) Mortgage finance if provided by an
    institution (without equity participation)   14%
(h) Actual net rents on first rent reviews   £99,000 p.a.

Details of the scheme shown in the accompanying plan are
summarised below, which is a new development to serve a
surrounding population of some 25,000 people (i.e. within 2–5
miles or 5–15 minutes driving time). Details of the project are
as follows:

	sq ft
Gross commercial floor, ground floor	54,000
First floor	26,000
	80,000
Malls and square	6,000
Total gross building area	86,000

Land Areas

	sq ft	acres
Ground floor area of building (inc. malls)	60,000	1·38
Service areas	37,000	0·86
Car parking @ 6 spaces per 1,000 sq ft of gross commercial area = 480 car spaces, at average of 250 sq ft per car	120,000	2·76
Total gross area	217,000	5·00

THE CLIVESVILLE DISTRICT CENTRE

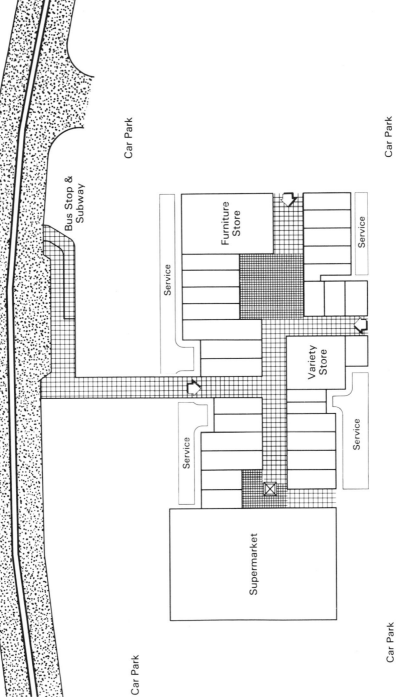

Merchandising of the District Centre

	Floor area (sq ft)		
Stores:	Ground	First	Total
Supermarket	20,000	10,000	30,000
Furniture	4,000	2,000	6,000
Variety	3,000	2,000	5,000
Total Stores	27,000	14,000	41,000

Shops:

A. Convenience Goods

	Ground	First	Total
Butcher	900	450	1,350
Green-grocer	900	450	1,350
Fishmonger	900	450	1,350
Fruiterer/Vegetables	900	450	1,350
Baker	900	450	1,350
Chemist	900	450	1,350
Hardware	900	450	1,350
DIY/Homecare	900	450	1,350
Newsagent	900	450	1,350
Tobacconist	900	450	1,350
Off-Licence	900	450	1,350
Sub Total	9,900	4,950	14,850

B. Comparison Goods

	Ground	First	Total
Electrical appliances	1,000	500	1,500
Womans wear	1,000	500	1,500
Mens wear	1,000	500	1,500
Carpets and floor coverings	1,000	500	1,500
Gas/Electrical	1,000	500	1,500
Shoes	1,000	500	1,500
Baby/Youth wear	1,000	500	1,500
Toys/Gifts/Leather goods	1,000	500	1,500
Sub Total	8,000	4,000	12,000

C. Services

	Ground	First	Total
Fish & Chips/Take away	900	450	1,350
Shoe repairs	900	450	1,350
Cafe	900	450	1,350

Launderette/Dry cleaner	900	450	1,350
Ladies' hairdresser	900	450	1,350
Betting shop	900	450	1,350
Men's hairdresser	900	450	1,350
TV rental	900	450	1,350
Sub Post Office	900	450	1,350
Sub Total	8,100	4,050	12,150
Total Standard Unit Shops	26,000	13,000	39,000
Grand total of retail space	53,000	27,000	80,000

Analysis of distribution (as a (rounded) percentage of total floor areas).

Shops	50%	
Stores and supermarkets	50%	100%
Comparison goods	30%	
Service trades	15%	
Convenience goods	55%	100%

Rent schedule (actually achieved)

Unit	£ p.a. per unit	Total £ p.a.
28 Standard shops	1,300	36,400
Supermarket	20,000	20,000
2 Stores	4,400	
	5,200	9,600
Total rental income		£66,000

Costs of development
Construction Costs

Demolition and site works	16,000
Car park and access roads	52,000
Landscaping, paving	10,000
Service yards and roads	15,000
Building	283,000
Malls and squares, pavements and canopies	20,000
	396,000

		B/f	396,000
Allowance for increase @ 10%			39,600
			435,600
Contingency say,			20,000
			455,600
Professional fees @ $12\frac{1}{2}$%			56,900
			512,500
Building finance			31,500
			544,000

Development Costs

Two agents fees and promotion		7,000
Sub Total	(£6·90 per sq ft)	551,000

Acquisition Costs

Site finance	12,000
Legal and agents fees	2,000
Net site cost	75,000
Total Costs	£640,000
Price per acre (5)	£15,000

The project is now used to demonstrate how the various forms of funding, had they all have been available, might have been applied:

1. Bank Loans

So far as the developer is concerned there are an increasing variety of ways in which finance can be made available from the banking sector. These include overdrafts, revolving credit, fixed term loans and the more recent "multi option facilities" which offer the developer a wide choice in the period, interest rate, currency, repayment schedule and security required. The choice is further extended by such factors as whether the loans will be at a fixed rate or floating rate, and if the latter to which index will it be linked – for example the bank's own base rate or LIBOR. Is it to be in domestic or a foreign currency? Will the loan be amortised over a period, or will interest only be paid, or "rolled up" and added to the outstanding debt together with the bank's own fees?

For most developers, bank finance is typically required for the period of the development (and letting) or for a somewhat longer, fixed term, for example until the first rent reviewers.

(i) Bridging Finance

Bridging, or interim finance, is required to meet the costs of the development as it proceeds. It is essentially short term and is repaid when the project is either sold, following the completion of the building works and a successful letting of the resultant accommodation, or when permanent re-financing takes place.

Unless the end financier, usually an institution, is also providing the interim finance, the lender will often be a clearing or merchant bank. This in itself highlights the difference in perspective between the borrower and the lender. A developer sees a proposed development in terms of opportunity whereas the banker sees it as a potential risk investment. The relationship will blossom on growing confidence based on mutual profitable experiences.

One of the many consequences of the "new era" in the City, after the "Big Bang", has been the introduction of a range of new, sophisticated, techniques of bank based finance. These are principally concerned with minimising the risk to the borrower of unexpected fluctuations in interest rates and, or, foreign currency exchange rates.

Initially, the bank will require detailed feasibility studies and cashflow forecasts. Above all they will want to be assured of their loan being repaid. In addition to a variety of project orientated questions, the bankers will enquire into:

(a) How much of the total cost is to be loaned, e.g. 60 to 80% (if not 100%!).
(b) The proposed rate of interest, e.g. 2–5% over the Bank's own base rate or indexed to LIBOR (London Inter-Bank Offered Rate) and it will be at a fixed rate or floating rate.
(c) The duration of the loan, i.e. the total development period.
(d) Whether interest will be paid at stated intervals, or "rolled-up", i.e. added at monthly or quarterly intervals to the outstanding loan balance (this of course means paying interest on interest).

(e) What additional collateral and guarantees will be required; (a personal guarantee by the developer concentrates his mind wonderfully).

(f) The additional charges to be made by the bank, e.g. commitment/facility fees, service charges, standby fees, etc. These can amount from 3 to 10% of the loan and may or may not be added thereto. Some lenders will require part of these charges to be paid as and when they fall due.

(g) What monitoring procedure will be operated, e.g. cashflow statements, architects certificates, periodic progress inspections, etc.

(h) Depending on how well the developer and lender know each other, there will be questions about the financial well being of the borrowing company. Frequently these can simply be answered by providing an updated set of accounts.

Essentially bankers are concerned with credit risks, rather than equity risks. They will therefore want to be assured that the potential cash flow from the completed project can comfortably cover the interest charges and at all times the outstanding debt is less than the capital value of the investment. As will be appreciated difficulties arise when, due to an upward movement in yield, the project is down valued and the margin between cost and value is eroded.

Example of bridging finance loan

Sale price, net before tax, of the completed project (i.e. actual rental income of £66,000 p.a. valued on a 5½% yield)		£1,200,000
less total costs of project including		
interest charges	£640,000	
bank's fees @ 3% of loan	19,200	
selling costs @ 2% of value	24,000	683,200
Net profit before tax		£516,800

In this exceptionally successful development, the sale proceeds will most adequately repay the bridging loan and fees thereon in addition to providing the developer with a substantial profit. However, unless the developer has a well established relationship with his banker, a full bridging loan will usually be difficult to arrange in the absence of prearranged long term funding for the project, on completion, or a contract for its sale. (This simplified first example should not be regarded as reflecting current levels of development profits.)

(ii) *Term Loans*

As implied by the title these are bank loans for an agreed period of time, or "term". For larger value projects these are often provided via a "tender panel" of competing bankers who will between them supply the necessary development funding. A recent innovation of this approach is the "multiple option facility". Under this arrangement a developer is able to choose from one or more different options in which his loan and/or credit facilities are to be arranged. Thus he can opt for fixed or floating rates of interest (with or without a "drop lock" facility); similarly with currency choice e.g. sterling, swiss francs, yen, etc. He may also wish to include a variety of technical refinements, such as caps, collars and floors which are methods of limiting future fluctuations in interest rates.

Another significant import from American funding practices is the "non recourse" loan under which the lender is limited in his remedies to the development itself, if there should be a default under the terms of the loan. True, full non recourse loans have not yet been incorporated into facilities in the UK as the bankers invariably require some essential commitments/ guarantees from the developer, for example that he will actually complete the project in accordance with the approved specifications and plans. Nevertheless an increasing number of (limited) non recourse loans have recently been written, including the £76 m to Greycoat Properties with which to undertake the redevelopment of Lutyen's House in the City.

(iii) *Revolving Credit*

Under this arrangement a developer will agree with the banker a ceiling to the loan. During the currency of the loan period (previously agreed with the bank) the developer can "draw down" funds for his project as it proceeds. As and when units or phases are sold, or refinanced on a long term basis, the developer will use these receipts to reduce his debt. This can subsequently rise, and fall, as further borrowings are made to meet progress payments and more sales take place, thereby reducing the debt until the revolving facility comes to an end.

2. Project Management by the Developer

This is the simplest way for the developer to arrange for all of the finance to be provided from the start and to be assured of a small profit (with the potential of an additional bonus if the scheme lives up to its original forecast). By this method the funding institution acquires the site, employs the professional team with the developer acting as project manager for a fee, and bonus, and provides all the development finance.

The attraction of this method to the developer is that his financial liability is minimal and he will be paid an attractive fee for managing the project. This fee will reflect also an element of commission or reward for introducing the project to the institution. The introduction will often include the identification of the site, having agreed a price with the owners for its purchase; testing the planner's reactions to the proposal and preparing the relevant feasibility studies. This latter item usually involves a friendly architect and quantity surveyor who will work on a contingency basis, i.e. "no deal, no fee". Here the developer displays his creative and entrepreneurial skills; probably the only things that the institution itself is lacking? As an added bonus, or incentive, to the developer and to avoid protracted argument over the anticipated rental value on completion, he is offered an agreed share in any improvement he can make on the project's profitability, for example through better than expected rents.

More mature and financially established developers with a track record would of course be far less eager to pass on a good project, so early, for what they would regard as crumbs from a rich man's table!

Example

The developer will be paid a project management fee of £25,000 plus 50% of any income in excess of the agreed estimated rental value, as an additional incentive bonus. The institution will capitalise this on a $6\frac{1}{2}$% basis, either on completion of the project or at a future date, to be decided by the partners.

Each party's interest on completion of the Clivesville project will be as follows:

(a) *The Institution*

Total net rents	£66,000 p.a.
less 50% share of excess rents	3,000 p.a.
Net income	£63,000 p.a.

As the total cost to the investor has been increased by the developer's fee, to £665,000 the return to the institution is now 9·47%.

(b) *The Developer*

50% share of excess rents	£3,000 p.a.
which will be capitalised @ $6\frac{1}{2}$% ∴ ÷ by	0·065
Capital value of income, say	£46,150
Plus fee	£25,000
Total profit for developer	£71,150

As will be seen from the calculation above of the developer's profit, the value of his minority share in the investment will alter the institution's position thus:

(c) *The Institution* (after purchase)

Total net income		£66,000 p.a.
Total costs	£640,000	
Plus fee	£25,000	
Plus purchase of developer's share	£46,150	£711,150

$$\therefore \text{yield} = \frac{£66,000}{£711,150} \times 100 = 9.28\%$$

Although their expenditure has been increased by a further £46,150 and the yield has now fallen to just under 9·3%, they are now the absolute owners, untroubled by an outside partner. Prior to acquiring this minority interest the investment value of their income, previously at £63,000 p.a., and valued at $5\frac{1}{2}$%, was £1,145,500. The new value, based on the increased income of £66,000 p.a. is now £1,200,000. Thus for an expenditure of £46,150 they have improved the value of their holding, in this example, by almost £55,000. Whereas in the early days of this method the developer was not obliged to sell out to his partner, it is now customary for this to be obligatory as soon as the project is completed. Obviously the formula for valuing the developer's interest is a matter of negotiation, as part of the overall financing agreement. It will not have gone unnoticed that the developer has created a profit before tax of £71,150 at no personal financial exposure! While in simple profit on cost terms, mathematically, the developer clearly scores the highest rate of return, at infinity, the institution has recorded a satisfactory capital profit of £488,850 or a yield of

$$\frac{£1,200,000 - £711,150}{£711,150} \times 100 = 68 \cdot 74\% \text{ on cost}$$

(before legal and any agents fees associated with the transaction).

3. A Forward Sale

Most short term lenders are interested in the answer to one question above all others. How are they going to be repaid and when? In American banking terminology this is known as the "take-out". Vague but enthusiastic assurances by a developer about a future sale, when the project is completed are insufficient. What the lender is looking for is either an irrevocable commitment by someone-else to re-finance the project when completed, or an unconditional contract to purchase it. From the lender's perspective he will have the deposit of the title deeds together with the benefit of the building works in progress as security for his loan but he will invariably insist on knowing where the "take-out" is coming form, and when, before agreeing to the short term bridging loan.

The easiest way to satisfy the lender will be for the developer to produce a contract for the forward sale of the completed project. In order to conclude a satisfactory negotiation for the forward sale i.e. at a price agreed now, for delivery at a future date, the possibilities of construction/development delays, and poorer than projected lettings will all have to be recognised

and legislated for. Usually these uncertain matters are anticipated by a previously agreed formula being triggered to deal
with them. In this way repayment of the short term loan capital
will be protected but invariably at the expense of part of the
developer's profit.

An alternative to a third party bridging loan is, of course,
to negotiate the interim development funding direct from the
purchaser of the completed project. This may have advantages
for the developer if he can obtain a more favourable rate of
interest to be charged on the bridging finance. It also gives
the purchaser a more direct involvement with, and control
over, the project throughout. However, as is repeatedly emphasised, the alternatives need to be carefully rehearsed and
tested. The provision of (cheaper) bridging finance may only
be offered on the condition that the developer will concede
a higher capitalisation yield to the purchasing institution, as
it is now increasing its risk exposure. The net consequence
will be a lower developer's profit. Indeed the effect of changes
in capitalisation rates (ignoring any changes in bridging finance
rates of interest) can be dramatic as the following table shows:

| Investment yield changes | Original target profit on cost | | |
| | 15% | 25% | 25% |
	Reduced profit, (rounded) after change in yield		
From 5 to 5½%	4·5	9·0	13·5
From 5½ to 6%	5·5	10·0	14·5
From 6 to 6½%	6·0	14·5	15·5

Source: Office Development by P. Marber (Editor), Estates Gazette
Books 1985.

Example
The developer enters into a contract to sell the proposed
Clivesville development when it is built, in accordance with
agreed plans and specifications and fully let in accordance with
a draft rack rent occupation lease attached to the contract.
The purchaser is to have the right to approve any proposed
letting by the developer. This is especially important in the
context of the tenant's financial status, the proposed rent,
review terms and the permitted uses.

The terms of the forward sale are that the buyer will pay a price based on an investment yield of $6\frac{1}{2}\%$. This higher yield reflects the fact that the project is unlet, the uncertainties as to how investment rates will change by the time the project is completed and let, and the provision of interim bridging finance by the purchaser. The purchase price is therefore calculated as follows:

Net actual project income		£66,000
Capitalised @ $6\frac{1}{2}\%$	$\therefore$	$\div 0\cdot065$
Capital value of investment	say	£1,015,000

The developer will therefore make a capital profit of £375,000 providing he is able to build within the estimated cost and that he can in fact achieve the letting of the accommodation within the time limit and at the better than original forecast rental. The value to him of achieving the very best level of rent i.e. £66,000 as opposed to £60,000 is significant, being an added £92,000, or over 24% of the overall profit. This also demonstrates the dramatic effect in capital terms of striving for the highest rent. For every additional £1 of net annual rent achieved the capital of the investment appreciates by £15·38. Some care, however, must be exercised in pushing this endeavour to extremes as a letting in excess of the full open market rental value may well depreciate the quality of the investment and thereby increase the required investment yield. This reduces the capital value of the investment!

4. Mortgage Finance

Historically fixed interest finance was the normal practice for the long term funding of any property development. As a result of rapidly appreciating property values and spectacular development profits, more frequent (upward) movements in interest rates and the decline in the real value of money, full mortgage finance rapidly lost its appeal to investors, as it became impossible to support from project income alone. However as with most techniques of funding, their popularity flows and ebbs over time depending on the fundamentals that determine their availability and suitability. Currently, (in 1987) mortgage finance is enjoying a more promising renaissance. This is due to a narrowing of the yield gap, as long term borrowing rates decline and property yields rise. However, it is unlikely that lenders will be prepared to advance more than two-thirds of the end value, although exceptionally this may be increased to four-fifths, especially if acceptable guarantees are forthcoming from the developer.

Example
In the comparatively financial tranquil and calm years of the 1950s and early 1960s a conventional mortgage could have been arranged on the following basis:

Value when completed

Net rents received		£66,000 p.a.
Capitalised @ $6\frac{1}{2}$% (the yield then applicable)	∴ ÷ by	0·065
Capital value	say	£1,015,000

Mortgage loan required to recover costs	£640,000
Mortgage repayments	
Repayment over 25 years @ $8\frac{1}{2}$%	£62,535 p.a.
Less net rents received	£66,000
Surplus income to developer	£3,465 p.a.

The above method has provided 100% finance; indeed it could have provided 106% of cost if the advance were made at 66·6% of the investment value. This would involve higher repayments, eliminating current surplus income, until the first rent reviews.

Benefits of Fixed Interest Mortgage Finance
The availability of fixed interest mortgages, and inflation even on the very modest levels of the late 1950s and 1960s, presented property developers with an effortless and spectacular increase in their equity interests in a development. The diagram below shows how the developer's equity income increased after each seven yearly rent review on a conventional fully amortised mortgage, during the 1960s. With annual inflation for that period in the 4–5% region, the current value of

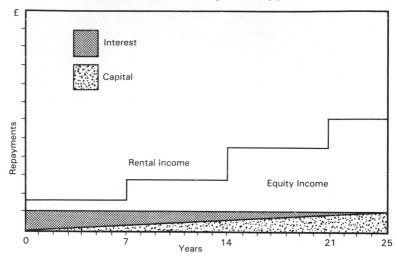

the property would increase by 100% over about 15 years merely if it kept pace with inflation. The debt under the mortgage was fixed at the time it was granted, and so the developer's equity will have risen by 400%, assuming he took a mortgage of two thirds the value of the project at the outset. The effect of a fixed interest mortgage on the developer's equity, through gearing, is demonstrated below:

Example

Assuming a project with an investment value of £1 million, producing a net income of £100,000 p.a. is financed by a fixed interest mortgage for 25 years at various rates:

Basic % cost of borrowing	Annual mortgage constant	Ratio of loan to value of project				
		60%	65%	70%	75%	80%
		Yield on the developer's equity capital				
6·0	7·82	13·3	14·0	15·1	16·5	18·7
7·0	8·58	12·1	12·6	13·3	14·3	15·7
8·0	9·37	10·9	11·2	11·5	11·9	12·5
9·0	10·18	9·7	9·7	9·6	9·5	9·3
10·0	11·02	8·5	8·1	7·6	6·9	5·9
12·0	12·75	5·9	4·9	3·6	1·7	(−1·0)

The above example indicates that with a project yield of 10% the developer will only achieve positive gearing with a loan restricted to 60% of value at a maximum borrowing rate of 8%. If the basic borrowing rate is 12% then a loan of 80% of value will result in a negative equity return for the developer on his own risk capital of £200,000 (20% of £1 million).

The project will be yielding	£100,000 p.a.
less mortgage repayments	£102,000
Project cashflow deficit	£ (2,000) p.a.

Not only would the developer be required to invest £200,000 of his own capital but he will have to contribute a further £2,000 p.a. towards project debt service, at least until the first rent review.

The Basic Forms of Mortgage Schemes

As seen previously the conventional mortgage for a viable funding operation was repaid from the net pre-tax income produced by the development. Whilst investment capital values of a project will influence the total amount of money loaned, the ability to fully service the debt often limits the size of the mortgage. There are three alternative schemes of arranging repayments.

(1) The equal level instalments, or annuitised repayment, method which involves equal regular repayments comprised of part capital and part interest.
(2) The capital and interest method requires equal annual repayments of capital plus interest on the diminishing outstanding debt. Thus instalments are higher in the earlier years as the loan interest element is higher than in the later years. Though the initial net costs even after interest tax relief are high, they decrease uniformly over the period.
(3) A non-profit endowment policy can be taken out so that at the end of the loan period, the amount produced by the policy will be sufficient to repay the original loan. During the intervening period interest is paid on the debt and regular annual premiums are invested into the endowment policy. The costs remain high throughout as the outstanding capital remains constant, but full tax relief is usually available on the interest payments.

These three alternatives can be illustrated thus:

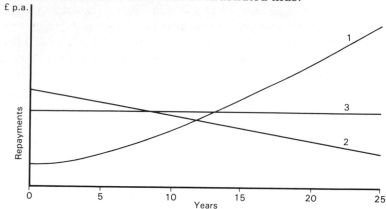

Comparative Costs

A comparison of these three alternatives is summarised below for a loan of £1 million over 25 years @ 15% p.a.

	Gross repay- ment	Interest paid	Capital repaid	Premium paid	Tax relief @ 52%	Net costs for 1st year
	£	£	£	£	£	£
(a) Annuitised	154,700	150,000	4,700	—	78,000	76,700
(b) Equal capital	190,000	150,000	40,000	—	78,000	112,000
(c) Endowment	180,000	150,000	nil	30,000	78,000	102,000

For simplicity it has been assumed that all alternatives would be at the same rate of interest. On this rather artificial assumption it can be seen that the total net cost for the first year is highest for the equal capital mortgage even if there is tax relief on the payment of interest. However, although the annuitised mortgage is lowest in the earlier years, the net cost will increase steadily in later years as the interest element of the repayments reduces and consequently so will the amount of tax relief available on that interest element also fall.

Mortgage Funding at High Interest Rates

At the date of the Clivesville project there was a borrowing rate of 14% p.a. Even if it were agreed that the rate would be a floating one, based on a suitable bench mark, e.g. 2% over gilts, there were comparatively few developments, if any, able to service a conventional mortgage on an annual repayment basis. Even if a lender were found, the cashflow, especially prior to the first review of the rack rents, renders this method virtually unworkable without some fairly fundamental changes to the basic formula. Although the borrower's ability to offset the interest against tax will influence his net position, the before tax relief picture is highlighted if one now applies an interest rate of 14% to the basic example, as follows:

Capital value, as previously	£1,015,000
Amount of loan, as previously	£640,000
Annual repayment of interest and capital over 25 yrs @ 14%	£93,119 p.a.
less net rents received	£66,000 p.a.
Annual deficit	£(27,119) p.a.

In theory, at least, there are a number of amendments that can be adopted to make this method financially viable. Assuming both parties are willing to re-negotiate the terms and depending upon the projected growth rate in rental values, the "solutions" might include:

(a) *Payment of interest only* for x years (i.e. no capital repayment during the period of x years).

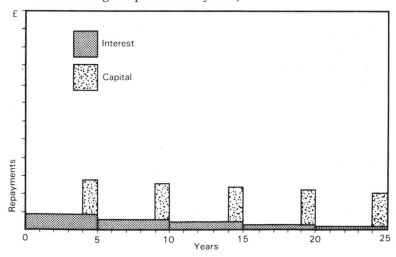

(b) A *"holiday"* for z years (i.e. no interest or capital is repaid for z years).

(c) A *"ballon"* is added at the end of term (i.e. a large final repayment is made at the end of the mortgage to redeem fully the debt partly repaid, together with added compensation for incomplete repayments having been made throughout the term of the loan). A variation of this is the "bullet" mortgage where the whole of the principal is not repaid until the end of the period of the loan.

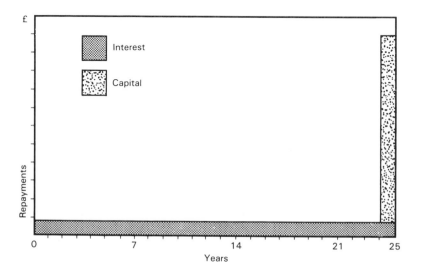

(d) A *variable rate of interest* which increases as the rental income grows.

(e) A *smaller loan and an extension of the period of repayment* but at a higher rate of interest:

Amount of reduced loan	£430,000
Annual repayment of interest and capital over 35 years @ 15%	£64,990 p.a.
Less rents received	66,000
Surplus	£1,010 p.a.

(f) *By mortgage with equity participation to the lender.* In this example the mortgage interest rate might be maintained at $8\frac{1}{2}$% if the mortgagee is given a 30% participation in the equity income.

Net rents received	£66,000 p.a.
Less mortgage repayments for 25 yrs @ $8\frac{1}{2}$%	62,535
Equity income	3,465
Less 30% share to mortgagee	1,040
Surplus to developer	£2,425 p.a.

The inducement of the equity participation is only likely to be successful in conditions of high interest rates if there is a confident expectation of strong rental growth with frequent rent reviews.

Pre-payment Penalties and Capital/Income Ratios

Some loan agreements will carry penalty clauses for early repayment of loans, possibly on a sliding scale related to the maturity date. They may also require that the amount of the outstanding loan will never exceed, say, 70% of the value of the asset on which it is secured; similarly with the ratio of repayment to project income. Where these or other terms are contravened they automatically "trigger" higher penalty rates of interest until the terms are complied with, or even give the lender the right to call for immediate repayment of all sums outstanding.

Tax Relief

Interest payable on loans is normally allowable for tax purposes. This is important, especially when the corporation tax rate is high. At a tax rate of 52% the net cost of a loan of £1 million at 14% was reduced to £67,200 per annum as a result.

Care is needed to ensure that any associated fees and bank charges are expressed in the formal agreement in such as way as they too will be eligible for tax relief, as well as interest. This was often done by increasing the rate of interest by an amount which is equivalent to the cost of the fees etc.

Tax relief does not of course extend to the repayment of capital which has to be made out of taxed income. This means that the higher the tax rate, the larger must be the pre-tax income. For example, an annual capital repayment of £10,000 requires a pre-tax income of £20,833 (at a tax rate of 52%), i.e.

$$£10,000 \times \frac{100}{100-52} = £20,833$$

After tax @ 52% was deducted from the gross of tax income the net sum remaining would still be sufficient to make the required capital repayment of £10,000.

The different taxation implications for the two elements of conventional mortgage repayments should be remembered when reviewing pre or post tax cashflow.

Example (based on alternative (e) previously but for 25 years @ 14%) before tax

Net project income, before tax		£66,000 p.a.
less Interest @ 14% gross	£60,200	
Repayment of capital	2,365	62,565
First year surplus		£3,435 p.a.

The after tax position, however, can change the position quite significantly and give a different perspective on the true net position, especially in an era of high taxation, as in 1973.

Example

Net project income before tax	£66,000 p.a.
less tax @ 52%	34,320
Net project income, after tax	31,680
less net, after tax, cost of interest	28,896
	2,784
less repayment of capital, (no tax relief)	2,365
Surplus income, after tax	£419 p.a.

It will be appreciated that in the above example it is assumed that no other tax reliefs or allowances are available to offset against the sole source of income.

5. Sale and Leaseback

The history of this method of financing can be traced back to the late 1920s and early 1930s. It was first used as part of more conventional property related investment, rather than for new development projects. During the 1930s a few enterprising retail companies used the technique as a means with which to raise capital to expand their trading operations. An ambitious expanding company would identify a local established family retailer, perhaps selling shoes and which occupied its own freehold premises. The acquiring company would agree to purchase the business and its assets, on a "going concern" basis. In order to raise the necessary, long term, capital with which to finance this investment, the new owner would approach one of the large financial institutions such as the Prudential Assurance Company and offer to sell the recently acquired freehold shops(s), subject to a long lease, back to the now expansionary retail group. The price extracted for the property alone was often more than sufficient to cover the acquisition price of the entire business. Thus the new owners had recovered their initial outlay in one fell swoop, expanded their retailing operations and obtained a valuable High Street presence in a new town. The rent payable under the leaseback was in turn funded from the sales turnover achieved by the business which continued to be carried on, as before, in the same shop.

Some of the early exponents of the method include Isaac Wolfson and the Norwich Union in 1937, with Hugh Fraser and Charles Clore also being credited among the pioneers. Meanwhile in the USA Tishman Realty concluded an early leaseback transaction for $9 million with the Prudential of Chicago. By 1953 Charles Clore made a spectacular take-over of Sears who, through their principal trading company, the True Form Boot Company owned a significant portfolio of shops, which he subsequently disposed of through sale and leaseback transactions to various insurance companies.

Other commercial companies also began to discover that they could raise capital, for example to increase or modernise their manufacturing operations, by selling the underlying operational property, such as a factory, – and simultaneously leasing it back. Within sensible limits it was possible to balance the rent to be paid against the capital raised, depending on whether maximum capital realisation or minimum rental payments were the overriding objective.

Example

The open market rental value of a shop was £5,000 p.a., on a full repairing and insuring lease. The freehold investment could be sold at a 6% yield, and the capital raised would be £83,300. Alternatively the sale and leaseback rent might be agreed at £4,580 p.a., i.e. below its true full rental value but with an early rent review. Because the investment would be seen as very secure indeed, the yield reflected this and the growth, and might be reduced to $5\frac{1}{2}$%. The net result was that the capital raised would be unaltered. In addition, the business turnover of the shop received a modest subsidy, by not having to pay the full rental, during the period when the new management is building up the retail business, before the rent review.

Evolution

During the 1950s property developers were discovering that mortgage and other fixed interest finance was no longer a suitable, or indeed easily available method of funding new developments. (The government restrictions on credit, progressively tightened during the late 1950's, were reinforced by controls on the raising of equity capital, bank lending and commercial mortgages.)

As a result of these difficulties over finance, developers had been fostering a closer relationship with the insurance companies. Joint development companies were established, for specific sites, often where the two partners held adjacent or interlocking interests. The insurance companies were also actively "in the market" for office accommodation themselves as their post war expansion programme gathered momentum and more space was needed. Additionally the funds available for investment by them had grown substantially, more than doubling during the 1950's. The Stock Exchange had run out of steam by the end of 1955 and the equity share price index did not permanently break through the closing 1955 level again until the middle of 1959. Fixed interest government stock, such as Consols were also stuck at a below 5·0% yield (until 1960) and bank rate similarly averaged the sub 5·0% throughout the 1950s. But because interest rates on mortgage finance were increasing (by the early 1960's they were $6\frac{1}{2}$%, by 1965 they had risen to 8% and at the end of the decade rates were over

10%) the property "reverse yield gap" had arrived! This meant that there was an adverse difference between the higher costs of borrowing and the lower yields from property.

Paradoxically, investment yields on property were being kept low by the demand from the institutional investors themselves. And competition between developers was also squeezing their own profit margins. The stimulus for the improvement in popularity of property was caused by the apprehension of the investing institutions over the effects of escalating inflation. (By the end of 1968 the annual increase had risen to nearly 6% and then with hardly a faltering step it rose steeply to 25% by the end of 1975.)

The Move Towards Leaseback Finance

The sea change in financing techniques which had already started to take place by the beginning of the 1960s was further encouraged by the institutions themselves who became disenchanted with mortgages – due to the erosion of the real value of their capital, as a result of inflation. Developers also found that the returns from property developments were insufficient to service mortgage debt finance which in any event was becoming significantly more expensive, and difficult to obtain. The move was thus well under way for sale and leaseback transactions to provide the long term funding for new projects, encouraged by a variety of circumstances:

(a) The institutions were favourably disposed towards property and developers were both active and in need of long term development finance. Their need was being frustrated by the government controls on credit and new issues. However the proverbial camel did squeeze through the eye of the needle in the form of what was to be the dominant force in the funding market for over a decade – the sale and leaseback. Its subsequent rapid acceptance, and implementation, was in no small-measure due to the fact that, surprisingly, it did not fall under the credit control measures then in force, and was thus the most available method of funding.

(b) A further influence arose in 1965 when major changes in the tax regime were introduced. These radical reforms included the introduction of capital gains tax and corporation tax. The consequence of these new taxes was a disincentive for developers to sell their properties, especially as unrealised gains, (or paper profit) could remain untaxed. It also became more effective for institutions to receive their share of development profits directly, in the form of rents (which did not suffer any tax charge before they were received) rather than through dividends from a company, including of course, a property company. In the latter case, dividends were (and still are) taxed twice. Firstly, on the profits (by the company) and secondly, on the dividends (paid from taxed profits). Although any tax deducted at source on the payment of dividends is reclaimable, the non tax paying investor, particularly the pension funds were still worse off than had they received their income directly in the form of rent.

(c) The legal framework used for leaseback funding, that of Landlord and Tenant, was also a well established and widely accepted relationship. It was subject to specific and clearly defined legislation without many of the ambiguities and grey areas of Company law. Also rents ranked high on the list of creditors – above debentures and dividends – on company insolvencies by tenants.

(d) A major source of additional funds appeared through the rapidly expanding pension funds and the emerging Property Unit Trusts.

During the 1960's and early 1970's the technique was refined and modified as the pendulum of negotiations – reflecting supply and demand – swung backwards and forwards between the developers and the suppliers of long term funds. The result was that the method became more sophisticated and complex as both parties sought on the one hand, to try and forsee all possible eventualities and on the other, to obtain compensating advantages in return for concessions over aspects of each agreement. The consequence was that the legal documentation also became more complex and more bulky! This was, and is again, proving a nightmare for valuers and other professional advisers who have to try to understand – and implement – the relevant provisions, as they are triggered, years later, by the happening of some event or change in circumstances. Typically, the need to renegotiate the terms, for example, by an injection of more capital to deal with unexpected obsolescence, is now commonplace.

Nevertheless the method became an established technique of funding new developments and for many developers it was the principal, indeed often the only way in which they could build up permanent equity participation in the project, with little, if any financial investment of their own.

The Pros and Cons of Leaseback Finance

These can be summarised as far as the developer was concerned as follows:

(i) The advantages include:
   (a) The provision of total permanent finance.
   (b) The creation of an immediate profit rent and a continuing future participation therein.
   (c) The possible elimination of the need to find bridging finance from a third party.
   (d) The creation of saleable interest which can be used to provide capital for other projects.
(ii) However, the disadvantages may include:
   (a) Onerous rental commitments which can result in a negative cashflow, especially if the leaseback is geared.
   (b) A possible absence of sharing in future income growth after certain bench-marks are reached.
   (c) A legal interest which by its very nature must be limited in time and fettered by a formidable range of leaseholder's covenants and frequent rent reviews.
   (d) The inability to re-finance the project at some later date if market conditions improve.
   (e) Unforeseen tax consequences and complications.
   (f) The basic rate of return used to calculate the institution's return is usually higher than the comparable investment yield.
   (g) The requirement that a minimum return be guaranteed by the developer to his funding partner.

As mentioned previously, over the years the method has undergone a number of refinements and modifications, as the pendulum of advantage swung back and forth between the developers and their institutional partners. These changes in advantage largely followed a feeling of injustice by one side, taking the view that the other had got the better end of the bargain, usually tempered by the underlying changes in supply and demand for new projects and for finance.

After the property crash in 1974, when many developments turned sour, and developers' guarantees were found to be worthless, the majority of institutions turned their backs on new leaseback transactions. Gradually confidence has returned, at least to a minority of institutions willing to enter into new commitments on this basis. However their criteria are much more demanding and speculative schemes funded in this way are very much the exception, being reserved for trusted and proven developers with first class projects in prime locations.

The Mechanics of Leaseback Funding

Originally these were simple and straightforward with the developer offering to sell his proposed building (fully described in the accompanying plans and specifications) subject to the investor agreeing to lease the building back to the developer (in accordance with the detailed terms contained in the appended draft lease) when the development was physically completed. This enabled the developer to prefund his project, often covering the entire development costs with his profit coming from the difference between the rent he had agreed to pay to his funding partners, and the rents he was able to charge the occupying tenant(s) for all or part(s) of his new building. However there are a number of major issues to be considered including:

(i) *The Legal Vehicle to be used*

Sale and leaseback are based on a landlord and tenant relationship, although some were effected in the form of a partnership where there was a tenancy in common, (i.e. an undivided interest) held behind a trust for sale. (A tenancy in common could only exist in Equity and not at Law because of Section 34 of the Law of Property Act 1925.) Thus each tenant in common holds a concurrent interest and has a distinct but not yet divided interest. Although each party owns a share in the project, and which do not have to be equal, the shares are not physically divided. The legal estate rests in the parties upon trust, with an ultimate power of sale.

The Law of Property Act also restricted to four, the number of partners that could jointly own the legal estate in a property.

(ii) Sharing the Income

In the early years of leaseback funding the investor would usually agree to provide 100% of the total finance required to carry out the project. The site, or the contract to acquire it, would be transferred to the investing landlord and all subsequent development costs would be reimbursed to the developer in accordance with a previously agreed procedure and in accordance with previously approved plans and specifications. The developer would therefore enter into a finance agreement and an agreement for a lease with the investor/landlord. The rent to be paid under the lease, typically for 99 or 125 years, would be calculated by a simple formula whereby the landlord will receive a rent representing an agreed percentage return on his total capital invested. Rent reviews, initially, were at comparatively infrequent interviews of every 21 years. They were calculated on the basis that the landlord would receive a previously agreed share of the difference between the initial rent and the actual rents received by the developer from the under lettings, at the time of each review. It is of course this difference in rents i.e. the rent paid by the developer, and the rents received from subletting the accommodation in the completed project, that provides the developer with his profit. However, this is not an absolute guarantee of future profits, as many developers discovered, when property proved difficult to let, or when the tenants moved out and voids arose. Indeed in the zenith of sale and leaseback many projects were being introduced for funding on a speculative basis with no specific tenant legally committed to lease the building, when it is completed, at an agreed rent. Hence there was uncertainty about the prospects of letting the project and its rental income. (By contrast, if a pre-letting is arranged, one of the major areas of uncertainty is removed and this will be reflected in the capitalisation rate used to value the investment.)

If the situation was less secure, with no forward letting agreement, this hardened the attitude of the investor who was influenced by such factors as:

(a) The quality of the building and its location.

(b) The general level of demand for, and availability of, similar accommodation to rent in the locality.
(c) The prospects of a successful letting to as suitable tenant.
(d) The projected rate of increase in rental values and construction costs during the actual development period.
(e) The anticipated future levels of supply for the type of accommodation proposed, at completion date, i.e. the competition.
(f) The strength of any guarantee (if any) offered by the developer and the period of time that it will remain in operation.
(g) The "track record" and experience of the developer and his professional team.
(h) The investment demand of the project, if it should have to be sold.

Whether the institution required a 1%, 2% or more, additional increase in its rate of return depended on the particular circumstances. Indeed in some cases of high demand, and rapidly rising rental values, in a good location there was a positive preference not to pre-let but to proceed on the basis of a yield which reflected the strong letting confidence shared by the developer and funding source. At the other extreme a project may well be unfundable at any price without a secure pre-let. In other cases a project may be partly let, sufficient to generate confidence by the funding source, notwithstanding an element of uncertainty over the ability satisfactorily to let the remaining space; there a guarantee by the developer would often be expected.

One of the key issues in a sale and leaseback transaction is how the partners are to share in any future changes in the rental income flowing the property. Because property development is a risk bearing exercise some arrangement is essential for the treatment of income sharing. This raises two important issues. The first is how each party's share is calculated or determined. The second is the order in which each is to receive his share. As will be seen, each party's share can be made up from a number of different components, or tranches, and these are paid out in a previously agreed order of priorities. In the early years of funding through sale and leasebacks, the parties to the transaction were not anticipating any significant, or dramatic, increases in rental values. Furthermore the fact that inflation was also to become such a powerful and devaluing force on the real value of investment returns had not been foreseen. The result was that little, if any, thought was given to what the effects of these two factors would be when the first and subsequent rent reviews were implemented.

The first wave of leaseback funding transactions took place on a "geared" sharing formula and the income was distributed on a "horizontal" (or "top slice") basis.

(iii) *"Geared" Rental Sharing Formula*

Unfortunately there still persists a measure of confusion in the use of the term "geared" and another basis, that of "proportionate" sharing arrangements. Surveyors and valuers tend to refer to leasebacks as being "geared" when they describe the situation where each partner's share is fixed (often by reference to a simple formula) in agreed proportions; for example it will be shared in the ratio of 7:3, irrespective of the level of the total income. Here there is no true gearing of the developer's share; he cannot improve his percentage "slice" of the income. It is therefore more accurate, in investment analysis terminology, to refer to this as a "proportionate" sharing leaseback which is in fact "ungeared". To misuse carelessly the technical language of another profession merely confuses everybody.

In the UK one of the early major sale and leaseback arrangements was the initial £25 million reserved for Town & City Properties Ltd. by the Prudential Assurance Company. The basis was that the developers could call on their institutional partner to buy a site, pay for the construction of a new building and lease it back to Town & City at a return of 6% plus 20% of income growth at 33 rent review intervals.

Example

The institution purchases the site, provides the interim finance, and then leases the completed development to the developer (who acted as project manager) on the basis that the funding institution will receive a return of 6%, plus 20% of all net rental income achieved in excess of the anticipated rental value of £60,000 per annum. Thus it is providing 100%

of the total costs required for the development, and will be the freeholder subject to a 99 years lease "back" to the developer of the Clivesville project.

Actual rent received		£66,000 p.a.
Less		
(a) Leaseback initial rent @ 6%	£39,600 p.a.	
(b) 20% share of excess rent	1,200	
Institutional share		40,800
Residual profit rent for the developer		£25,200 p.a.

(iv) *"Top slice" Arrangements*

Having determined the basis on which the rental income is to be shared, by the application of a previously agreed formula, the question arises as to the order in which each party receives his allocated share. Contrary to what might be assumed from this piece of technical jargon, the developer does not receive the first or best slice of the project income. In fact, quite the reverse, as he receives the last "slice" after the institution has received its prior guaranteed share; this typically was the basis for "geared" sharing arrangements.

Diagrammatically this can be illustrated thus:

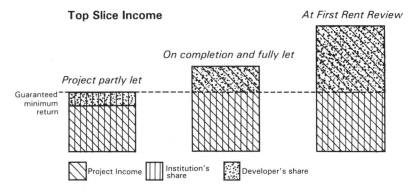

Top Slice Income   *At First Rent Review*

On completion and fully let

Project partly let

Guaranteed minimum return

Project Income   Institution's share   Developer's share

As will be appreciated from the above diagram, if the total project income falls below the guaranteed rate of return it is the developer who will suffer first, and most, through the sacrifice of his "top slice" in order to protect the institution's guaranteed rate of return on their investment of capital in the project. Whether this return is guaranteed (by the developer) was, like many other aspects, a matter of individual negotiation. Where the agreed return is guaranteed, it will be the developer's responsibility to make good any deficiency in the rents actually received, up to the guaranteed yield.

The "geared" leaseback gave a distinct advantage to the developer in the sale and leaseback transaction. "Gearing", it will be recalled implies that a movement at one level (i.e. the net project income) will cause a much larger movement at another level (i.e. the developer's share).

Example

Consider the following where the yield to the institution was agreed to be $5\frac{1}{2}\%$ on costs of the Clivesville project and all surplus income thereafter is to be shared equally. (The lower yield of $5\frac{1}{2}\%$ reflects that in this example the project is assumed to be fully pre-let at £66,000 p.a.)

	Project income on completion and fully let	On first rent reviews of underleases
Institution	£38,200 (57·9% of income)	£54,700 (55·3% of income)
Developer	£27,800 (42·1% of income)	£44,300 (44·7% of income)
Total	£66,000 (100% of income)	£99,000 (100% of income)

From the above it will be seen that although the total income from the development has increased by 50%, the developer's share has grown from 42·1% to 44·7% (i.e. an improvement of some 6·2%). On the other hand the institution's overall share has decreased by some 4·7% even though its income has grown from £38,200 to £54,700 p.a. This shows the dramatic effects of "gearing" and the benefit it can bring to the developer.

The downside risk to the developer should not be overlooked. Consider his dilemma if the total income were to fall, perhaps through voids to £28,500. This will result in a shortfall of £6,700 on the institution's guaranteed return which will have to be made good by the developer from his other income (if any!).

Notwithstanding the theoretical downside risk to the developer and the protection of his guarantee of a basic rate of return to the institution, the decreasing share of an appreciating income is now seldom entertained by institutions. They will invariably insist on proportionate sharing arrangements, even if they have to concede the absence of a minimum guaranteed return.

(v) *"Ungeared" (or "Proportionate") Sharing Arrangements*

As indicated previously, for many years leasebacks did not involve any element of equity sharing as between the developer and the institution. The vendor/lessee merely paid an agreed rent, being a previously determined rate of return on the purchase price with comparatively infrequent rent reviews. In the late 1960s it became increasingly common for the institutions to try and maintain their relevant position *vis à vis* the developer. From the developer's point of view, however, an ungeared leaseback is generally less attractive than a geared arrangement. This is because he will not be able to increase his percentage share of the overall rental income from the project that he himself has created. Experience showed that in some cases the institution's percentage share of the total income actually declined over future years to the obvious benefit of the developer. In other cases the situation was reversed. It soon became apparent that a basis was desirable whereby each party's share could be calculated by reference to a previously agreed formula and that on the appointed day the application of that formula would determine the precise share in which all present and future income will be divided.

The proportions in which the net rents from the investment are to be shared is of course a matter of individual negotiation. Sometimes the institution's share is built up by a number of components, of slices, some of which may or may not be guaranteed by the developer.

The important characteristic is that the application of whatever formula or sharing arrangement which was agreed, determines each party's share on the appointed day. Thereafter both will share the income from the project, in that agreed proportion.

Example

The institution will receive a return of $5\frac{1}{2}\%$ on its total costs of £640,000 plus 50% of any excess rents actually received over the anticipated rental, on completion of the Clivesville project.

The proportionate sharing is calculated as follows:

On completion and fully let	£66,000 p.a.	
Developer receives	£27,800	(representing 42% of income)
Institution receives $5\frac{1}{2}\%$ on £640,000 + 50% of £6,000 p.a.	38,200	(representing 58% of income)
Total	£66,000 p.a.	

As will be seen from the above the proportions in which the project income is shared are approximately 6:4 with the developer being allocated 42% and the institution 58%. These proportions become fixed and form the basis for all future sharing arrangements. Although this means that the developer's share is ungeared and remains fixed at 42% he will be sharing on a more equitable basis as both parties will participate in the agreed proportions in whatever income is received, whether it goes up of down. Thus the developer is no longer in the exposed "top slice" position but is sharing, although not equally, at least side by side with his institutional landlord/partner through the "vertical slice" or "side by side" leaseback.

The position when the first rent reviews take place of the occupational leases will not alter the proportions.

Example

Total net rents received after rent reviews		£99,000 p.a.
The institution's proportionate share @ 58%	£57,420	
and the developer's proportionate share @ 42%	£41,580	£99,000 p.a.

If on the other hand the net income was to
drop by a substantial amount, after the
rent review, because of large voids, to   £34,000 p.a.
The institution's proportionate
share @ 58%   £19,720
and the developer's proportionate
share @ 42%   £14,280 £34,000 p.a.

In these rather unfortunate circumstances this arrangement
would be particularly unattractive to the institution.

If the development were revalued just after the first rent
reviews, i.e. £99,000 p.a., at a yield of 5½% to produce a capital
investment value of £1,800,000, the institution's share at 58%
is thus £1,044,000. Subsequently their income of £19,720
would be only a 1·9% return. However, as the original investment cost only £640,000 their actual exposure is somewhat
reduced as they are achieving a 3% return on costs, following
the fall in income, due to the unexpected voids.

To safeguard their position an institution often sought to
introduce either a rental guarantee from the developer or the
right to suspend or modify the sharing agreement when minimum rates of return were not being achieved. One of the ways
in which the method became modified, in the light of experience, was to incorporate a third element to the formula. Thus,
in addition to a basic yield and an agreed division of any better
than anticipated initial rents, a different (often higher) share
of future rents (typically from rent reviews in the occupational
leases) was also incorporated into the formula.

Example

A sale and leaseback with a fixed base rent, plus a 40% share
of initial surplus and 50% equity participation in future
increases for the institution.

(a) *Developer's share*
Net rent received   £66,000 p.a.
Less base rent @ 6½% on costs   41,600

Initial profit rent   24,400
Less 40% share of initial profit rent   9,760

Surplus to developer   £14,640 p.a.

(b) *Institution's share*

Net rents received	£66,000 p.a.
Less developer's share	14,640
	£51,360 p.a.

At the first rent review of the occupational lease the position is assessed to be:

(c) *Developer's share*

Net rents, after reviews	£99,000 p.a.
Less base rent, as above	41,600
	£57,400
Less 40% of initial profit rent, as above	9,760
	£47,640
Less 50% of increase i.e. $\dfrac{£99,000 - £66,000}{2}$	16,500
Surplus to developer	£31,140 p.a.

(d) *Institution's share*

Net rents, as above	£99,000 p.a.
Less developer's share, as above	31,140
Institution's share	£67,860 p.a.

Note that at the first lettings the developer received some 22% of the net rents. After the first rent review his share of total rents has increased to over 31% (i.e., a 41% improvement). Although the rent received has grown by 50% the institution's share has fallen from 78% to 68% and this trend will continue as long as rack rental values increase. This example again underlines the need to rehearse, in advance of the funding negotiations, the various scenarios that might exist in the future and the effect of the application of various formulae to those circumstances. Obviously from the institution's point of view the above example was an unfortunate arrangement.

(vi) *"Vertical" or "Side by Side" Sharing*
Having witnessed the often devastating effect of the "top slice" or "horizontal" sharing approach in hard times the developers fought back in the evolving cut and thrust of subsequent

funding negotiations and a more equitable sharing arrangement known as "side-by-side" sharing of income emerged. This is preferred by both parties, and is illustrated, graphically, below. As the name implies, the project rental income is shared in agreed proportions simultaneously by each party. Unless otherwise agreed neither has priority to any part of the income. In its simplest version the arrangement applies to whatever income is actually received, irrespective of whether it goes up or down. It also enables the developer's share to be valued more readily as compared to the valuation of a top slice interest, which is difficult to value because of the very limited demand for this type of investment, and its uncertain future performance. This vertical sharing arrangement usually applies to "ungeared" i.e. proportionate sharing of income.

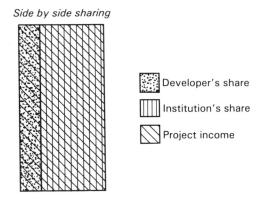

Side by side sharing

Developer's share

Institution's share

Project income

(vii) *Priority Yields*

These are used as an alternative to the developer's guarantee, to protect the institution's required minimum return on capital invested. For example the institution has priority to that part of the income which is required to provide, say, a 6% return on its funds. The next tranche will be allocated to the developer up to say, a, 7% yield and the balance divided in an agreed ratio between the two parties. This arrangement has the advantage of avoiding arguments over whether actual rents received, or rental values, should be used for the base calculations. It also allows a measure of flexibility whereby additional funds can be provided, to deal with cost overruns for example, if matched by an expectation that higher rents will be achieved when the project is completed. These considerations make it particularly appropriate for larger schemes involving lengthy and high value building contracts.

Example

Actual rents received			£66,000 p.a.
Priority yield @ 6% to institution	£38,400		
Next 1% yield to developer		£6,400	
Balance agreed to be divided equally between institution and the developer	10,600	10,600	
	£49,000	+ £17,000 = £66,000 p.a.	

(viii) *Profit Erosion*

After the traumatic property crash in 1974 the worth of many developers' guarantees was put to the test, and found to be either wanting, or more often than not, worthless. As a consequence the institutional partner was left with the problem and the property! Once again the dynamics of the evolution of funding took over and yet a further refinement was incorporated. Under a profit erosion arrangement the developers anticipated "paper profit" – if all goes well with the proposed development – is held as a hostage until the final (financial) outcome of the development is known. Thus his "profit" will be eroded by the shortfall in rental income following completion of the project and accumulating interest on the total development costs, until either the development is fully let or his "profit" is wiped out, whichever is the earlier.

Example

Anticipated rental income	£60,000 p.a.
Actual rents on completion	7,000
∴ shortfall in income	£53,000 p.a.

Thus yield to institution $\dfrac{7,000 \times 100}{640,000} = 1{\cdot}094\%$

∴ shortfall on guaranteed yield = 6·5% *less* 1·094% = 5·406%

Developers' anticipated profit based on a sale
@ 6½% (on £60,000 − £41,600 p.a.)   £283,000

Assuming that the building remains largely unlet, the developer would loose all his potential profit after 8 years i.e.

$$\frac{£283,000}{£37,600} = 8{\cdot}18$$

Although there are a number of important assumptions implied in the above calculations, as emphasised before, there are few if any absolutes in the various refinements. It is a dynamic, innovative and financially entrepreneurial field of business. Hence the negotiating strength and skills are of major importance in this economically imperfect market where freedom of information does not exist. It is, therefore, appropriate to identify beforehand the more important and fundamental aspects of sale and leaseback agreements where the balance of advantage is often won or lost, before entering into negotiations. This is best achieved by testing a variety of scenarios and applying each contemplated formula to all of the alternative future possibilities.

(ix) *Legal Issues*

There are also a host of important subsidiary issues, that will be formally incorporated in the legal documentation. This documentation will include such matters as:

(a) The contract and conveyance for the sale of the property to the landlord/investor.
(b) The finance agreement.
(c) The building agreement and the draft lease "back" to the developer, including detailed plans and specifications.
(d) "Approved" underleases to occupying tenants.

The number of clauses, covenants and schedules which have to be agreed, and incorporated into the legal documentation is often formidable. The result is invariably a weighty, lengthy and bulky bundle of papers. While many are fairly routine and standard clauses, there are a number which are of particular relevance to the negotiations. Among these are the following:

(x) *Rent or Rental Value*

Many institutions will seek to have the sharing arrangements calculated by reference to the rental value of the project at the relevant date, rather than the actual income. This applies particularly to top slice arrangements to the disadvantage of the developer, for example in a project where part is vacant and thus not revenue producing, or where the rent reviews against the occupying tenants are at infrequent intervals, or where leases were granted with fixed rent increases which are below the now current rental value; here the institution will use the current rental value as their base, rather than actual net income, unless the agreement provides otherwise.

(xi) *Guarantees*

Notwithstanding the somewhat complex sharing arrangements of income, the institution may in addition insist on a minimum guaranteed rent in a totally speculative scheme. In the example this is £41,600 p.a. which represents the basic return of $6\frac{1}{2}\%$ on the total cost of the scheme. Where institutions are being called upon to fund a totally speculative scheme with no firm underletting by the developer then understandably they are anxious to limit the downside risk as much as possible by insisting on this minimum, no matter what, basic return. A common compromise is for the developer to limit his rental guarantee until the project is fully let. However, some institutions concluded that after the collapse of the property development sector in 1974, many such guarantees were worthless! This was the final nail in the coffin for many institutional top slice arrangements and their replacement by reverse leasebacks or more popularly, the side by side or proportional sharing arrangement. Profit erosion provisions further reinforced the position of the institution.

(xii) *Rent Reviews*

The basis on which rental income from the development is

to be shared has been previously discussed, as was the way in which it is distributed i.e. through a "horizontal" or "vertical" arrangement. The parties to the deal will also need to agree how frequently this will be done. In the pioneering days of leaseback where a geared formula was used, the head rent was reviewed every 33 or 25 years. Since then both the formula has been refined to a "proportionate" basis and the intervals between reviews has consistently dropped until, under a "vertical" distribution, the income is shared on a continuous basis as each partner receives his proportionate share of all receipts of rents.

Developers were however persuaded in the formative stages of leaseback to accept upward only rent reviews. This was an attempt by institutions to "peg" each rent review on an imaginary cribbage board. The purpose here is to ensure that on each and every rent review against the developer, the new rent shall never be less than the last one. These upward only reviews can of course prove catastrophic if the project income should fall substantially at some future date. The practical consequences of these clauses is not always self evident, especially if the institution's participation is made up of a number of separate components.

As far as the occupational leases are concerned, clearly it is in the interest of both developer and investor to try and impose frequent reviews against their tenants. The frequency will be determined by market forces at the time that the leases are negotiated.

(xiii) *Prior Approval of Lettings*

In cases where the underlettings are not yet completed by the developer at the date of the agreement with the institution, there will invariably be a requirement that the approval of the institution must first be obtained to the proposed tenant and the lease. Generally a standard draft underlease is annexed to the sale and leaseback agreement. The institution will be particularly adamant that all leases are at full rack rental value and will prohibit the developer granting underleases for a capital premium or with inadequate rent reviews. Problems also arise as to the permitted use of the premises which among other things tend to cause difficulties with rent reviews against the occupying tenant. To overcome this some institutions now insist on a lease back to them, from the developer thus:

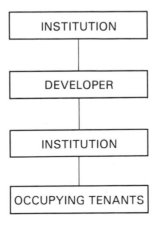

(xiv) *Use of Tax Relief and Allowance*

It is often the case that the institution itself is exempt from tax or suffers a reduced rate of tax. This will render in their hands, tax allowances on the project of little, if any, benefit. However, if the funding is advantageously structured for the developer it is he and not the institution who can benefit from such tax reliefs as capital allowances which relate to plant and machinery (e.g. air conditioning plant) and to industrial and agricultural building allowances. Indeed the prospect of being able to write off a significant proportion of the construction costs by the developer is obviously attractive and will improve his net, after tax, profits. It should be noted, however, that great care must be exercised to comply with the relevant statutory conditons as to the timing of purchase by the institution to preserve these rights. During periods of high tax rates and, or large capital allowances, there is a noticeable upturn in a specialised sector of the funding market, that of the "finance lease". In suitable cases this type of lease can be applied to property developments where there is a substantial potential tax allowance due to the nature of the building, its plant and machinery and its location (most especially within an Enterprise Zone with its enhanced tax allowances and reliefs). This is a separate, and very specialised sector of the funding market and when used is subject to its own individual documentation.

(xv) *Capital Contribution by the Developer*

It may be possible for the developer or the institution sometimes to improve their equity participation in a sale and leaseback relationship by contributing some, or more funds towards the total project costs.

Example

Original costs of project		£640,000
Original proportionate sharing of income		
Institution	67·5%	
Developer	32·5%	100%
Rents as a percentage return on costs		10·3%

However, it has been agreed that both parties will invest as follows:

Capital to be contributed by developer	£128,000
Balance by institution	£512,000
	£640,000

The problem is how to renegotiate the original proposals. The developer will now invest £128,000 towards the estimated costs of the scheme. The negotiating base can be established by changing the original sharing proportions by the ratio of each party's capital investment, in this case 4:1.

The existing sharing arrangements, altered mathematically by this ratio, would change the proportionate sharing thus:

Institution	61%	or £40,260 p.a.	giving a 7·86% return on capital invested
Developer	39%	or £25,740 p.a.	giving a 20·11% return on capital invested
Total	100%	£66,000 p.a.	which is 10·31% yield on total cost

As in all funding arrangements the revised basis will have to be a matter of some skilled negotiations! The developer, before this investment was to receive £21,450 p.a. as his equity share, representing 32·5% of the £66,000 net income. By contributing £128,000 his income is increased by £4,290 (or a modest 3·4% return on his capital). He has, however, improved his proportionate share of the total income by 20% and would thereby achieve nearly two fifths of all future income from the project. Clearly his opinion as to the growth of rental values will be a deciding factor as to whether or not the purchase of a further $6\frac{1}{2}$% share of the total revenue will be justified.

(xvi) *Valuation of the Developer's Interest and "Put" and "Call" Options*

Of critical importance to both parties is that the agreement between them should regulate the valuation of the developer's interest in the project if and when it is to be sold to the institution. The RICS valuation guidance notes are a helpful background to the approach to be taken by the valuer. However, the first question to be answered is whether or not there exists a legal obligation for the institution to buy-out the developer. Some agreement will carry a "put" option whereby the developer can "put" his share to the institution who must than acquire it. If there is no mandatory requirement for this to be done, then the developer is, of course, at the mercy of the market as to who, if anyone, wishes to acquire his interest. As mentioned previously, a top-slice share is difficult to value and generally even more difficult to sell; there being few interested buyers at anything other than a sacrificial price. The institution is often the only prospective purchaser, but very much on its own terms. Therefore developers will always press for some legal commitment by their partner to purchase the minority interest in the project. This legal right in itself will be of little practical value unless the basis on which the interest is to be valued is recorded in the documents. Typically this will be the application of an appropriate multiplier to the then current project income attributable to the developer's share.

Most institutions have a strong preference to be the sole owner of an investment, especially once it has been proven.

They are therefore only too willing to buy out their partner from the venture, indeed some will insist on it! The prospect of accumulating some capital is also an attractive proposition to the smaller developer although participating in an increasing rental income, especially if the gearing is favourable, can present a dilemma of choice to him.

If the agreement includes a "call" option then the developer's choice is limited by the right of the institution to "call" or require, that the developer sells his interest to them.

Where neither "put" or "call" options have been incorporated then there normally is included a mutual right of first refusal for the benefit of both partners.

Example

It has been agreed that the leaseback rent will for the Clivesville project be by reference to the respective proportions attributable to each party on a side-by-side basis with a guarantee by the developer of a minimum rent on completion. This guarantee was extinguished as soon as the actual rack rents receivable from the underlettings reached the minimum level agreed. In the event the actual rents exceeded £60,000 on completion and the surplus was divided equally. The basic leaseback rent was calculated on a 6% basis to reflect: (i) bridging finance at a cost of 8% was provided by the institution; (ii) the project was not pre-let; but (iii) the leaseback rental is guaranteed by the developer. Valuation of developer's interest (based on the right to require the institution to acquire his interest):

Actual net rents achieved	£66,000 p.a.
less 6% on the costs, (£38,400) plus a 50% share on initial surplus (£3,000)	£41,400
Surplus income to developer	£24,600 p.a.
Valued on an agreed 6% yield	÷ 0·06
Capital value of developer's interest on completion	£410,000

If the developer had not exercised his "put" option the future rents would be shared as to

$$\frac{£41,400}{£66,000} \times 100 = 62 \cdot 7\% \text{ to the institution}$$

and
$$\frac{£24,600}{£66,000} \times 100 = 37 \cdot 3\% \text{ for the developer}$$

(xvii) *The use of leaseback in local authority partnership schemes*

Sale and leaseback funding has played, and continues to play, a major, indeed pivotal role, in the funding of many local authority sponsored developments. It was a method extensively used to raise the necessary funding to carry out the central area redevelopments of the 1960s and 1970s. This usually involved an extension of the basic agreement, between a developer and institution, to accommodate a third party, i.e. the land owning local authority. (Developments are also carried out by local authorities themselves acting as the developer, under the conventional two party arrangement.)

(xviii) *Treatment of leaseback transactions in property company accounts*

It is extremely difficult to ascertain the extent that property developers have funded their projects through the use of sale and leasebacks. This is because they are not separately identified or reported upon, in the developer's Annual Accounts. The rents payable under a sale and leaseback, to the institutional lender, are "buried" with other rents payable, e.g. ground rents and leasehold rents, in the Accounts. Similarly rents receivable from projects funded by this method are "lost" within the other property rental receipts.

One of the worrying aspects over this lack of disclosure is the difficulty in gauging the extent of the borrower's "contingent liabilities" (for he will in all probability have to continue paying the head rent under a leaseback even if the project becomes non revenue producing through voids or obsolescence). Many sale and leaseback transactions, it will be recalled, are also partly guaranteed in terms of a basic return, by the developer.

6. Reverse Leaseback

The conventional sale and leaseback had the major disadvantage of sometimes leaving the developer with a relatively highly geared leasehold equity, which was virtually unmortgageable and furthermore, often could only be valued at a relatively high yield of 10% or more.

However, so long as the margins are satisfactory, the developer may be able to retain the freehold and grant a long lease to the institution, i.e. a reverse leaseback is used to fund the project. He retains his legally superior position and has a more valuable interest.

Typically a 125 years lease is granted to the institution at a £nil or peppercorn rent during the period of the development. The institution appoints the developer as their project managers, it then being the latter's obligation to carry out the development as agents for the institution and arrange the first lettings on terms approved jointly.

As and when the development is completed and fully let, the ground rent payable to the developer, in its capacity as freeholder is calculated to ensure that the institution has first priority to a sum, being the agreed return on the total outlay, plus 50% of any part of the rent in excess of a $6\frac{1}{2}$% yield achieved on initial letting. Thus the developer would retain the freehold but receive a proportionate ground rent subordinated to the first charge on the project income of £41,600 p.a. in favour of the institution (i.e. £640,000 × 0·065).

Example

It is agreed that the institution will receive $6\frac{1}{2}$% return on total capital employed, plus 50% of all income achieved in excess of the estimated rental of £60,000 per annum, as the first charge on the income. The residual income is received by the developer by way of a ground rent reviewable yearly upwards or downwards, to restore the ratio between initial ground rent and head rent. It is also agreed that the developer can call on the institution to purchase his interest at the same rate as that used to value their own interest, i.e. $6\frac{1}{2}$%, when completed and fully let.

Initial Value of Developer's Interest

Actual rents received		£66,000 p.a.	
Less (a) 6½% on cost	£41,600 p.a.		
(b) 50% of difference between £66,000 and £60,000	3,000 p.a.		
		44,600 p.a.	(67·58% on total income)
Residual ground rent (variable)		21,400	(32·42% of total income)
Capitalised @ 6½% ∴		÷ 0·065	
Initial value of developer's freehold interest – say		£329,000	

Value of developer's interest after rent review

Rents received after first reviews	£99,000 p.a.
Less share to institution of 67·58%	66,900
Residual ground rent (variable)	£32,100
Capitalised @ 6½% ∴ ÷ by	0·065
Value of developer's freehold interest	£494,000

Here it will be seen that as this is an ungeared (or proportionate) sharing arrangement and the net rents from the project have increased by 50%, the value of the developer's interest has also risen by one half as well.

7. Sale and Leaseback Coupled with a Mortgage

This rather more complex method of direct development funding involves the developer in selling the *site* of the Clivesville project to an investor and then leasing it back, subject to a mortgage being granted to him, by the same investor in the leasehold interest that he, the developer, has created by the leaseback. The process usually follows the format outlined below:

(a) The institution enters into a contract with the developer to purchase the freehold interest in the *site* when the development obligations have been discharged, for a sum typically between 30% to 60% of the estimated freehold value of the completed development when let; this sum is payable when the building has been completed. The developer undertakes the proposed scheme in accordance with the previously agreed drawings, specifications etc. Upon completion the developer agrees to take a lease for a term of, say 125 years.

(b) The payments by the institution during the building contract are limited to a total of the agreed purchase price of the freehold interest, together with a further sum to represent two thirds of the estimated value of the head leasehold interest in the completed building, when let and valued for mortgage purposes.

(c) The above advances are made by way of instalments, upon production of architects' certificates, or, in the case of professional fees, upon production of receipted accounts.

(d) The payments are subject to the approval by the institution's surveyors of plans, specifications, building contract and of the architects' certificates.

(e) All monies paid by the institution bear interest at 2% above LIBOR, calculated on a day to day basis and compounded quarterly until the grant of the lease.

(f) Upon practical completion of the building, a lease is granted to the developer for a term of 125 years. The initial rent represents an agreed return on the institution's expenditure in acquiring the freehold including legal and all other costs. The yield on the sale and leaseback could be typically, 1 to 2% above the interest rate that the income of the completed project would be valued in the open market as a freehold investment.

(g) All lettings by the developer are required to be at full open market rental value, with no fine or premium. In the event of the estimated income from the scheme, agreed at the outset, being exceeded, then the rent payable to the institution would be increased by an agreed proportion of the amount that the net income actually achieved is in excess of the originally estimated net income.

(h) The ratio between the net rents receivable by the developer and the total rent payable to the institution is calculated on completion and at agreed periods throughout the term of the head lease, so that the leaseback rent is revised in order to restore the initial ratio.

(i) It is agreed that should any space be unlet twelve months after the practical completion of the building, the rental value of the vacant space will be decided by the institution's surveyors, acting as an expert.

(j) The developer's and institution's expenses in connection with the lease and stamp duty thereon are borne by the developer.

(k) On practical completion of the scheme, the freehold interest is conveyed to the institution and the outstanding debt is reduced by the amount of the purchase price of the freehold. The residue of the debt, namely the difference between the purchase price of the freehold interest, and the total development costs will be due for repayment not later than twelve months after practical completion of the building.

(l) The institution, agrees from the outset to mortgage the created leasehold interest held by the developer and will advance the capital sum when agreed rental levels are achieved.

Example

(a) One third of development costs will be covered by sale and leaseback of the freehold.

(b) Two thirds of the development cost will be covered by a mortgage secured on the "created" head leasehold interest.

(c) The institution will receive 2% above the freehold investment yield for the project, i.e. a $7\frac{1}{2}$% return on the purchase price of freehold, subject to leaseback to developer, plus 20% of all income in excess of the estimated rental value. The leaseback rent will be reviewed, proportionately every 15 years.

(d) The institution will receive interest on the money advanced by way of mortgage at 3% above the completed investment yield for the project subject to one third of the loan being paid back equally over 25 years with the balance repayable in one final payment at the end of the 25th year.

(i) The Leaseback

(a) *Calculation of Head Rent Payable*

Purchase price of site, including fees etc.	£213,000
Head lease rent @ 7½% on cost £213,000 (inclusive of fees)	× 0·075 say, £16,000 p.a.
Plus 20% of difference between £66,000 and £60,000	1,200 p.a.
Total head lease rent paid by developer	£17,200 p.a.

(b) *Valuation of leasehold interest held by developer*

Actual rent achieved	£66,000 p.a.
Less head rent (as above)	17,000
∴ Profit rent:	£48,000 p.a.
Capitalised at 7½% ∴ ÷	0·075
Value of leasehold interest	£650,650

(ii) The Mortgage

(a) *Basic Terms*

Principal: £427,000 (640,000 less £213,000)

Interest: 8½%

Pay-back: 33⅓% of capital over 25 years

Mortgage security: the head leasehold interest valued as above at £650,650. (Note £427,000 is just under two thirds of the capital value of the leasehold interest.)

(b) *Calculation*

The profit income of head leasehold interest held by the developer is £66,000 less £17,200 =	£48,800 p.a.
less Interest on principal of £427,000 @ $8\frac{1}{2}\%$	36,295
	12,505

$$less \text{ pay-back } \frac{£427,000 \times 0.333}{25} = £5,693$$

grossed up, i.e. $\dfrac{£5,693 \times 100}{100 - 52}$	11,860
Before tax surplus income	£645 p.a.

(iii) Summary

(a) *The net project income, before tax,* has been apportioned thus:

Net rental income		£66,000 p.a.
Less Payable to institution:		
Head rent	£16,000	
20% of initial surplus	1,200	
Mortgage interest	36,295	
Mortgage pay-back of capital (grossed up)	11,860	65,355
Residual surplus to developer		£645 p.a.

(b) The capital funding has provided:

Total required		£640,000
Sale of site	£213,000	
Mortgage	427,000	640,000
Shortfall		Nil

The advantage to the developer is that he retains greater control and although in the initial years this technique will produce a very minimal net, before tax, surplus, the excess will grow steadily. As the rents receivable from the occupying tenants are increased the developer's income is further enhanced by the declining interest payments on the reducing amount of the outstanding loan. Thus he does not have to share the anticipated growth in rental income with the institution until the first rent review under the leaseback and his annual debt servicing costs will also decline throughout the 25 years of the loan.

Basic Comparison of Methods of Funding

An initial comparison is given in the following table which sets out the capital value and first years income position, from the developer's viewpoint, of seven methods of funding illustrated previously, for the Clivesville District Centre. (Not all the figures are truly comparable because of the different underlying rates of interest and sharing arrangements assumed for each case. However, in practice different terms etc. would indeed apply as between the various methods.)

Method of funding	*Capital value of developer's interest or profit*	*&/ or:*	*Income position of the developer*
1. Bridging finance	£516,800		N/A
2. Project management	£71,500		N/A
3. Forward sale	£375,000		N/A
4. Mortgage			
(a) Conventional	£375,000*		(£27,119) p.a. deficit
(b) Equity share	£262,500**		£2,425 p.a.
5. Sale and leaseback	£410,000		£24,600 p.a.
6. Reverse leaseback	£329,000		£21,400 p.a.
7. Leaseback/mortgage	£223,650***		£645 p.a.

   * This represents the encumbered freehold investment value which has been reduced by the amount of the loan of £640,000.

  ** This represents 70% of the investment value of £1,015,000 (as 30% will be charged to the lender as security for his equity participation) after deducting the amount of the loan of £640,000.

*** This represents the encumbered leasehold value which has been reduced by the amount of the mortgage, namely £427,000, thereby resulting in a net asset of £223,650.

Comparison of Methods of Funding by DCF Techniques

A cashflow approach can usefully be employed to compare alternative forms of long term finance such as a mortgage as against a leaseback. Traditional valuation methods cannot be used effectively. The essence of any comparison must be of the different equity shares that the various methods give to the investor and these are dependant on expectations of rental growth. In any form of proportionate financing arrangement traditional appraisal methods, which allow for rental growth *implicitly* in the initial yield, are inadequate.

Example

(a) The first example assumes a 25 year mortgage at 14% with the loan repaid at the end of the period.

(b) The second example illustrates a conventional repayment mortgage at 12%.

(c) The third is a geared 125 year leaseback at 6·5% with the financial institution taking 40% of the initial profit rent and 50% of subsequent increases in the rack rent income.

(d) The fourth example assumes a highly geared leaseback at 10% plus 50% of the initial profit rental income and a further 25% of future profit rentals arising from rent reviews of the occupational leases.

(e) The final example shows an ungeared (or proportionate) 125 year leaseback at 5·5% with all income apportioned in the ratio of 60 to the institution and 40 to the developer.

An essential preliminary step before the comparison can be made is a calculation of expected rental growth as obviously the whole comparison rests on this expectation. A 5·5% free-hold initial yield was used previously and if the opportunity cost of capital is taken to be 15% then this suggests an expected rental growth of 10·5% p.a. assuming 5 year rent reviews (obtained from any DCF growth tables). This figure therefore is used in the following comparisons together with a high discount rate of 18% to emphasise further the added risks inherent in this type of projection.

(a) The Interest Only Mortgage

Year	FRV*	Repayments (interest)	Cashflow to developer	YP @ 18%	PV @ 18%	YP def'd @ 18%	Net present value
	£	£	£				£
0	66,000	89,600	(23,600)	3·127		3·127	(73,800)
5	109,000	89,600	19,400	3·127	0·4371	1·3668	26,500
10	179,000	89,600	89,400	3·127	0·1911	0·5976	53,400
15	295,000	89,600	205,400	3·127	0·0835	0·2611	53,600
20	486,000	89,600	396,400	3·127	0·0365	0·1141	45,200
25	801,000		801,000	18·18	0·016	0·2900	233,000
		640,000**	(640,000)		0·016	0·016	(10,200)
					Net present value		327,700

* The anticipated FRV is derived by increasing the initial FRV by 10·5% p.a.
  receivable every 5 years.
** After the mortgage has been repaid in year 25, the developer would be
  able to sell the freehold interest and so the income has been capitalised
  at the initial yield of 5·5%.

(b) The Repayment Mortgage

Year	FRV	Mortgage repayable over 25 yrs @ 12%	Cashflow to developer	YP def'd @ 18%	Net present value
	£	£	£		£
0	66,000	81,600	(15,600)	3·127	(48,781)
5	109,000	81,600	27,400	1·3668	37,450
10	179,000	81,600	97,400	0·5976	58,206
15	295,000	81,600	213,400	0·2611	55,719
20	486,000	81,600	404,400	0·1141	46,142
25	801,000	81,600	719,400	0·2909	233,010
				Net present value	381,746
				Say	382,000

(c) The Conventionally Geared Leaseback

Year	FRV	Leaseback rent @ $6\frac{1}{2}\% + 40\%$ of initial profit rent	50% rental increase	Cashflow to developer	YP def'd @ 18%	Net present value
	£	£	£	£		£
0	66,000	51,360*	N/A	14,640	3·127	45,800
5	109,000	51,360	21,500	36,140	1·3668	49,400
10	179,000	51,360	56,500	71,140	0·5976	42,500
15	295,000	51,360	114,500	129,140	0·2611	33,700
20	486,000	51,360	210,000	224,640	0·1141	25,600
25	801,000	51,360	367,500	382,140	0·1780	68,000
				Net present value		265,000

* £51,360 represents initial repayments @ $6\frac{1}{2}\%$ (41,600) plus 40% of the initial profit rent, i.e. $0.4 \times (£66,000 - £41,600)$.

(d) The Highly Geared Leaseback

Years	FRVs	Leaseback rent @ $10\% + 50\%$ of initial profit rents	Plus 25% of profit rents	Total to institutions	Cashflow to developers	YP def'd @ 18%	Net present values
	£	£	£	£	£		£
0	66,000	65,000	N/A	65,000	1,000	3·127	3,127
5	109,000	65,000	11,000	76,000	33,000	1·3668	45,104
10	179,000	65,000	28,500	93,500	85,500	0·5976	51,095
15	295,000	65,000	57,500	122,500	172,500	0·2611	45,040
20	486,000	65,000	105,250	170,250	315,750	0·1141	36,027
25*	801,000	65,000	184,000	249,000	552,000	0·1780	98,256
					Net present value		278,649
						say	279,000

* To simplify the example the calculations have been terminated at year 25 on the assumption that the developer's income receivable then is maintained at this level thereby enabling it to be capitalised in the traditional way for the remainder of the lease (say 100 years). The assumption used above of $10\frac{1}{2}\%$ p.a. rental growth and a discount rate of 18% are the same as valuing traditionally with an initial yield of 8·95% in perpetuity assuming 5 year reviews. Thus the YP deferred figure of 0·1780 is obtained by multiplying YP @ 8·95% for 100 years by PV £1 @ 18% for 25 years.

(e) The Proportionate Leaseback

Year	FRV	Leaseback rent @ 60% to institution	Cashflow to developer	Y.P. def'd @ 18%	Net present value
	£	£	£		£
0	66,000	39,600	26,400	3·127	82,553
5	109,000	65,400	43,600	1·3668	59,592
10	179,000	107,400	71,600	0·5976	42,788
15	295,000	177,000	118,000	0·2611	30,810
20	486,000	291,600	194,400	0·1141	22,181
25	801,000	480,600	320,400	0·1780	57,031
				Net present value	294,955
				say	295,000

The full DCF valuation given above is, in fact, unnecessary. Because the initial profit rent is proportionate (or ungeared), it can be capitalised in the traditional manner using an initial yield of 8·95% as explained above. The developer's interest is valued thus:

Initial net project income		£66,000 p.a.
Less Leaseback rent @ 60%		39,600
Developer's share		26,400
Capitalised @ 8·95%	∴	÷ 0·0895
Value of developer's interest	say	£295,000

(f) Summary

	Mortgage (25 years)		Leasebacks		
	Interest only	Conventional repayment	Conventionally geared	Highly geared	Proportionate sharing
	£	£	£	£	£
Developer's initial income p.a.	(23,600)	(15,600)	14,640	1,000	26,400
NPV	327,700	382,000	265,000	279,000	295,000

(g) *Conclusion*

Based on the assumptions adopted above the conventional mortgage provides the highest NPV whereas initially the proportionate leaseback provided the highest net income and on the face of it may have seemed the preferable alternative. It might have been expected in times of high mortgage interest rates that the mortgage would have the lowest NPV. However, in spite of the problems caused to the developer by the large initial income deficit (which will have to be borne effectively for the first few years) it nevertheless produced the highest NPV. Surprisingly the conventionally geared leaseback here is less profitable than the proportionate sharing leaseback. The above demonstrates the need to apply more sophisticated techniques to various possible simulated scenarios when considering which method, in the longer term, is in fact the most advantageous.

In practice the rental growth expectation will be derived from an analysis of market expectations using the initial yield and cost of capital. In an ungeared arrangement, if expectations of rental growth change in the future, then it is probable that the cost of capital will also change, therefore resulting in a similar answer. But in a geared situation this will not be so, and a lower rate of rental growth can give a markedly different answer. Therefore it is again emphasised that comparative calculations should be undertaken on different assumptions, using probability factors. In the simplified examples used above, rather than examine various alternative assumptions, a higher discount rate was adopted to make an allowance for the simplified assumptions involved. It would be advisable to build up a table of resultant NPVs using a variety of rental growth and discount rate assumptions so that a more complete picture can be provided to enable a better informed development funding decision to be reached. This is of course a form of sensitivity analysis similar to that normally used in appraising viability.

8. Finance Leases and Tax Based Methods of Funding

A finance lease is, in practical terms, a type of mortgage although the major distinction is that the rent paid under the lease (which includes interest and repayment of capital) is fully allowable for tax purposes. Under these "amortised leases" the principal motivation is to utilise any tax allowances in such a way that lenders can obtain the tax relief on the assets which they lease (and thereby reduce their tax bill); because of this, lessees are able to benefit, indirectly, from a reduction in the rate of interest charged (as the tax relief is afforded to the lessor). This "sharing" of tax relief is all the more important if the lessee himself does not have sufficient profits against which to offset the full tax allowance, had he purchased the asset himself in the first place. Although industrial buildings and plant and machinery are still eligible for capital allowances, albeit at a reduced rate (up until 1984 it was 100%!) the expenditure on the construction of buildings for letting in Enterprise Zones still carries full relief. Finance leases have therefore been used increasingly to provide a significant part of the funding package used to finance new projects located within Enterprise Zones. However, as with all tax related schemes considerable care is needed to ensure that there is full compliance with all of the relevant regulations associated therewith, especially the length of lease, the use of the property and the holding of a "relevant" interest in it. Finance leases are, for tax reasons, usually split between a primary period (during which there is a full pay-back of capital) followed by a long secondary period where only a nominal or peppercorn rent is paid. A recent example of the use of this funding technique in an Enterprise Zone is provided by the Gateshead Metro Centre which was partly funded by the Church Commissioners and the Royal Bank of Scotland. It now remains to be seen, if as a result of successive reductions in the amount of tax relief on industrial buildings and plant and machinery, partly compensated by successive reductions in corporation tax, whether finance leases *outside* Enterprise Zones will continue to provide a viable funding vehicle.

9. Government Grants

The range and availability of central and local government grants and development incentives frequently change, as do the percentage amounts eligible for assistance and the qualifying conditions that must be met. It is therefore essential to ascertain whether part or all of the costs of a project might be met through one of the grant aid programmes as they can be a useful component of the overall funding package, especially for more difficult-to-fund projects. Apendix 1 contains a summary of the various grant schemes which are of potential interest to developers.

CLIVE DARLOW

BIBLIOGRAPHY

"Property Development," Cadman D. and Austin-Crowe L. [Spon 1984].
"Urban Land Administration," Ratcliffe J. [Estates Gazette 1978].
"The Property Development Process," CALUS [CEM 1976].
"Future of the Development Industry," RICS [1979].
"Property Development Library," Jolly B. (Ed.) [CEM 1984].
"Investment in Property," CALUS [CEM 1974].
"Principles of Property Investment and Pricing," Fraser W. [Macmillan 1984].
"Financial Services Act," HMSO 1986.

CHAPTER 10
Tax and Property Development

INTRODUCTION

The general principles of the taxation of income and capital are applicable equally to income and gains arising from land as to those arising from any other source. However, the application of the general principles is in many circumstances subject to particular rules reflecting the complexity and the multiplicity of interests in land.

Successive governments must necessarily look to the state of the commercial climate before deciding how to raise revenue through the annual budget. Hence, as in the late seventies we witnessed an avalanche of new legislation concerning the taxation of oil as the full commercial benefits flowed from oil drilling in the North Sea and elsewhere. However, continual efforts have been made to tax the significant profits that can arise from property transactions throughout this century, either within the existing rules, or by changing the rules.

The first full-blooded attempt to tax the development value of property was the Town and Country Planning Act 1947 but this led to a withholding of land from the market and was repealed in 1953 although the planning provisions of the 1947 Act remained. Public authorities continued to acquire land at a price virtually excluding development value but sales between private persons continued at full market value. The two price system was abolished in 1959 and full market value then applied to all transactions.

This position continued until the Land Commission Act 1967 introduced Betterment Levy with effect from 6 April 1967. The levy was effectively abolished in July 1970.

However, the extraordinary increase in property values during the early seventies meant that it was not long before extensive legislation regarding the taxation of property development was introduced. This was in the form of a tax on development gains under Case VI of Schedule D under the Finance Act 1974 but within a short period of time it was announced that other proposals to tax development value would be introduced and the new tax was outlined in a Government White Paper entitled "Land" in September 1974. As a result the Community Land Act was given the Royal Assent in November 1975, the general objectives of which were:

(a) to enable the community to control the development of land in accordance with its needs and priorities; and
(b) to restore to the community the increase in value of land arising from its efforts.

The intention at that time was that Local Authorities would purchase land at current use value and all development land would be sold to Local Authorities who would then sell it on to developers at a price including development value, or would develop it themselves. Development Land Tax (DLT) was supposed to last for a transitional period until the government prevented this. The Development Land Tax Act 1976 was substantially mollified by succeeding Finance Acts but the provisions were complicated.

It survived for nine years, being repealed by the Conservative Government in 1985. However, all development gains continue to be liable to capital gains tax, income tax, or corporation tax, as may be appropriate. Due to the demise of DLT it is not the author's intention to discuss the provisions of this tax any further. If necessary reference should be made to the first edition of this book.

When considering the taxation of property development it is also necessary to examine the tax consequences that flow from retaining the completed development property and part of the chapter is therefore taken up with the taxation of rental income.

Although the chapter looks at the taxation of property developments principally from the corporate viewpoint various factors which affect individuals are also included where appropriate. A complete over view of the taxation of all types of UK property investors is contained in Appendix 2.

The principal areas with which the chapter is concerned are:

1 Income from land – Schedule A
2 Tax relief on interest payments
3 Capital allowances
4 Tax consequences of property dealing
5 Capital gains tax
6 Inheritance tax
7 Property Rates
8 Value Added Tax
9 Stamp Duty
10 Finance
11 Grants and Incentives

Abbreviations Used

CGTA	Capital Gains Tax Act
FA	Finance Act
ICTA	Income and Corporation Taxes Act
SA	Stamp Act
VATA	Value Added Tax Act

Glossary of Terms
A glossary of terms used is provided at the end of this chapter.

1 INCOME FROM LAND – SCHEDULE A

Income arising from the ownership of interest in land is assessed under Schedule A and the basis of assessment is common to all taxpayers whether they are companies, partnerships, individuals or trusts. The chargeable income is based on the rents or receipts to which a person becomes entitled in the chargeable period. (Furnished lettings are normally assessed under Schedule D Case VI and are not the subject of this chapter.)

(a) *Expenditure*
The expenditure which is allowed as a deduction from rents falls under the following categories (Section 72 ICTA 1970):

(i) maintenance, repairs, insurance and management,
(ii) services which the landlord must provide under the lease but for which no separate payment is received,

(iii) rates or other occupier's charges which the landlord is obliged to pay,
(iv) any rent, rentcharge, ground annual, feu duty or other periodical payment reserved in respect of, or charged on or issuing out of the land.

The rules relating to the deduction of interest from rents is dealt with under (b) below.

(b) *Losses and classification of leases*

There are complicated rules concerning the setting off of any excess of expenditure of one lease against another and it is therefore necessary to examine the lease classifications and also the currency of a lease.

Leases are divided into three groups:

(i) leases at full rent, which are not tenant repairing leases,
(ii) tenant repairing leases at full rent,
(iii) leases not at full rent.

A lease at a full rent is defined (Section 71 ICTA 1970) as one where the rent "is sufficient, taking one year with another, to defray the cost of the lessor of fulfilling his obligations under the lease and of meeting any expenses of maintenance, repairs, insurance and management of the premises subject to the lease which fall to be borne by him".

A tenant repairing lease is one under which the lessee is obliged to maintain and repair the whole, or substantially the whole, of the premises.

Expenditure is generally not deductible until actually paid, and paid by the person chargeable. The deduction is made in the year in which payment is made, any unrelieved expenditure may be carried forward (subject to the loss offsetting rules below). Relief will not be given for expenditure relating to a period before the currency of the lease, e.g. repairs and maintenance as a result of dilapidations occurring before the currency of the lease. With one exception, the currency of the lease is the period of the lease itself. The exception being a lease at full rent which may include earlier periods (Section 72 ICTA 1970).

Expenditure on improvements, additions or alterations are not allowed.

Where a loss arises on a landlord repairing lease at full rent it can only be offset against profits on leases within this class. Effectively all leases within this class can be pooled in a composite computation. Net losses of the pool cannot be offset against profits on leases of a different class. Losses on tenant repairing leases may be offset against the pool but not against profits arising on other tenant repairing leases. There is no provision for any set off of losses arising on leases not at full rent.

Summary:

Tenant Repairing Lease		Landlord Repairing Lease		Leases not at full rent	
Profit	*Loss*	*Profit Pool*	*Loss*	*Profit*	*Loss*
Must be assessed unless loss on same lease brought forward	Carry forward against same lease to same tenant or to new tenant if within currency of lease OR POOL	Assess net income	Carry forward against same lease or any other lease at full rent (not a tenant repairing lease) OR POOL	Assessed unless loss brought forward on same lease to same tenant	Carry forward against profits on same lease to same tenant

(c) *Depreciation*

Depreciation of a building or any of its fixtures will not qualify as a deduction for tax purposes but in certain circumstances a claim for capital allowances may be available (see Section 2 below – Capital Allowances).

(d) *Grant/Assignment of Leases*

The income and capital gains tax legislation in respect of the grant or assignment of leases is complex. However, the following are the basic principles:

(i) the assignment of a long or short lease (less than 50 years duration on disposal) is an outright disposal of the entire leasehold interest. The normal capital gains tax principles for disposal of assets therefore apply, including a requirement to "waste" the base cost of a short lease.

(ii) The grant of a long or short lease out of a freehold constitutes a part disposal.

(iii) in theory a premium paid for the grant of a short lease is similar to rent, whereas a premium paid on grant of a long lease is more closely related to the capital value of the underlying property. The income provisions of Section 80–85 ICTA 1970 adopt this theory by treating part of the premium paid on grant of a short lease as if it were rental income. The balance of the premium being dealt with separately under the capital gains tax provisions for leases. The amount treated as rent is the whole premium less 2% for each complete year of the lease other than the first. There is no Schedule A assessment on the assignment of a lease.

Example

Grant of lease out of a freehold (ignoring indexation):

The part disposal formula (see Section 4b) below – Capital Gains Tax) is modified to find the cost of the part disposed of i.e. the A/(A + B) formula becomes:

$$\frac{\text{the premium (for short leases the premium not subject to Schedule A)}}{\text{the premium + capital value of rent + value of reversion}}$$

Bob grants a 30 year lease for a premium of £15,000. The building had cost £20,000, the value of the reversion, including the right to receive rents is £10,000.

Premium received	£15,000
Less: 2% per annum (30–1)	8,700
Schedule A assessment	£6,300
Proceeds	£8,700
Less: $20,000 \times \dfrac{8,700}{15,000 + 10,000}$	6,960
Capital gain (before indexation)	£1,740

Example

Assignment (ignoring indexation):

Arthur acquired a 21 year lease for a premium of £20,000. Seven years later he assigns it for £18,000.

Proceeds of disposal		£18,000
Less: cost of lease	£20,000	
wastage during life		
(see below)	(4,198)	(15,802)
Capital gain (before indexation)		£2,198

The wastage is calculated using percentages taken from the Table in Schedule 3 CGTA 1979 (See Table 1) and placing them in the following formula:

$$\frac{\text{percentage applicable to lease at acquisition} - \text{percentage applicable to lease at disposal}}{\text{percentage applicable to lease at acquisition}}$$

$$\frac{\text{\% for 21 years} - \text{\% for 14 years}}{\text{\% for 21 years}} = \frac{74 \cdot 635 - 58 \cdot 971}{74 \cdot 635} = 20 \cdot 99\%$$

Therefore cost wasted is £20,000 × 20·99% = £4,198.

The purpose of the formula is to reflect the fact that a lease is a wasting asset.

(f) *Anti-avoidance*

Anti-avoidance legislation has been introduced to deal with circumstances such as the granting of a lease to a connected person at a nominal rent and premium, the lease then being assigned to a third party for a premium and full value rent (Section 81 ICTA 1970).

Example

John grants a lease to his brother Bill for £2,000. The lease is for a period of seven years and if the lease had been granted on an arm's length basis it would have been valued at £15,000. Bill then assigns the lease to the third party for £15,000.

In accordance with Section 81 ICTA 1970 the Inland Revenue

are entitled to recoup the tax lost through a Schedule A assessment on the £13,000 profit which would otherwise only have been liable to Capital Gains Tax.

Summary:
Capital Gains Tax and Leases

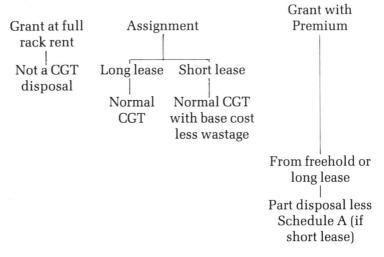

Note: the grant with premium of a sub lease out of a short lease is not considered in this chapter.

2 RELIEF FOR INTEREST

The rules governing relief for interest are complicated but are principally governed by Section 75, Finance Act 1972 and Schedule 1, Finance Act 1974. Where a property developer (company or individual) borrows money for use in his business, the interest paid in any period ending after 31 March 1982 will be an allowable deduction against the profits. Any resulting loss can be carried forward to a future year. For periods prior to 31 March 1981 a deduction was only allowed to a company if it charged the interest in its Profit and Loss Account. If the company charged it to capital then there was no relief, although, in certain circumstances, there would be relief for capital gains.

Interest on a loan to purchase, develop or improve a property which is to be let is only allowed if the property during a period of 52 weeks is let at a commercial rent for more than 26 weeks and, when not so let, is available for letting or is not available due to works of construction or repair. In the case of an individual, relief may also be given in certain other circumstances. In addition, a property investment company may be able to claim a tax deduction for interest paid against other income.

3 CAPITAL ALLOWANCES

(a) *General*

The depreciation of a capital asset charged in the Profit and Loss Account of a business is not an allowable deduction in computing taxable profits, but is replaced by tax depreciation allowances called "capital allowances" at statutorily prescribed rates. The effect of the allowances is to permit capital expenditure on a qualifying asset to be deducted from taxable profits.

The 75% initial and 100% first year allowances (see Table 2) previously available on industrial buildings and plant and machinery respectively were gradually phased out over the period 14 March 1984 to 1 April 1986. The straight line writing down allowances of 4% on industrial buildings and the 25% writing down allowance (calculated on a reducing balance basis) for plant and machinery have been retained. (It should be noted that since 1945 successive Governments have varied the rates from time to time of both first year allowances and writing down allowances).

(b) *Industrial Buildings Allowances*

Land

Land, excluding buildings on it, are excluded from eligible expenditure for industrial buildings allowances (IBAs) (Section 17 CAA 1968).

Buildings

Capital expenditure on the development of a building to be used as an industrial building qualifies for IBA. An industrial building is broadly one which is used to house a manufacturing process but also includes a building in use for purposes of transport and in certain circumstances a building which is used for storage. The allowances consist of an initial allowance of 75% for expenditure incurred before 31 March 1986 (increased from 50% with effect from 10 March 1981), and an annual writing down allowance of 4% per annum until the residue of the expenditure has been reduced to nil. Legislation was introduced in the Finance Act 1978 to allow expenditure on hotels to qualify for IBA although the initial allowance was restricted to 20% until 31 March 1986. To encourage investment in small businesses the Finance Act 1980 contained legislation granting an initial allowance of 100% of the expenditure incurred before 27 March 1985 on the construction of small workshops where the gross internal floor space of the whole building did not exceed 1,250 square feet.

Lessor

If a person incurs expenditure on construction of a building which is to be used by a lessee as an industrial building, the landlord will be able to claim IBA.

Lessees

The lessee of an industrial building may incur capital expenditure on the building either under the terms of the lease or with the consent of the landlord. He is entitled to the relevant interest in the building in respect of the expenditure he incurs and will therefore be entitled to IBA. It is therefore possible that two or more persons hold different relevant interests in the same building at the same time in respect of different expenditure.

Joint Election

The lessor and lessee may jointly elect for the grant of the lease to be regarded as a sale of the lessor's relevant interest to the lessee, so that any capital sum paid by the lessee is regarded as the purchase price of a relevant interest enabling the lessee to claim IBA (Section 37 FA 1978). The election is only applicable to leases in excess of 50 years and must be made within two years from the commencement of the lease.

Such an election is likely to be of use when the lessor is not in a tax paying position and cannot take avantage of the IBAs available. The lessee, on the other hand, may be in a tax paying situation and would be prepared to pay an increased rental in return for the IBAs.

Disposal

When the relevant interest in a building is disposed of, a comparison is made between the residue of expenditure (cost less allowances already claimed) and the proceeds. Any excess of the former will produce a balancing allowance, while surplus proceeds will produce a balancing charge. The amount of the balancing charge cannot exceed the total of the allowances given immediately before disposal to the owner of the relevant interest.

See Table 2 for the rates of allowances applicable to industrial buildings.

(c) Fixtures in leased properties

A person claiming capital allowances on plant and machinery must demonstrate that the machinery or plant on which he has incurred expenditure "belongs" to him (Section 41, Section 44 FA 1971). The possession of a limited interest in the assets e.g. a lease, was not sufficient as the 1971 Act required absolute ownership. The Stokes v. Costain Property Investments Ltd 1984 case highlighted this fact. The decision reached in that case was that fixtures affixed to the land or buildings e.g. lifts, central heating etc. "belonged" to the freeholder and not to the lessee irrespective of whether the lessee incurred the expenditure. Accordingly, the lessee was not entitled to the capital allowances.

In the past, before the Costains case, the Revenue by concession had granted capital allowances to lessees on their expenditure if it was incurred for the purposes of a trade. This situation was clearly unsatisfactory and in light of the Costain decision legislation was introduced in the 1985 Finance Act (Schedule 17 FA 1985). The basis of the new rules is that fixtures will be treated as "belonging" to the person who pays for them provided that he has an interest in the relevant land or building at the time the fixtures are installed and incurs the expenditure for the purpose of a trade or of property letting.

Any balancing adjustment required on cessation of trade or letting etc. will correspondingly fall on the person who obtained the allowances.

See Table 2 for the rates of allowances applicable to plant and machinery.

(d) *Very small workshops and enterprise zones*

A very small workshop is an industrial building qualifying under the normal rules, but which has a floor space not exceeding 1,250 square feet. For expenditure incurred between 27 March 1983 and 26 March 1985 a 100% initial allowance will be given wherever the building is situated (Section 73 FA 1982). Previously 100% initial allowances were available for expenditure incurred between 26 March 1980 and 27 March 1983 where the gross internal floor space did not exceed 2,500 square feet (Section 75 FA 1980). Alternatively, the claimant may elect to take a smaller initial allowance followed by a 25% writing down allowance on a straight line basis for the following years (Schedule 13 para 3 FA 1980).

The IBA provisions have been modified in respect of enterprise zones (EZ) so that any industrial or commercial building built in such a zone will qualify for the 100% initial allowance. The benefit is available for a 10 year period from the date on which each zone is designated an EZ. A commercial building is just about any building which would not already qualify for IBAs other than a dwelling house (Section 74 FA 1980). The initial allowance continues to be 100% notwithstanding the reduction in the normal rate of initial allowance for industrial buildings built outside the zone (see Table 2). No allowances are given on the capital cost of land on which the building stands. As with small workshops, a lower initial allowance may be claimed with 25% writing down allowance being given in subsequent years.

An important avantage of being within an EZ, and one which benefits the occupier, is the exemption from local authority rates on industrial and commercial property for a ten-year period from designation as an EZ.

See Table 3 for areas which have been designated as an EZ.

(e) *Agricultural Building Allowances (ABA)*

Expenditure on the construction of farmhouses, farm or forestry buildings, cottages, fences or other works qualifies for agricultural buildings allowances. However, no more than one-third of the cost of constructing a farmhouse qualifies for the allowance.

The initial allowance of 20% on agricultural land and buildings was withdrawn with effect from 1 April 1986 and from that date the rate of writing down allowance was reduced from 10% to 4% still to be computed on a straight line basis (Section 62 FA 1985). Also from that date a system of balancing adjustments will be available, for the first time, at the option of the taxpayer, when an agricultural building is demolished, destroyed or sold. Any balancing charge will not exceed the amount of writing down allowances already claimed (Schedule 15 paragraph 6 and 7 FA 1986).

Example

A farmer built a farmhouse in November 1986 which cost £72,000 to construct. In January 1987 fences and other works costing £20,000 and qualifying for ABA were erected. In May 1988 the farmhouse, fences and other works were sold for £120,000.

ABA available to the developer

(a) Year ended 5 April 1987
     Writing down allowance

4% of £24,000 ($\frac{1}{3}$ of cost of farmhouse)	£960
4% of 20,000	800
£44,000	£1,760

(b) Year ended 5 April 1988
     Writing down allowance

4% of £44,000	£1,760

(c) Year ended 5 April 1989

Balancing charge	£3,520

ABA available to new owner

(a) Year ended 5 April 1989
Writing down allowance available

$$\text{for 23 years} = \frac{£44,000}{23}$$ £1,913

4 TAX CONSEQUENCES OF PROPERTY DEALING

(a) *Types of property company*

The most common forms of property companies are:

(i) A property dealing company: one which buys speculative land or buildings and then sells them (possibly having obtained planning permission) but without otherwise adding value.

(ii) A property investment company: one which buys land with the intention of holding it as an investment and renting out that property so as to service its capital with rental income.

(iii) A property development company: one which buys virgin land, obtains planning permission, builds houses etc. and then sells on the properties freehold, or on long leases.

There have been cases where companies have tried to maintain that certain properties are held as investments and some as dealing stock. The courts have usually held that where any of the property is dealing property it is all to be treated in the same way. The holding of land as both an investment and as trading stock has been successfully contended in two cases both involving individuals but it is more difficult for a company to contend that it is acting in a dual role (Hudson v. Wrightson and Harvey v. Caulcott).

In a group of property companies it is normally advisable to have separate dealing companies, developing companies and investment companies.

(b) *Taxation of a property dealing company*

If the company is a property dealing one then it is assessable to corporation tax under Schedule D Case I. For corporation tax rates applicable to different financial years see Table 5.

The general rules for arriving at the amount of profit assessable under Case I of Schedule D are broadly the same for property dealing companies as for other trading companies. Since a considerable period of time may elapse before sales take place or transactions yield income it is important to establish that a trade has commenced so that expenditure is not disallowed on the ground that it occurred before the trade began. Considerable help has been given in this connection by Section 39 of the Finance Act 1980 whereby expenditure incurred within three years of the date of commencement of trade is treated as incurred on the day on which the trade is first carried on.

Stock relief, which was available to a property dealing company was abolished with effect from accounting periods beginning after 12 March 1984 (Section 48 FA 1984).

If properties forming part of the stock-in-trade are let, pending sale, any rents (including premiums) are to be dealt with under the rules of Schedule A. The amount of any premium taxed under Schedule A is excluded from the calculation of the trading profits under Schedule D Case I which therefore will reflect only the balance of premium received.

(c) *Taxation of a private dealer*

There are no major differences between the rules for taxing a private dealer as compared to a property dealing company other than that a private dealer will be subject to income tax on a sliding scale between 27% and 60% rather than corporation tax at 35% (or 27% if the small companies rate is applicable). For income tax rates applicable to different income bands see Table 6.

The taxation of profits arising from dealing in land follows the normal rules for taxing trading profits under Schedule D Case I. Other income is included with dealing profits and then deductions are made for expenses, interest costs and any losses are brought into the calculation. It is unrealistic therefore to give an example of the tax payable on one dealing transaction in isolation. A pro-forma computation of a dealer is illustrated below:

Example

	(£'000)	(£'000)
Sales		1,000
Less: Cost of properties sold	400	
Expenses of sale	60	
Improvements during the year	100	
Overheads	40	
Interest costs	90	690
Amount liable to income tax		£310

(d) *Taxation of a property investment company*

Sales of property are subject to capital gains tax at a rate of 35% (or 27% where the small profit rate applies). Gains realised before 17 March 1987 were charged at a rate of 30%.

Income from rents and premiums are assessable under Schedule A. There is no charge under Schedule D for that part of the premium not taxed under Schedule A since by definition no trade is being carried on. However, there is a part disposal for capital gains tax purposes whenever a premium is received, and accordingly the balance of the premium not taxed under Schedule A will be taxed as a capital gain at 35%.

A property investment company will make a claim under Section 304, ICTA 1970 for expenses of management. The Section 304 claim must exclude expenses already deducted in computing Schedule A income. Management expenses are treated as a deduction from total profits.

For "close companies" there is no requirement for any part of a capital gain to be distributed to the shareholders. However, the Revenue have the power to apportion all the relevant income, that is estate (Schedule A) and investment income, of an investment company, to the individual shareholders whereas the trading income of a property dealing company is not apportionable (Schedule 16 FA 1972). Also for a property dealing company allowable expenditure is governed by a fairly wide definition (expenditure must be incurred wholly and exclusively for the purposes of the trade, Section 130 ICTA 1970) but expenditure allowed as a deduction on a disposal by a property investment company under Section 304 is more restrictive.

Where enhancement expenditure is incurred then under the capital gains tax rules it must be reflected in the state or nature of the assets at the time of sale to be allowed as a deduction in the computation of the gain (Section 32 CGTA 1979).

(e) *Taxation of a private investor*

A private investor will be subject to income tax on his rental income for years of assessment ending on 5 April each year.

Sales of property will be subject to capital gains tax at 30%. Individuals are allowed an annual exemption of £6,600 (1987/88) from net chargeable gains.

Summary:
Corporation and Capital Gains Taxes

	Dealing Company	Investment Company	Development Company
Sales of property liable to Corporation Tax on profits at 35% (small companies rate 27%)	Yes	No	Yes
Sales of property liable to Capital Gains Tax at 35%	No	Yes	No
Rental income liable to Corporation Tax at 35% (small companies rate 27%)	Yes	Yes	Yes

(f) *Anti-avoidance*

There is a very widely drawn anti-avoidance section (Section 488 ICTA 1970) which requires that certain gains of a capital nature, not otherwise treated as income and arising on the disposal of land, may be assessed as income under Case VI of Schedule D. Gains taxed as income will suffer tax at a rate of 35% in the hands of a company, and at rates up to 60% in the hands of individuals. However, the importance of this section will diminish with the rate of tax on capital gains for companies increasing from 30% to 35% for gains realised after 16 March 1987. Section 488 is applied where a person acquires land or buildings or any interest therein with the sole or main object of realising a gain from disposing of it or developing

it. It is unlikely that the Section would apply to property dealing companies as sales of properties are already taxed as
income.

There are other anti-avoidance sections (Section 491 ICTA
1970, Section 80 FA 1972) which deal with certain abuses by
means of sale and leaseback arrangements. Briefly, Section 491
limits the deduction allowed for tax purposes to a commercial
rent for the premises. Section 80 treats part of the consideration on sale of a short lease as taxable income and not capital
where it is leased back for a term not exceeding fifteen years.

(g) *Appropriations to and from trading stock*
It is possible that a taxpayer will transfer assets originally held
as an investment to his trading stock. The asset is not actually
sold but is deemed to have been disposed of at market value
for capital gains tax. However, the taxpayer can elect to take
the asset into his trading stock at its original cost and so no
capital gain will arise. The election (Section 122 CGTA 1979)
is available to groups of companies as well as to an individual
tax payer and has the effect of converting a capital gain into
a trading gain.

A person may also appropriate trading stock for investment
purposes giving rise to a notional disposal for trading purposes.
The deemed trading profit is calculated on the market value
prior to the transfer and becomes immediately taxable.

5 CAPITAL GAINS TAX

(a) *General*
The rate of capital gains tax for individuals and companies
is 30% and 35% respectively. For gains realised before 17 March
1987 the rate for companies was 30%.

The computation of the gain on the disposal of a freehold
interest in a property follows the same basic rules as for other
assets. The gain is calculated by deducting from the sale proceeds the disposal costs, the original cost and the costs of
acquisition. Financing costs are not allowable.

Individuals are entitled to exemption from capital gains tax
for the first £6,600 (1987/88) of net chargeable gains in any
fiscal year. The exempt amount is linked to the retail price

index so that it will automatically be increased each fiscal year (5 April).

No capital gains tax is payable on a deemed disposal on death. Under the provisions of Section 79 Finance Act 1980 two individuals can elect to roll over a gain from one to the other on a transfer between the two.

(b) *Indexation*

A further deduction is made for the indexation allowance. The Finance Act 1982 introduced an indexation allowance in an attempt to solve the problem of inflationary gains. The allowance is calculated on the original cost, or market value at 31 March 1982 if purchased prior to that date, and is deducted from the gross gain to give the chargeable gain. The values of the retail prices index for March 1982 and subsequent months are given in Table 8.

Example

Sale price (31 March 1987)		£1,000
Less: Cost of sale		(15)
		985
Less: Original cost (31 March 1972)	£295	
Cost of acquisition	5	300
Capital gain before indexation		685
Indexation allowance		
Market value at 31 March 1982	£700	
Retail price index 31 March 1982	313·4	
Retail price index 31 March 1987 (say)	396·1	

$$\frac{396·1 - 313·4}{313·4} = ·264$$

·264 × £700		(185)
Chargeable gain		£500

(c) *Enhancement*

Enhancement expenditure is allowed as part of the cost so long as it is reflected in the state or value of the asset at the time of the disposal.

Example

Sale price	£1,000
Less: Cost of sale	(15)
	985

Less: Original cost	£295	
Costs of acquisition	5	
Costs of improvement	60	(360)
Capital gain (before indexation)		£625

(d) *Part disposals and acquisitions*

One common feature of transactions in land is that an interest may have been built up from several different acquisitions over the years. Similarly one asset may be sold off in a series of part disposals.

Where there is a part disposal the original cost is apportioned between the part disposed of and that part retained. The cost of that part disposed of is given by the formula:

$$\text{Cost of part disposed} = \text{Total cost} \times \frac{A}{A+B}$$

Where A = disposal value of part disposed
B = market value, at the date of disposal, of the part retained.

Subject to certain possible relaxations of the formula there are special rules governing disposals and part disposals out of interests acquired before 6 April 1965. The gain arising before 6 April 1965 is exempt from tax. As an oversimplification of the rules the taxpayer can elect to time apportion the gain between the pre and post 6 April 1965 periods or treat his acquisition as having been made on 6 April 1965 at its then market value.

6 INHERITANCE TAX

The Finance Act 1975 introduced capital transfer tax (CTT) as a replacement for Estate Duty, which had for the previous

80 years been the main charge on a person's capital assets at death.

CTT was not only payable by reference to a person's capital assets at death but also all lifetime dispositions unless specifically exempted.

The structure of CTT was then substantially changed in the Finance Act 1986, and as a consequence is to be known as Inheritance Tax (IHT). In relation to events occurring on or after 18 March 1986 the main features of IHT are:

(i) lifetime transfers between individuals are potentially exempt transfers (PET) and no tax arises when the transfer is made.
(ii) If death occurs within 7 years the PET becomes a chargeable transfer. Tax is then charged at death rates with a tapering of the charge for transfers made more than 3 years before death.
(iii) The rate of tax applied to any chargeable transfer is determined by reference to the cumulative total of transfers made in the previous 7 years.
(iv) chargeable lifetime transfers are charged to tax at half the death scale rates. Where death occurs within 7 years of the date of transfer additional tax may be payable.

Chargeable transfers during one's lifetime or on death are still eligible, under the old CTT rules for exemptions such as the £3,000 annual exemption, the transfers between spouses exemption (See Table 4), and reliefs (e.g. business and agricultural property relief).

Interaction of inheritance tax and capital gains tax

Inheritance tax and capital gains tax are separate taxes. One or other, or both, may be payable on the transfer of an asset. The fact that one of the taxes may or may not be payable on a transfer may affect the quantum of the other tax payable.

Example

A makes a gift to B and they elect to role over the chargeable gain under the general relief for gifts (Section 79 Finance Act 1980). A dies shortly afterwards and the potentially exempt transfer proves to be a chargeable transfer for IHT purposes. The subsequent disposal by B will crystalise a CGT liability but in computing the gain he will be able to deduct the IHT paid by the donee, A in arriving at his gain.

7 PROPERTY RATES

(a) *History*

The origin of the present rating system lies in the Poor Relief Act of 1601 which directed overseers (the predecessors of the rating authority) to levy a tax on "every occupier of land and houses ... towards the relief of the poor" in the parish. Occupiers were to contribute according to their means, but there was no specific or common method of assessment laid down. It gradually came to be accepted that the most satisfactory basis of assessment was the annual value of a person's real property within the parish, and this has continued until the present day. The present law on rating is found in the General Rate Act 1967. This made no major change to the existing system but consolidated almost all the statute law on rating. It gives every rating authority (district councils and the London borough councils) the power to make and levy rates applying the proceeds to local purposes of a public nature.

To prevent the worst excesses of the rating system, the 1984 Rates Act requires the local authorities to consult with representatives of the business community before determining their rates. Also, in the same Act the Conservative Government introduced the controversial "rate-capping" legislation with effect from 1 April 1985.

The Government has recently issued a consultative paper, "Paying for Local Government", on the future of the rating system.

The Green Paper proposes that the rating system be divided into two sections, the domestic and non-domestic. In the domestic sector a new "community charge" would be a flat rate charge payable at the same rate by all the adult residents of a local authority. In the non-domestic sector several options have been advanced but the preferred one is for a uniform national business rate which would be set centrally and levied on all businesses. The rate would be linked to the rate of inflation. One of the advantages of this proposal is avoidance of the current distortion in the rates payable from one local authority to another.

(b) *Liability*

In 1985–86 rates are expected to raise £13·6 billion (of this business pays £8·3 billion) and fund approximately 1/3 of local government expenditure. Rates are the fourth most highly yielding tax after income tax, national insurance and value added tax.

Each ratepayer's liability is made up of the rate in the pound levied by the local authority on the "rateable" value of the property, which is independently fixed by the Valuations Office of the Inland Revenue.

The rate in the pound is set by the local authority at a level which will meet its expenditure after allowing for Government grants, fees and charges of other authorities such as the County Council and police for whom it acts as the revenue collecting body. To arrive at the rate in the pound, the total cash required is divided by the total rateable value of all the property in the authority's area.

The main liability to pay rates falls upon the occupiers of land, houses and other buildings and structures. (However, in some cases the owner of the land or building can be liable to pay rates on unoccupied property – see (c) – (iv) below). As it is the occupiers, and not the property which is rateable, then in general, when there is no occupier, no rate can be levied.

(c) *Reliefs*

The general rule is that property rates are always payable. There are hoewver reliefs and exemptions to this, some of which are applicable to property development:

(i) New buildings and other works in the course of construction are not rateable because there is no "occuper" of the building within the meaning of the Act. However, parts of the building or site may be used in such a way as to render them rateable. Builders' huts have, for example, been held to be rateable when they are in one place for a sufficient length of time (usually more than six months).

(ii) When structural alterations are made to existing buildings, as in refurbishment, and the occupiers move out for the duration of the construction work, then relief from the liability to pay rates may be available. For this to be effective the construction work must be of such an extent that the Valuation Officer is of the opinion that the property is not capable of being occupied. If this is the case the assessment in the Valuation List will be reduced to a nominal value of £1 for the duration of the work. The mere fact that the occupier moves out during the refurbishment does not guarantee relief as the Valuation Officer may still consider that the property is physically capable of being occupied.

(iii) When structural alterations are made to a building which continues to be occupied whilst the work is being carried out, then the building remains rateable. However, the carrying out of alterations may constitute grounds for a reduction in the assessment of rateable value for the duration of the alteration work. The amount of the reduction, if any, is a matter to be agreed with the Valuation Officer.

(iv) As already stated the general rule is that where there is no occupation then there is no liability to pay rates. However, if commercial and industrial property remains unocupied for 3 months then the owner of the property will be liable to pay the unoccupied rate. Since 1 April 1981, except for dwelling houses, the rate on unoccupied premises is limited to 50% of that which would normally be payable. From 1 April 1984 empty industrial premises are exempted from paying the unoccupied rate, but it is a requirement that all plant and machinery be moved. This relief was extended, as from 1 April 1985, to included industrial premises which still contained plant and machinery, and also empty warehouses and storage buildings.

8 VALUE ADDED TAX AND LAND

(a) General

Value Added Tax (VAT) is charged on any supply of goods and sevices made in the United Kingdom, where it is a taxable supply made by a taxable person in the course or furtherance of any business. A person who makes or intends to make taxable supplies is a taxable person, and a taxable supply is a supply of goods or services made in the United Kingdom other than an exempt supply (Section 2 VATA 1983).

Within taxable supplies there are two rates of VAT, the zero rate and the standard rate of 15%. The amount of tax on zero rated supplies is nil, but they are still called taxable supplies. Making exempt supplies for VAT purposes is much worse than making taxable supplies from the supplier's point of view in that input VAT cannot be recovered.

Example
The consequences of a supplier of goods or services being zero-rated, exempt or standard rated may be illustrated as follows:

	Outputs		
	Zero rated	Exempt	Standard rated
Cost of purchases (inc VAT)	115	115	115
Less VAT recovered	15	NIL	15
	100	115	100
Supplier's Profit	30	30	30
Sales Price (exc VAT)	130	145	130
Add VAT	NIL	NIL	*19
Total Sales Price	£130	£145	£149

* The supplier's output VAT will represent recoverable input VAT to the customer assuming that he is registered and fully taxable.

If a business makes both taxable and exempt supplies, it may suffer partial exemption problems i.e. a restriction on the amount of its deductible input tax (see (c)).

Supplies in relation to land can be exempt, zero-rated, and standard rated. Land includes buildings, walls, trees and other structures attached to land (Notice 742 para 7).

(b) *Exempt Supplies*
The grant, assignment or surrender of any "interest in or right over land" or any licence to occupy land is exempt, i.e. in

general rents for accommodation and consideration for property disposals are exempt (Group 1 Schedule 6 VATA 1983). There are a number of exceptions which are standard rated as excepted items (e.g. provision of sleeping accommodation in a hotel, inn, boarding house, or similar establishment, Group 1 Schedule 6 VATA 1983), or which are zero rated as newly constructed buildings (see (d) below) or substantially reconstructed "listed buildings" (see (f)) below, Group 8 and Group 8A Schedule 5 VATA 1983).

The term "interest" would include:

– sale of freehold
– grant of lease
– sale of mineral rights

A "licence to occupy" comes about when the supplier allows someone to use the land or buildings in question without actually creating a lease. A licence would not normally be transferable, it dies with the garantee. The licence must give the licencee exclusive rights to occupy the land or buildings, rather than mere permission to use the property in question. The case of J. A. King (1980 VATTR 60) provides an illustration. A farmer allowed others to graze horses with his own animals in his field. As sole occupation was not granted sums received for the permission to graze the horses could not be for a licence to occupy. Accordingly, the charge for grazing was liable to VAT at the standard rate (if a supply is neither specifically exempt or zero rated then it is standard rated).

Likewise groups of companies have been caught out by the distinction between exclusive right of occupation and mere licence to use when sharing out the costs of a building occupied by a number of the companies. If one company holds the freehold or leasehold and is therefore legally responsible for paying rent, rates etc. then the rate of tax applicable to the costs recovered from the other occupiers will depend on the status of their occupancy. If a particular company does not occupy a defined area then there is a standard rated supply when rent is recharged (unless there is a VAT group registration). Standard rating will also apply to amounts billed for lighting, heating, salaries etc. as it cannot be argued that these amounts are merely being reallocated as no individual company has an exclusive right to occupy the land. This is irrespective of the nature of the underlying costs.

(c) *Partial exemption*

The sale of a piece of land or a building used by a business will be an exempt supply (assuming that the seller has not previously constructed it – see (d) below). The proceeds could be substantial and under the old partial exemption rules (existing before 1 April 1987) this could lead to a restriction on the recovery of input tax. This is because the de-minimis rules were based on the value of exempt outputs.

The above inequity was catered for by Statutory Instrument 1985/886 Regulation 32 (a). Where a capital sum is received for the exempt grant, assignment or surrender of an interest in (but not a licence to occupy) land or buildings which have been habitually occupied by the grantor in the course of carrying on his business then the transaction may be disregarded for the purpose of the partial exemption rules.

However, from 1 April 1987, Regulation 32 (a) will cease to exist, as will all de-minimis rules based on values of exempt outputs. From the above date a business will be unable to recover any input tax that is either directly or indirectly attributable to exempt supplies (known as "exempt input tax"). There are a number of provisions which can, given the appropriate circumstances mitigate any potential cost in respect of irrecoverable input tax. For example, Regulation 31 (1) prescribes that any input tax that is attributable (directly or indirectly) to the exempt supply of a lease, tenancy, or licence to occupy any premises may be treated as if it were attributable to taxable supplies. This is provided that;

- the input tax attributable to all such supplies is less than £1,000 per year, and
- that such supplies do not constitute, in effect, a separate business in its own right, and
- that there is no other input tax attributable to other exempt supplies (with certain exceptions).

Furthermore, Customs and Excise under the new rules may grant permission to use a Special Method of input tax attribution for the residue of input tax that cannot be directly attributed to outputs. In these instances a method may be approved based on the ratio of taxable supplies made to the total supplies made by a business. The residue of input tax that is recoverable is determined by applying this ratio to the unallocated input tax. If input tax is apportioned in this way the value of "incidental real estate" transactions must be excluded. As these are invariably exempt (however see (d) below) a measure of relief will be obtained through their exclusion when calculating the ratio (i.e. a greater ratio will result leading to a higher recovery of input tax). This Special Method is essentially the same as the Standard Method under the old rules (see partial exemption, glossary of terms).

(d) *Zero-rated supplies*

Through the zero rating mechanism VAT is not included in the cost of new buildings. There is some considerable doubt being expressed in the European Community as to whether it was ever intended that zero rating should apply to non-residential property and therefore whether the UK should have included the construction of industrial and commercial property under the zero rting provisions. A case is expected to be heard before the European Commission in September 1987 with a decision being reached in the following year.

Despite this the UK zero rating provisions apply equally to both residential and non residential property. The granting by a person "constructing" a new building on his own land of a "major interest" in that building or its site being zero rated (Group 8 Schedule 5 VATA 1983).

"Constructing" does not include converting, reconstructing (but see protected buildings – (f) below), altering or enlarging an existing building. Only new construction can be covered by zero rating. However, if the new building merely makes use of existing foundations or a single wall of an old building, Customs and Excise will accept that as new construction. If the building being constructed includes anymore of the previous building then it will be standard rated.

"Major interest" is the freehold interest or a lease which exceeds 21 years when granted (Section 48 VATA 1983). A major interest must be granted by the person who did the construction. Hence the buyer of a new building cannot zero-rate its subsequent sale, instead it will be an exempt supply.

A building need not be complete to constitute something that can be supplied at the zero rate. Custom's view is that the building must be constructed above foundation level for zero rating to apply.

A "site" may include:

(i) a reasonable plot of land, and
(ii) roads etc, forming part of a development and dedicated to a highway authority.

(e) Services

The granting, assignment or surrender of a major interest in land is a supply of goods under para 4 Schedule 2 VATA 1983. Anything which is not a supply of goods but which is done for consideration is a supply of services (Section 3 VATA 1983). Therefore Mr J. A. King's supply of grazing rights ws a supply of services as no major interest was granted.

Services in relation to land include the supply of construction (or demolition) services. These supplies must be distinguished from the final grant of the major interest in a constructed building. The supply of such services, other than those of any architect, surveyor etc, can be zero rated if they relate to the construction of a new building or civil engineering work or the demolition of a building or civil engineering work. The materials used and certain other goods installed in connection with the zero rated services can also be zero rated. However some goods installed are specifically excluded. A new building could be fitted out with all sorts of extras e.g. carpets, curtains, furniture etc. which could then be supplied as part of the overall zero-rated supply of a new building. However, Group 8 Schedule 5 VATA 1983 stops this possibility by zero-rating only the supply of "materials or builder's hardware, sanitary ware or other articles of a kind ordinarily installed by builders as fixtures" (e.g. fitted kitchen furniture, central heating and (with effect from 21 May 1987) carpets).

Services in relation to alterations are standard rated (as from 1 June 1984), together with repairs and maintenance.

(f) Rental accommodation including service flats

Following on from the principles established in (b) and (d) above, rental income from the lease of a building or a room in a building which exceeds 21 years ("major interest") is zero rated provided the landlord constructed the building. Otherwise the rent will be exempt. It should be noted that the inclusion of provisions for periodic rent reviews or for the termination of the lease within 21 years will not prevent a lease qualifying as a major interest. The essential requirement being that the lease is capable of exceeding 21 years.

Common services

Where flats or offices are let to several tenants it is not uncommon for the landlord to provide common services under the lease agreement e.g. heating and cleaning common parts. Such service charges if under an inclusive rental are not regarded as a supply of services separate from the rent. Instead they are regarded as part of the consideration for the grant to the tenants of their right to occupy the premises, and accordingly follow the VAT treatment applicable to the rent. If the rent is exempt then the landlord will have to absorb the input tax on the various expenses as he cannot pass it on to the tenants. However, if there is a separate service agreement then the supply of such common services will be standard rated.

If the landlord operates a common fund where tenants pay into the fund but no more than is necessary to meet the costs of maintaining the building, then such payments out of the fund are treated as disbursements by the landlord on behalf of the tenants. VAT will be borne on the proportion that applies to the underlying payments. The landlord will however be unable to recover the input tax as the fund does not belong to him. The tenants in turn cannot recover the input tax as the invoices are addressed to the fund administrator rather than to themselves.

Specific charges to tenants

Services supplied to individual tenants within their particular areas (rather than common areas) are regarded as separate from the grant of any right to occupy the premises. The rate of VAT follows the type of supply e.g. zero on heating and lighting, standard on cleaning. The rationale being that the tenant is receiving electricity etc. not services.

Service flats let short term

As noted in (b) above the provision of sleeping accommodation in a "similar establishment" is standard rated rather than exempt. From 1 November 1986 the meaning of "similar establishment" was extended to include furnished sleeping accommodation (with or without board facilities for the preparation of food) and which are heldout as being suitable for use by visitors or travellers.

(g) Protected buildings

A protected building is a listed building or a scheduled monument. Services in connection with all repair and maintenance and all alterations except "approved" alterations are standard rated. Architect fees etc. are always standard rated. "Approved" alterations are zero rated and cover all alterations to protected ecclesiastical buildings, and for other protected buildings for which "listed building" consent under the relevant legislation has been given.

The grant of a major interest in a substantially reconstructed building may be zero rated if only the original external walls remain or 60% of refurbishment costs (including materials) consist of zero rated approved alteration work (Group 8A Schedule 5 VATA 1983).

(h) Grouping

Two or more companies, but not individuals, who are resident in the UK may elect to be treated as a single group for VAT purposes if one of them controls the others, or one person, who may be an individual or a partnership as well as a company, controls all of them.

Where there is an election for group treatment all the companies in the group are treated as carrying on the same business with a consequence that any supply of goods or services by one company in the group to another company is disregarded for VAT purposes. This could be beneficial to the extent that charges which were being made to partly exempt group companies, or exempt supplies which are being made between group companies would be ignored under a group registration.

There are obviously accounting implications in this in that invoices to other copanies in the group have no VAT on them but that invoices to third parties must have VAT on if appropriate.

9 STAMP DUTY

Stamp duty was first imposed in 1694 during the reign of William and Mary. The forecast yield for 1985–86 is £1·1 billion which exceeds the yield from capital transfer tax (£760 m) and capital gains tax (£790 m).

Stamp duty is a tax on documents and not transactions and thus providing a transaction can be carried out without using documents no duty is payable. There is no stamp duty on moveable chattels, the ownership of which may pass with the property, because transfer may be by delivery and need not therefore be the subject of an instrument. The duty normally falls to be paid by the purchaser, it being in his interest to ensure that a document is validly stamped, as it cannot be produced as evidence in a court of law, to prove title for instance, unless it is duly stamped.

The other unusual feature of stamp duty is that it is not an assessed tax. The Inland Revenue wait for a document to be presented to be stamped and then the tax is paid. Accordingly, its collection costs are low in comparison with other taxes.

The duty is either charged at 1% (ad valrum) of the value of the transaction or is a fixed duty of £0·50p.

(a) *Sale of land*

In the case of the sale of land, the document requiring to be stamped is the conveyance, not the contract of sale. The rate is 1% and is applied to the consideration given subject to an exemption threshold of £30,000; on or, below which no duty is payable (Section 55 FA 1963).

(b) *Leases*

Where a new lease is created or agreed to be grnted the level of duty depends upon a combination of the length of the lease, the premium payable on the grant and the rent payable over its life.

Where a lease is granted for a premium the premium will attract a 1% duty, unless it does not exceed £30,000 and the rent does not exceed £300 per annum (Section 55 FA 1963).

Stamp duty is payable in respect of rent in accordance with the Table shown in Schedule 1 SA 1891. See Table 7.

10 DEVELOPMENT FINANCE AND TAX RELIEF

A developer who raises finance through loans or deep discount loans may be entitled to tax relief.

(a) *Loans*

A trading company is entitled to relief for interest paid to a UK resident where the loan ws obtained for the purposes of the trade. Interest paid is generally allowed against the profits for the year in which the interest was paid (Section 248 ICTA 1970).

(b) *Deep discount loans*

A deep discount security (DDS) is any redeemable loan stock, whether secured, or unsecured, issued by a company where the issue price is less than the amount payable on redemption by (Section 36 FA 84) and is either:

(i) more than 15% of the redemption amount, or

(ii) more than $\frac{1}{2}$% of the redemption amount per complete year between issue and redemption dates (so that if a 10 year bond is redeemable at 100, it will be a DDS if the issue price is less than 95).

The return to the lender can be in the form of regular interest payments plus an element of interest which is "rolled-up" until redemption. This rolled up interest element is the discount. Alternatively a DDS may be a "zero-coupon" stock where no interest is payable throughout its life with the lender obtaining his return wholly from the recovery of the initial discount, on the redemption of the DDS.

There is a beneficial tax treatment for the borrower in that the discount will be deducted as a charge on income as it accrues during the period from issue to redemption even though the discount does not have to be borne until redemption. Any interest actually payable on the DDS will be deductible in the normal way.

Example

A zero-coupon DDS is issued at £2,000 and redeemable after 10 years at £4,000 and offers the lender a redemption yield in maturity of 7·18% p.a. (i.e. the internal rate of return). The income element for each income period can be determined using the following formula:

$$\frac{A \times B}{100} - C$$

Where A = the issue price plus the income element of previous income periods

B = the yield to maturity

C = the amount of interest, if any, attributable to the income period

Using the above formula the income element for the first income period will be:

$$\frac{2,000 \times 7 \cdot 18}{100} - 0 = £144$$

(c) Finance leases

Finance leasing is basically a form of lending and the rental paid by the lessee effectively represents capital and interest. For all practical purposes, but not for legal or for tax purposes, the equipment is owned by the lessee to whom all the risks and rewards of ownership have been transferred. The market is a relatively recent one which was started by the accepting houses in the early 1970s. It experienced dramatic growth in the late 1970s and the early 1980s as the clearing banks moved in, partly as a means of avoiding credit control legislation.

Finance leasing is particularly attractive to banks and borrowers for tax reasons. The banks are able to defer payment of their tax liabilities through the purchase of leased assets which attract tax allowances and are able to pass on part of this benefit to the lessor in the form of reduced rentals. In addition, the banks have been able to achieve a higher return on funds employed in leasing than in conventional lending.

In contrast, many UK companies in recent years have had little or no mainstream corporation tax liability and were therefore unable to take advantage of the high first year allowances on buildings, plant and machinery. As already noted, the essence of a leasing transaction is that (a) the bank buys the plant and machinery and so obtains the benefit of the capital allowances which it can offset against its taxable profits, therefore deferring the payment of taxation, and (b) then passes on part of the benefit to the lessee by way of reduced interest charges. However, with the abolition of first year allowances (see Table 2), but not writing down allowances, the benefits are not so great as they were.

There are restrictions on the availability of capital allowances and care needs to be exercised in ensuring that not only the original cost of providing assets, both for the building and the plant and machinery in the building, is incurred by the right person. Again it is essential to ensure that additions and/or improvements are also borne by the right person.

11 GRANTS AND INCENTIVES FOR DEVELOPERS

In addition to the various tax reliefs available to developers, further government assistance is available through a large number of incentive schemes including various grants, soft loans, etc. There are now close to 300 UK and EEC grants and loans available to help industrial and agricultural development in the UK. Some of these grants are specifically aimed at property, such as urban development grants and derelict land reclamation grants. There are others aimed at capital projects, in particular manufacturing industries, which, for example, assist employment in those industries. Details of the current, more relevant to property, incentives available are contained in Appendix 1. The majority of schemes change frequently with regard to qualifying conditions, level of grant, etc., and further information can be obtained from the awarding departments and agencies about the individual incentives which fall within their responsibilities.

D. J. WESTCOTT

TABLE 1
CAPITAL GAINS TAX
Depreciation of leases

Years	Percentage	Years	Percentage
50 or more	100	25	81·100
49	99·657	24	79·622
48	99·289	23	78·055
47	98·902	22	76·399
46	98·490	21	74·635
45	98·059	20	72·770
44	97·595	19	70·791
43	97·107	18	68·697
42	96·593	17	66·470
41	96·041	16	64·116
40	95·457	15	61·617
39	94·842	14	58·971
38	94·189	13	56·167
37	93·497	12	53·191
36	92·761	11	50·038
35	91·981	10	46·695
34	91·156	9	43·154
33	90·280	8	39·399
32	89·354	7	35·414
31	88·371	6	31·195
30	87·330	5	26·722
29	86·226	4	21·983
28	85·053	3	16·959
27	83·816	2	11·629
26	82·496	1	5·983
		0	0

TABLE 2
CAPITAL ALLOWANCES

Since 1945 successive Governments have varied the rates from time to time. The most recent rates are set out below.

Industrial Buildings
Initial allowance: available on qualifying capital expenditure before 31 March 1986 as follows:

Date of expenditure	Initial allowance
Before 14 March 1984	75%
14 March 1984 – 31 March 1985	50%
1 April 1985 – 31 March 1986	25%
After 31 March 1986	Nil

Writing down allowance: available at a rate of 4% per annum (where building in use for a qualifying trade) for balance of expenditure.

Plant and Machinery
First year allowance: available on qualifying expenditure before 31 March 1986 as follows:

Date of expenditure	First year allowance
Before 14 March 1984	100%
14 March 1984 – 31 March 1985	75%
1 April 1985 – 31 March 1986	50%
After 31 March 1986	Nil

Writing down allowance: given at the rate of 25% per annum on a reducing balance basis on the residue of expenditure.

TABLE 3
ENTERPRISE ZONES

The following have been designated—

Enterprise zone designation order	Number	Coming into operation
The Lower Swansea Valley	SI 1981/757	11 June 1981
Corby	SI 1981/764	22 June 1981
Dudley	SI 1981/852	10 July 1981
Langthwaite Grange (Wakefield)	SI 1981/950	31 July 1981
Clydebank	SI 1981/975	3 August 1981
Salford Docks	SI 1981/1024	12 August 1981
Trafford Park	SI 1981/1025	12 August 1981
City of Glasgow	SI 1981/1069	18 August 1981
Gateshead	SI 1981/1070	25 August 1981
Newcastle	SI 1981/1071	25 August 1981
Speke (Liverpool)	SI 1981/1072	25 August 1981
Belfast	SR 1981/1309	21 October 1981
Hartlepool	SI 1981/1378	23 October 1981
Isle of Dogs	SI 1982/462	26 April 1982
Delyn	SI 1983/896	21 July 1983
Wellingborough	SI 1983/907	26 July 1983
Rotherham	SI 1983/1007	16 August 1983
Londonderry	SR & O 1983/ 226(NI)	13 September 1983
Scunthorpe (Normanby Ridge and Queensway	SI 1983/1304	23 September 1983
Dale Lane (Wakefield) and Kinsley (Wakefield)	SI 1983/1305	23 September 1983
Workington (Allerdale)	SI 1983/1331	4 October 1983
Invergordon	SI 1983/1359	7 October 1983
North West Kent	SI 1983/1452	31 October 1983
Middlesbrough (Britannia)	SI 1983/1473	8 November 1983
North-east Lancashire	SI 1983/1639	7 December 1983
Tayside (Arbroath)	SI 1983/1816	9 January 1984
Tayside (Dundee)	SI 1983/1817	9 January 1984
Telford	SI 1983/1852	13 January 1984
Glanford (Flixborough)	SI 1984/347	13 April 1984
Milford Haven Waterway (North Shore)	SI 1984/443	24 April 1984
Milford Haven Waterway (South shore)	SI 1984/444	24 April 1984
Dudley (Round Oak)	SI 1984/1403	3 October 1984
Lower Swansea Valley (No 2)	SI 1985/137	6 March 1985

TABLE 4
INHERITANCE TAX AND CAPITAL TRANSFER TAX

Rates of tax

(a) Transfers from 6 April 1985 to 17 March 1986

Portion of value		Tax	
		Rate	Cumulative tax
Over	Not over	per cent	at upper limit
£	£		£
Transfers on death			
0	67,000	Nil	Nil
67,000	89,000	30	6,600
89,000	122,000	35	18,150
122,000	155,000	40	31,350
155,000	194,000	45	48,900
194,000	243,000	50	73,400
243,000	299,000	55	104,200
299,000	—	60	—

The above rates apply to transfers made on or within 3 years preceding death. Lifetime transfers are taxed at half the death scale rates.

(b) (i) Transfers from 18 March 1986 to 16 March 1987

0	71,000	Nil	Nil
71,000	95,000	30	7,200
95,000	129,000	35	19,100
129,000	164,000	40	33,100
164,000	206,000	45	52,000
206,000	257,000	50	77,500
257,000	317,000	55	110,500
317,000	—	60	—

(ii) Transfers from 17 March 1987

0	90,000	Nil	Nil
90,000	140,000	30	15,000
140,000	220,000	40	47,000
220,000	330,000	50	102,000
330,000	—	60	—

The above rates apply to transfers made on or within 3 years preceding death. Reduced rates apply to transfers made more than 3 years but less than 7 years preceding death. The reduced rate is expressed as a percentage of the full charge at death rates as follows:

Years between gift and death	Percentage of full charge at death rates
3–4	80%
4–5	60%
5–6	40%
6–7	20%

TABLE 4 (continued)

Chargeable lifetime transfers are taxed at half the death scale rates.

Main Exemptions	£
Transfers on death:	
To UK domiciled spouse	No limit
Charities	No limit
Chargeable transfers:	
To spouse	As above
Annual exemption per donor	3,000
Small gifts – annual amount per donee	
(but not available to cover part of a larger gift)	250
Normal expenditure out of income	Varies
Wedding gifts;	
– to child of donor	5,000
– to grandchild (or remoter issue) of donor	2,500
– to others	1,000
Charities	No limit

TABLE 5
RATES OF CORPORATION TAX

Year beginning 1 April	Full rate	Small companies rates
1982	52%	38%
1983	50%	30%
1984	45%	30%
1985	40%	30%
1986	35%	29%
1987	35%	27%

Capital gains are effectively taxed at 35% or (if small companies rate) 27% after indexation.

SMALL COMPANIES RATE – MARGINAL RELIEF
The small companies rate applies where a company's profits exceed £100,000 but are less than £500,000. The effective marginal rates for financial years 1985, 1986, and 1987 are as follows:

Financial year	Statutory fraction	Effective marginal rate
1985	1/40	$42\frac{1}{2}$%
1986	3/200	$36\frac{1}{2}$%
1987	1/50	37%

Where there are associated companies, which includes those overseas, the limits are reduced by dividing them by one plus the number of associated companies carrying on a business.

TABLE 6
RATES OF INCOME TAX

Year ended 5 April 1987
Basic and higher rates:

Over £	Not over £	Rate per cent	Cumulative tax at upper limit £
0	17,200	29 (Basic rate)	4,988
17,200	20,200	40	6,188
20,200	25,400	45	8,528
25,400	33,300	50	12,478
33,300	41,200	55	16,823
41,200	—	60	—

Year ended 5 April 1988
Basic and higher rates:

0	17,900	27 (Basic rate)	4,833
17,900	20,400	40	5,833
20,400	25,400	45	8,083
25,400	33,300	50	12,033
33,300	41,200	55	16,378
41,200	—	60	—

Currently there is no investment income surcharge.

TABLE 7
STAMP DUTY: RATES OF DUTY APPLICABLE TO RENTS FROM PROPERTY LEASES

Rent	If the term does not exceed 7 years or is indefinite £p	If the term exceeds 7 years but does not exceed 35 years £p	If the term exceeds 35 years but does not exceed 100 years £p	If the term exceeds 100 years £p
Not exceeding £5 per annum	Nil	0·10	0·60	1·20
Exceeding £5 and not exceeding £10	Nil	0·20	1·20	2·40
Exceeding £10 and not exceeding £15	Nil	0·30	1·80	3·60
Exceeding £15 and not exceeding £20	Nil	0·40	2·40	4·80
Exceeding £20 and not exceeding £25	Nil	0·50	3·00	6·00
Exceeding £25 and not exceeding £50	Nil	1·00	6·00	12·00
Exceeding £50 and not exceeding £75	Nil	1·50	9·00	18·00
Exceeding £75 and not exceeding £100	Nil	2·00	12·00	24·00
Exceeding £100 and not exceeding £150	Nil	3·00	18·00	36·00
Exceeding £150 and not exceeding £200	Nil	4·00	24·00	48·00
Exceeding £200 and not exceeding £250	Nil	5·00	30·00	60·00
Exceeding £250 and not exceeding £300	Nil	6·00	36·00	72·00
Exceeding £300 and not exceeding £350	Nil	7·00	42·00	84·00
Exceeding £350 and not exceeding £400	Nil	8·00	48·00	96·00
Exceeding £400 and not exceeding £450	Nil	9·00	54·00	108·00
Exceeding £450 and not exceeding £500	Nil	10·00	60·00	120·00
Exceeding £500: for every £50 or fraction of £50	0·50	1·00	6·00	12·0

Valuation and Development Appraisal

TABLE 8
CAPITAL GAINS TAX

The values of the retail prices index for March 1982 and subsequent months are

	1982	1983	1984	1985	1986	1987
January	—	325·9	342·6	359·8	379·7	394·5
February	—	327·3	344·0	362·7	381·1	396·1
March	313·4	327·9	345·1	366·1	381·6	
April	319·7	332·5	349·7	373·9	385·3	
May	322·0	333·9	351·0	375·6	386·0	
June	322·9	334·7	351·9	376·4	385·8	
July	323·0	336·5	351·5	375·7	384·7	
August	323·1	338·0	354·8	376·7	385·9	
September	322·9	339·5	355·5	376·5	387·8	
October	324·5	340·7	357·7	377·1	388·4	
November	326·1	341·9	358·8	378·4	391·7	
December	325·5	342·8	358·5	378·9	393·0	

TABLE 9
VAT

The limits for VAT registration (from 17 March 1987) are:

Future turnover:

Registration is required where there are reasonable grounds for believing that the value of taxable supplies for the next 12 months will exceed £21,300.

Past turnover:

A person must notify HM Customs and Excise if the value of taxable supplies has exceeded £7,250 in preceding quarter, or £21,300 in the preceding year. A person whose past quarter's value of taxable supplies has exceeded £7,250 may nevertheless seek not to be registered if there are grounds for believing that the annual value of taxable supplies will not exceed £21,300.

Standard rate (from 18 June 1979)   15%

GLOSSARY OF TERMS

Assignment

Generally, a transfer of property, e.g. of a lease, or mortgage.

Balancing allowance/charge

A balancing adjustment which ensures that the total allowances given equal the net cost of providing the asset and would occur on sale/disposal of that asset.

Close company

The principal definition of a close company is a company which is resident in the UK and under the control of;

 (i) 5 or fewer participators, or
(ii) the directors

A participator is any person who has any share or interest in the capital or income of the company.

Fixture

Plant or machinery which is so installed or otherwise fixed in or to a building so as to become part of that building.

Freehold

An interest in land which amounts to full ownership of the land.

Income period (DDS)

An income period means;

(a) in the case of an interest bearing security, any period to which an interest payment is attributable (so that, if interest is payable at six monthly intervals, each six months from issue to redemption represents an income period).
(b) in the case of a non-interest bearing security, each period of 12 months beginning with the issue date.

Indexation allowance

An allowance which is given as a deduction from the gross capital gain in computing the liability to capital gains tax. It is based on the fractional change in the retail price index between the month of disposal and month of acquisition, and is applied to the base cost of the asset.

Initial/first year allowance

A capital allowance which is given for the chargeable period related to the incurring of the expenditure.

Land

ICTA 1970 Section 488 "references to the land include references to all or any part of the land, and 'land' includes buildings, and any estate or interest in land or buildings".

Lease

A contract by which the owner of a building or land allows another to use it for a specified time, usually in return for payment.

Partial exemption (VAT)

Partial exemption will result in a restriction being placed on the amount of recoverable input tax.

Rules to 31 March 1987:

Standard method: a business will become partially exempt when its exempt supplies as a proportion of its total supplies (standard, zero, and exempt) are above certain de-minimis levels. Only that input tax attributable to taxable supplies as a proportion of total supplies will be recoverable.

The de-minimis limit below which partial exemption will not apply (i.e. treated as fully taxable) is where exempt outputs are less than 1% of the total annual outputs (5% up to 1 April 1984).

Rules introduced from 1 April 1987:

Standard method: Input tax must be identified and attributed to the greatest possible extent between taxable and exempt supplies. The remaining input tax which cannot be duly attributed is to be apportioned by reference to the use made of the goods and services to which it relates. Only that input tax attributable to taxable supplies will be recoverable.

The di-minimis limits below which partial exemption will not apply (i.e. treated as fully taxable) is where input tax attributable to exempt supplies amounts to less than any of the following:

(i) £100 per month on average;
(ii) both £250 per month on average and 50% of all input tax;
(iii) both £500 per month on average and 25% of all input tax.

For group registrations the provisions will apply to the group as a whole.

Relevant income

All income other than trading income is relevant income. The relevant income of a close company can be apportioned amongst the shareholders and regarded as their income for tax assessment purposes.

Relevant interest

The interest in a building to which the person who incurred the expenditure on its construction was entitled to when he incurred that expenditure. If the freeholder incurs expenditure on the erection of a building, the freehold is the relevant interest in relation to that expenditure. If a leaseholder incurs the expenditure, his leasehold interest is the relevant interest in relation to his expenditure.

Small companies rate

A reduced rate of corporation tax of 27% applies to the "income" of companies with "profits" of £100,000 or less.

Income: Profits chargeable to corporation tax, including chargeable capital gains.

Profits: Profits chargeable to corporation tax plus dividend income (except dividends from companies within the same group).

Known as the small companies rate, the reduced rate is applicable to companies with small profits, as explained above, irrespective of the turnover or net assets of the company.

Writing down allowance

A capital allowance which may be claimed for each chargeable period until the residue of expenditure has been reduced to nil.

BIBLIOGRAPHY

Accountancy Age Journal	"Community charge is a poll tax in disguise" C. Holtham 20.3.86
Chartac Taxation Guide	Handbook on Taxation of land J. G. Harrison

Financial Times	"Simple matter of a stamp"
	M. Gammie 30.11.85
	"Uniformity sought to prevent
	distortion by non-domestic rate"
	29.11.86
Price Waterhouse	Capital Gains Tax
	Corporate Earnings
	Taxation of Land
	Tax Memorandum "Landlords fixtures:
	proposed legislation", 20.2.85
	The Pocket Tax Book 1986/87
	The UK Finance Act 1984
	The UK Finance Act 1985
	The UK Finance Act 1986
	Value Added Tax
Simon's Taxes	3rd Edition
Tax Digest	Industrial Buildings Allowances
	P. Newbold
	Close Companies
	F. Smith
Taxation Journal	"Know your rate rights"
	M. Bull 20.4.85
	"Ships and fixtures"
	A. Sellwood 31.3.85
	"Reform of business rates"
	C. Hedley 11.10.85
	"Enterprise Zones"
	B. Williams 14.3.86
Taxation of land transactions	A. R. Mellows
Taxation Practitioner Journal	"Land and VAT"
	J. Whiting 12.84
Tolleys Income Tax 1985/86	
Tolleys Practical Tax	"A new finance opportunity"
	B. Armitage 28.11.84
	"Capital allowances on fixtures"
	C. Cox 30.1.85
	"Capital allowances for fixtures"
	T. Smith 28.8.85
	Budget Summary 1986
Tolleys Tax Planning 1986	
Tolleys Value Added Tax	

Grants, Loans and Assistance for Development

General Investment/Development

1 General investment support for major projects.
2 Urban development grant.
3 Urban regeneration grant.
4 COSIRA: Financial assistance to small businesses.
5 Welsh development agency; Loans in rural areas.
6 Local enterprise grants for urban projects. }Scotland
7 LEDU: Selective assistance for small firms
8 Standard capital grants scheme.
9 Urban development grant (Northern Ireland) } Northern Ireland

Land Reclamation/Urban Renewal

10 Derelict land reclamation grants (England).
11 Derelict land reclamation grants (Wales).
12 Inner Urban Areas Act 1978: Sections 2, 4, 5, 6, 9 assistance.

Countryside Development

13 Conservation and recreation in the countryside.
14 Grants for landscape conservation work.
15 Countryside grants.
16 Countryside research and development projects. }Scotland

Architectural Heritage/Conservation

17 EC Pilot conservation projects (architectural heritage).
18 Historic buildings (England): Conservation grants.
19 Historic buildings (England): Repair grants.
20 Historic buildings (Scotland): Conservation area grants.
21 Historic buildings (Scotland): Building repair grants.
22 Historic buildings (Wales): Repair/conservation grants.

1 GENERAL INVESTMENT SUPPORT FOR MAJOR PROJECTS

(Industrial Development Act 1982: Section 8)

Assistance is available, normally in the form of a grant, for major capital investment projects which are in the national interest.

Eligible project costs are principally those for new fixed capital investment in buldings and plant and machinery.

Projects should normally involve new investment of at least £500,000 including working capital and ancillary costs directly associated with the project.

The amount of assistance is negotiated on a case by case basis and is the minimum necessary to bring about the additional benefits associated with the project. Assistance is usually in the form of a grant and is taxable as a trading receipt. There is no maximum or minimum assistance level but over recent years grants have averaged around 10%.

Application must be made and approval given before the start of the project.

Further information from:
Department of Trade and Industry
Industrial Financial Appraisal Division
Room 527
Bridge House
89 Eccleston Square
London
SW1V 1PT
Telephone: (01) 212 4150

2 URBAN DEVELOPMENT GRANT (ENGLAND AND WALES)

A flexible scheme for providing financial assistance for urban development projects in England and Wales which will promote the economic and physical regeneration of run-down urban areas by encouraging private investment which would not otherwise take place in such areas and which will strengthen the local economy and bring land and buildings back into use. Almost any type or size of project is eligible provided that it meets these objectives. Assistance is normally in the form of a capital grant or a loan or a combination of both.

There is no restriction on the size of scheme which can be put forward, but the private sector contribution is expected to be significant in relation to total project costs and the project must make a demonstrable contribution to meeting the special social needs of the inner urban areas.

In England, priority is given to projects in the areas of the 57 authorities invited to submit inner area programmes. (See item 11 below).

Further information from:

(England)	(Wales)
Department of the Environment	Welsh Office
Inner Cities Division 1	Cathays Park
Room P2/127	Cardiff
2 Marsham Street	CF1 3NQ
London	
SW1P 3EB	

Telephone: (01) 212 5153 or 5281   Telephone: (0222) 825111

3 URBAN REGENERATION GRANT (ENGLAND)

The purpose of Urban Regeneration Grant is to promote the economic and physical regeneration of older urban areas affected by industrial change, by enabling the private sector to redevelop large sites and refurbish large groups of buildings, and by encouraging private investment in such areas. It differs from UDG by being directed to large sites.

URG is available in the form of an outright grant, a loan, or a repayable grant, depending on the type of assistance needed. It can bridge the gap between the cost of the development and its value on completion, or it can provide temporary finance before any income has been received from the development. URG is only available for schemes which bring about substantial private investment. Unlike UDGs it is paid direct by the Department to the firm or developer. It is not available for schemes which appear profitable and feasible without a contribution from the government.

Priority is given to schemes within urban areas which have suffered severe losses in employment in traditional industries and where there are substantial amounts of derelict or disused industrial or commercial property.

Further information from:
Department of the Environment,
Inner Cities Division 1
Room P2/126
2 Marsham Street
London
SW1P 3EB

Telephone: (01) 212 4077

4 COSIRA: FINANCIAL ASSISTANCE TO SMALL BUSINESSES

Financial assistance is available in the form of loans for new buildings, conversions and adaptions, plant and equipment and working capital, to small businesses in rural areas and country towns in England. The loan fund is used to top up finance from the private sector.

Eligible expenditure for building loans is the acquisition of buildings on freehold or long lease sites for business purposes; acquisitions of freehold or long lease sites, with or without buildings with a view to their improvement or development; and erection of new, or improvement, adaption or extension of existing buildings on land already owned or occupied on long lease, by the applicant.

Minimum size of loan in respect of buildings is £750. The maximum loan available to any one applicant at any time is normally £75,000. Rates of interest are broadly commercial with a 3% concession for job creation projects in the Rural Development Areas.

Further information from:
Councils for Small Industries in Rural Areas
141 Castle Street
Salisbury
Wiltshire
SP1 3TP
Telephone: (0722) 336255

5 WELSH DEVELOPMENT AGENCY: LOANS IN RURAL AREAS

Funds are available at reduced rates of interest for small businesses in rural locations in Wales which create new jobs. The loans are available mainly towards the purchase of buildings, equipment, or working capital. They are meant for new businesses starting up, and embryonic small businesses.

Eligible expenditure for building loans covers: the acquisition, adaptation, construction or renovation of buildings on freehold or long leasehold sites.

Loans are at a fixed rate of interest, approximately 3% below current commercial lending rates. A subsidised loan will not exceed 50% of the cost of the project or, in the case of an existing business, will no more than double existing finance.

Available to eligible businesses employing fewer than 10 people. Loans are available from £1,000 to £7,000. One new job must be created for each loan awarded.

Further information from:
Investment Department
Welsh Development Agency
Pearl House
Greyfriars Road
Cardiff
CF1 3XX
Telephone: (0222) 32955

6 LOCAL ENTERPRISE GRANTS FOR URBAN PROJECTS (SCOTLAND)

Financial assistance is available to promote economic development in urban areas of Scotland by stimulating private enterprise and investment activity that would not otherwise have occurred. Projects may be of any type – industrial, commercial, recreational or residential. Finance is tailored to the project and may take the form of a direct non-refundable subsidy, a low interest loan or some other suitable form.

Assistance is available in all urban areas of Scotland where there is an economic need. An urban area is broadly defined as a community of 15,000 people or more.

Further information from:
Colin Morris
Project Manager
LEG-UP
Scottish Development Agency
120 Bothwell Street
Glasgow
G2 7JP
Telephone: (041) 248 2700

7 LEDU: SELECTIVE ASSISTANCE FOR SMALL FIRMS

A financial "package" of assistance available to small manufacturing and service sector firms in Northern Ireland putting forward projects which will provide additional employment. The package consists of a variety of grants, loans and loan guarantees.

To be eligible for support, projects must provide additional employment in Northern Ireland, and not simply the transfer of existing jobs from one business to another.

LEDU offers a variety of financial aids for different purposes and includes capital grants for new buildings, extensions and renovations to existing buildings in the range of 20–50% depending on need and location:

Further information from:
Local Enterprise Development Unit
LEDU House
Upper Galwally
Belfast
BT8 4TB

Telephone: (0232) 691031 or Freephone LEDU

8 STANDARD CAPITAL GRANTS SCHEME

An item-related capital grant available to firms in Northern Ireland in the manufacturing sector. New buildings or previously unoccupied existing buildings used for most manufacturing processes are eligible items of expenditure.

To qualify for a grant, expenditure on individual buildings must exceed £5,000. The rate of award is a fixed 20% of eligible expenditure up to a maximum grant of £4 million paid to any one company in any single financial year. Payments of grants on eligible expenditure in excess of £5 million are subject to a cost per job limit of £15,000 for each job created by the grant-aided project. The grant is not subject to tax in any way. It is neither treated for tax purposes as an income receipt nor does it need to be deducted from the cost of assets for depreciation purposes.

Further information from:
Department of Economic Development
Aids to Industry Branch
22 Donegall Street
Belfast
BT1 2EP

Telephone: (0232) 221200

9 URBAN DEVELOPMENT GRANT (NORTHERN IRELAND)

A discretionary grant aimed at assisting economic development and revitalization in the inner city and enterprise zone areas of Belfast and Londonderry by stimulating private enterprise and investment activity that would not otherwise have occurred. UDG is intended to enable developers to bridge the funding gap which frequently exists because of the higher costs or lower rates of return on inner city projects. Projects eligible for assistance may be in respect of commercial developments, private housing, feasibility studies and non-commercial environmental/amenity schemes.

Eligible expenditure, on which financial need is assessed, covers total project costs including, acquisitions of land and premises, demolition costs, new building costs, fees, financing costs and other costs incurred in carrying out the project.

Further information from:
Department of the Environment for Northern Ireland
Room 204
Clarendon House
9/21 Aderlaide Street
Belfast
BT2 8NR
Telephone: (0232) 242486

10 DERELICT LAND RECLAMATION GRANTS (ENGLAND)

Central Government grants are available in England for the reclamation of derelict land both to local authorities and to the non-local authority sector for the purpose of bringing it into beneficial use or improving its appearance. A grant can be paid towards the works which the Department is satisfied are required primarily for the purpose of reclamation; as a general guide this would include all costs necessary to bring the land to the equivalent of a green field site. In the case of the local authority scheme these can include the acquisition of land and site surveys and investigations, whether or not reclamation works are subsequently carried out.

In the case of the non-local authority scheme, the grant is on a more restricted basis than for local authorities. It is payable on the net loss incurred by the landowner in carrying out the reclamation works only, i.e. the cost of reclamation less the betterment in the value of the land. Land acquisition, infrastructure, administration expenses or schemes for neglected or unsightly land are not eligible. Grant is paid at the rate of 80% of the net loss in the assisted areas and in designated derelict land clearance areas and at 50% elsewhere.

Further information from:
Department of the Environment
Inner Cities Directorate 4
P2/109
2 Marsham Street
London
SW1P 3EB

Telephone: (01) 212 8172

11 DERELICT LAND RECLAMATION GRANTS (WALES)

Grants are available to the local authority sector in respect of the improvement of derelict, neglected or unsightly land, and the non-local authority sector in respect of the reclamation of derelict land. The objective is to bring land into use or improve its appearance.

In the case of local authority schemes, eligible expenditure includes the cost of acquisitions of land required for a project, including the vendor's legal and valuation fees directly related to the purchase and works such as site investigation and ground exploration, site survey, demolition etc.

In the case of non-local authority projects, eligible expenditure includes the cost of reclamation works necessary to bring the site to a greenfield state and approved costs incurred in carrying out a survey of derelict land but only where a project of reclamation follows.

Further information from:
Land Reclamation Department
Welsh Development Agency
Treforest Industrial Estate
Pontypridd
Mid Glamorgan
CF37 5YT

Telephone: (044 385) 2666

12 INNER URBAN AREAS ACT 1978

Section 2 Assistance

Long term loans at commercial rates of interest are available to industry and commerce in designated districts for the acquisition of land or the carrying out of works on land. There is no restriction on the use to which the land and works may be put but this assistance is mainly intended to provide long-term finance for industrial and commercial projects for which finance cannot readily be obtained from other sources.

Section 4, 5, 6 Assistance

Loans or grants available to firms for environmental improvement and the provision of means of access and other facilities and grants avalable for the conversion, improvement, modification or extension of industrial or commercial buildings or the conversion of other buildings into industrial or commercial buildings. These loans and grants are only available within Improvement Areas declared by district authorities designated under the Inner Urban Areas Act 1978.

Section 9 Assistance

Concessionary loans available to firms in "Special Areas" designated under the Inner Urban Areas Act 1978, for site clearance works and for the servicing of sites. Qualifying activities include site preparation works, installation of services and provision of access roads.

Further information from:
The appropriate local authority or:
Department of the Environment
Inner Cities Directorate
2 Marsham Street
London
SW1P 3EB
Telephone: (01) 212 4077

The following authorities in England have been invited to prepare inner area programmes and it is in these areas that IUAA assistance may be available:

Barnsley	Liverpool
Birmingham	Manchester
Blackburn	Middlesbrough
Bolton	Newcastle
Bradford	Newham
Brent	North Tyneside
Bristol	Nottingham
Burnley	Oldham
Coventry	Plymouth
Derby	Preston
Doncaster	Rochdale
Dudley	Rotherham
Gateshead	St Helens
Greenwich	Salford
Hackney	Sandwell
Halton	Sefton
Hammersmith & Fulham	Sheffield
Haringey	South Tyneside
Hartlepool	Southwark
Islington	Stockton
Kensington & Chelsea	Sunderland
Kingston-upon-Hull	Tower Hamlets
Kirklees	Walsall
Knowsley	Wandsworth
Lambeth	Wigan
Langbaurgh	Wirral
Leeds	Wolverhampton
Leicester	Wrekin
Lewisham	

13 CONSERVATION AND RECREATION IN THE COUNTRYSIDE

Grants are available to private bodies and individuals, and voluntary bodies for projects which lead to the conservation and enhancement of the natural beauty of the countryside of England and Wales and the provision and improvement of facilities for the enjoyment of the countryside and for open-air recreation.

Support is only given to projects (or parts of projects) which benefit the general public. Projects which are only of benefit to organised sectors of the community (such as members of a club) are not normally eligible. Grants may also be awarded to voluntary bodies for the acquisition of land for access and/or conservation.

Development grants are also available for voluntary bodies who wish to further their work in line with the Commission's aims and priorities.

Eligible expenditure is normally the capital cost of the project and excludes any running or maintenance costs. Where revenue earning projects are grant-aided, the capital cost is offset by the District Valuer's estimate of income.

Further information from:

(England)
Countryside Commission
John Dower House
Crescent Place
Cheltenham
Gloucestershire
GL50 3RA

Telephone: (0242) 521381

(Wales)
Countryside Commission
Ladywell House
Newtown
Powys
SY16 1RD

Telephone: (0686) 26799

14 LANDSCAPE CONSERVATION WORK

Grants are available to farmers, landowners and managers towards the cost of conserving important landscape features which are already established in the countryside, or creating new ones. The scheme incorporates the former Grants for Amenity Tree Planting and Management Scheme.

To receive support the work to be undertaken must form part of a whole farm conservation project and not be merely a one-off task.

The Countryside Commission only consider grant-aiding a project after the applicant has received advice on the project from a Countryside Adviser (see 12) or from an equivalent acceptable source (e.g. amenity tree planting local authority agent).

The landscape conservation work which is eligible for assistance is considered under three categories:

- planting of trees and small woods using broadleaved species that are suitable for the locality and its soil and weather conditions;
- conservation of existing trees which includes: managing small woods by coppicing, selective felling, clearing, drainage, fencing and replanting and fencing to encourage natural regeneration; pollarding riparian willows and alders, particularly projects which include a substantial number of trees within a single land ownership or involving multiple land ownership within a single riparian zone; approved tree-surgery to extend the life of visually important single trees or groups of trees;
- conservation of other important landscape features; for example: pond works (e.g. desilting, fencing and/or vegetation management); restoration or rejuvenation of ancient hedgerows visually important in the landscape, green lanes with public access, visually important hedgebanks in western Britain and visually important stone walls in upland, hill or wold areas. Traditional hedgelaying or coppicing is encouraged as well as the use of local or original stone for walling.

Further information from:

(England)
Countryside Commission
John Dower House
Crescent Place
Cheltenham
Gloucestershire
GL50 3RA

Telephone: (0242) 21381

(Wales)
Countryside Commission
8 Broad Street
Newtown
Powys
SY16 2LU

Telephone: (0686) 26799

15 COUNTRYSIDE GRANTS TO BODIES OTHER THAN LOCAL AUTHORITIES

Grants may be available to any individual or organisation providing, developing or improving facilities for enjoyment of the

Scottish Countryside or conserving or enhancing the natural beauty and amenity of the countryside.

Eligible expenditure is normally the capital cost of the project and excludes any running or maintenance costs. Eligible items include the provision of picnic areas, viewpoint indicators, car park and lavatories, public footpaths and nature trails, crofter's caravan sites, signposting and waymarking, interpretative schemes, landscape conservation, ranger services, hostels and other low cost accommodation.

COUNTRYSIDE GRANTS TO LOCAL AUTHORITIES

Grants are available to local authorities in Scotland for projects which improve opportunities for the public to enjoy the Scottish Countryside and projects designed to conserve or enhance its appearance.

Eligible costs are as follows: the acquisition of land, or rights over land (including land covered by water); the erection or adaption of buildings; landscaping, including tree planting; the improvement of facilities for the enjoyment of waterways (including lochs, reservoirs, rivers and canals); the provision of car parks, picnic sites, interpretative facilities, footpaths or other means of access (including the cost of materials); the provision of public lavatories; the provision of camping and caravan sites for tourists and other accommodation, including facilities for the provision of meals and refreshments; the provision of litter bins or other equipment for the disposal of litter; other works designed to preserve or enhance the natural beauty of the countryside, such as conservation of natural resources (e.g. dune restoration scheme). Payment of compensation may also be eligible for support. Current expenditure eligible for support is the cost of providing ranger services, management and operational staff costs in regional parks, litter collection costs in country parks, the costs of access agreements, and maintenance costs of paths forming part of approved long distance routes.

Reasonable professional fees to outside consultants incurred in the design and execution of the project are also eligible for support.

Further information from:
Countryside Commission for Scotland
Battleby
Redgorton
Perth PH1 3EW
Telephone: (0738) 27921

16 COUNTRYSIDE RESEARCH AND DEVELOPMENT PROJECTS

The Countryside Commission for Scotland may enter into joint contracts with individuals, organisations or other authorities, thus jointly funding research and/or development projects which are likely to result in the provision, development or improvement of facilities for the enjoyment of the Scottish Countryside and/or the conservation and enhancement of its natural beauty and amenity.

The research and/or development project should be likely to lead to some immediately practical benefit in terms of subsequent action, better quality of advice, or the structured setting of ideas about how an area could be developed for public enjoyment of the countryside. Research and development projects related to informing and educating persons in the proper use of, and behaviour in, the countryside and in assisting in the provision of publicity and information services relating to the countryside can also be considered. The Commission also has a longer term review function in respect of its own aims and purposes which is undertaken within the framework of research and development activities.

Eligible costs are: the salaries of project staff; their accommodation and travel expenses; the costs of works on the ground which are of an experimental or small scale demonstration nature; and publications directly relating to the project.

Further information from:
Countryside Commission for Scotland
Battleby
Redgorton
Perth PH1 3EW
Telephone: (0738) 27921

17 EC: PILOT CONSERVATION PROJECTS

Financial assistance is available in the form of a grant for pilot projects to conserve the Community's architectural heritage. Support is confined to monuments and sites of European renown which illustrate some aspect of the national or regional architectural heritage of the Community by reason of their artistic value or historical interest in bearing witness to the living and working conditions of a given section of the population. Funding of 500,000 ECUs has been made available under this programme for 1986.

Calls for proposals in relation to the programme are published from time to time in the Official Journal of the European Communities.

To be eligible for a grant, the applicant must receive a subsidy from another public organisation at least equivalent to the Commission grant.

The public must have access to the monument or site once work has been completed.

The applicant must be agreeable to the implementation of the project being monitored.

Eligible expenditure covers the total approved costs of the project.

Further information from:

(England)
English Heritage
Historic Buildings and Monuments
   Commission
2 Marsham Street
London SW1P 3EB

Telephone: (01) 734 6010

(Wales)
Welsh Office
CADW
New Crown Building
Cathays Park
Cardiff CP1 3NQ

Telephone: (0222) 825111

(Scotland)
Scottish Development Department
20 Brandon Street
Edinburgh EH3 5DX

Telephone: (031) 556 8400
and ask for the Historic
Building Division

(Northern Ireland)
Historic Monuments and Buildings Branch
Department of the Environment for Northern Ireland
1 Connsbrook Avenue
Belfast BT4 1EH

Telephone: (0232) 653251

18 HISTORIC BUILDINGS (ENGLAND): CONSERVATION GRANTS

Under Section 10 of the Town and Country Planning (Amendment) Act 1972 (as amended by the Local Government, Planning and Land Act 1980) grants are available in England towards expenditure which will make a significant contribution towards preserving or enhancing the character or appearance of areas designated as conservation areas by local planning authorities. It should be noted, however, that funds available for these grants are limited and only certain types of project will be considered.

The type of projects likely to be acceptable for grant-aid include the following: works to a building in a conservation area of particular architectural or historic interest for which the local authority has been invited by the Commission to submit a programme of conservation work; where there is a town scheme in the conservation area concerned (in which the Commission will provide matching grants towards the cost of repairs to buildings included in a town scheme administered by a local authority); a conservation project (e.g. the restoration of buildings in a particular square, terrace, street or village). Where construction work is undertaken by a group of private owners, individual grants sought could be for relatively small sums provided that they are part of a scheme.

The repair of buildings which have been the subject of a notice under section 101 or 115 of the Town and Country Planning Act 1971 will also be considered for grant-aid especially if they have been acquired by a local preservation trust in order to preserve them.

Applicants must be capable of carrying out the scheme which

they are putting forward for approval and be prepared to demonstrate that they can do so. In financing any project, the fullest use should be made of all existing grants, gifts, voluntary contributions, income from sales and leases, etc.

Grants will not normally be offered for properties purchased within the last four years unless the purchase has been made for the express purpose of securing the restoration of the building (e.g. purchase by a preservation trust, local authority or housing association). If the building has been empty for some time and/or is in a deteriorating condition, especially if the local authority have encouraged an applicant to acquire it, grant-aid may be possible, but each case is considered on its merits.

Grants will not normally be given to commercial concerns whose financial resources appear (after examination of their last published annual balance sheet) adequate to meet the expenditure themselves.

Eligible expenditure normally includes structural repairs to the fabric of the building; repairs using natural or traditional materials; restoration of features of historical or architectural interest (e.g. door cases, windows, cornices and balconies). Grant-aid is not available for normal maintenance work or for painting and decorating.

Expenditure on professional services (e.g. architect's fees) will qualify for grant.

Further information from:
Historic Buildings & Monuments Commission for England
25 Savile Row
London W1X 2BT

Telephone: (01) 734-6010

19 HISTORIC BUILDINGS (ENGLAND): REPAIR GRANTS

Under the National Heritage Act 1983 grants are available in England towards the cost of structural repairs to buildings, including religious buildings, of outstanding historic or architectural interest. Grants are also available for the repair or maintenance of any objects (pictures, furniture, fittings, etc.) ordinarily kept in any such buildings provided these are also of outstanding interest and have a long association with the building in question.

It should be noted that the funds for grants are limited so that, even among outstanding buildings, financial help can be given only where it is most urgently needed.

ELIGIBLE EXPENDITURE

Eligible expenditure covers the costs of structural repairs (e.g. re-roofing, dry-rot). Alterations, improvements, redecoration (except where made necessary by the structural repairs), minor repairs or maintenance are not eligible.

In the case of the non-local authority sector, an allowance for professional fees and expenses will be made in the calculation on which the grant offer is based.

Further information from:
Historic Buildings & Monuments Commission for England
25 Savile Row
London W1X 2BT
Telephone: (01) 734-6010

20 HISTORIC BUILDINGS (SCOTLAND): CONSERVATION AREA GRANTS

Under Section 10 of the Town and Country Planning (Amendment) Act, 1972, grants are available in Scotland towards the cost of preserving or enhancing the character or appearance of designated conservation areas which the Secretary of State considers to be of outstanding architectural or historic interest.

Applications should be submitted before any detailed scheme of work is drawn up.

Works to the exterior of the buildings are eligible for grant consideration.

Types of work eligible for grant purposes include: environmental improvement; the repair and conversion of buildings not qualifying for other forms of grant; the demolition of unsightly structures; works not involving repairs to buildings (e.g. amenity street lighting, tree planting, landscaping). Expenditure on professional services and VAT could also qualify in appropriate circumstances.

Further information from:
Scottish Development Department, Historic Buildings Division
20 Brandon Street, Edinburgh EH3 5DX
Telephone: (031) 556-8400, and ask for the Historic Buildings Division

21 HISTORIC BUILDINGS (SCOTLAND): BUILDING REPAIR GRANTS

Under the Historic Buildings and Ancient Monuments Act 1953, grants are available in Scotland towards the cost of repair or maintenance of buildings of outstanding architectural or historic interest. It should be noted that since comparatively few of the statutory listed buildings qualify as "outstanding" the scope of these grants is limited.

Applications should be submitted before any detailed scheme of work is drawn up.

Before considering applications in detail, the Historic Buildings Council must decide that the building is of outstanding architectural or historic importance and that public funds are necessary for the proposed project to go ahead.

Any award of grant is subject to the following conditions: the Secretary of State must be notified of the actual starting date of the work; competitive tenders must be sought; the Council must approve the final scheme before any work is undertaken; the execution of the work must be supervised by an architect appointed by the applicant; any departure from the agreed scheme of work must obtain prior approval; the work must be completed to the satisfaction of the Council's architect who may inspect the work at any time.

Eligible expenditure covers the cost of repair of the historic fabric of the building.

Further information from:
Scottish Development Department, Historic Buildings Division
20 Brandon Street, Edinburgh EH3 5DX
Telephone: (031) 556-8400, and ask for the Historic Buildings Division

Appendix 2

AN OVERVIEW OF TAXATION

The following chart identifies the individual taxes and duties that can affect property developers.

Taxpayer	RENTAL INCOME Income Tax	RENTAL INCOME Corporation Tax	PROFIT ON DISPOSAL Income Tax	PROFIT ON DISPOSAL Corporation Tax	PROFIT ON DISPOSAL Capital Gains Tax	INTEREST RELIEF ON LOANS	VAT
Individual investors	27% to 60%	—	—	—	30%	If "qualifying" loan	"C"
Individual traders (eg hotelier)	27% to 60%	—	—	—	30% – can roll over	If loan used in trade	"B"
Property Investment Companies	—	35%	—	—	35%	If "close" needs to be "qualifying" loan	"A"
Property Trading Companies	—	35% on profits as adjusted	—	35% on profits as adjusted	If appropriate 35%	If loan used in trade	"B"
Trading Companies (eg hotels)	—	35%	—	—	35% – can roll over	If loan used in trade	"B"
Property Bonds	—	35%	—	—	35%	If "qualifying" loan	"C"
Property Unit Trusts	Subject to normal rules of trust taxation	—	—	—	30% unless all unit holders are exempt	If "qualifying" loan	"C"

| Taxpayer | RENTAL INCOME | | PROFIT ON DISPOSAL | | | INTEREST RELIEF ON LOANS | VAT |
	Income Tax	Corporation Tax	Income Tax	Corporation Tax	Capital Gains Tax		
Investment Trust Companies	—	35%	—	—	Exempt	Yes	"C"
Pension Funds	Exempt	Exempt	Exempt	Exempt	Exempt	No	"C"
Insurance Companies Life Funds	—	35%	—	—	30% – policy holders' funds 35% – shareholders' funds	Yes	"C"
General Funds	—	35% on profits as adjusted	—	—	35%	Yes	"C"
Charities	Exempt	Exempt	Exempt	Exempt (unless trading)	Exempt	N/A	"C"

NOTES: 1. Capital gains tax is payable after indexation allowance where appropriate.

2. Stamp duty – all the above are subject to stamp duty at 1% on conveyances over £30,000

3. Inheritance tax – companies with close company status and individuals are subject to inheritance tax in certain circumstances. The tax is levied on a sliding scale between 30% and 60%.

4. A Property Unit Trust cannot be Authorised but it is understood that this may change after 1987.

5. *Rates.* All the above will be subject to normal rules of rateable occupation of land and buildings but where charities occupy buildings for charitable purposes there is a 50% relief. Private individuals may be entitled to a rate rebate in certain circumstances. Agricultural land and buildings are exempt from rates. Unoccupied commercial property may be entitled to limited and partial relief.

CODES: "A" Majority of outputs are exempt, can only claim input VAT in proportion to standard or zero rated outputs.

"B" Can claim VAT inputs back unless restricted by exempt outputs.

"C" Outside scope of VAT but suffer input VAT at 15%

Index